Crucifixion
Fact or Fiction?

An Investigation of Crucifixion

Dr. Seyed Mostafa Azmayesh

Prefaced By Dr. W. Glaudemans

Mehraby Publications

Crucifixion: Fact or Fiction?

Dr Seyed Mostafa Azmayesh

Prefaced by Dr. Willem Glaudemans

London 2008

Mehraby Publishing House 2nd Edition 2016.

Printed in England

ISBN: 978-0-9935347-4-4

Info@mehraby.com

Acknowledgements:

This book is the result of many years of study, travel and investigations.

The process of finalising all the material into a book was completed by a small group of people.

The author wishes to thank Mehraby Foundation for publishing the book. The second edition has been redited, revised. The author also wishes to thank Mehrdad N. and Helmut G. for the support and ideas they offered during the compilation of this book.

Cover Design: Atbin E.

Cover photograph: Upper half image is a photo of a painting by Andrea Solario (1503) and lower half image is a photo of a wall painting by Da Vinci.

www.jesusfamilytomb.blogspot.com

From the same author:

The Teachings of a Sufi-master. 2nd Edition, Mehraby Publication, 2016

The Pearl of Sufism. 2nd Edition, Mehraby Publication, 2016

New Researches on the Quran, Why and how two versions of Islam entered the history of mankind, Mehraby Publication, 2016.

Een ontmoeting met Jezus in Christendom en Islam. Ten Have. Holland. 2008 / in collaboration with Dr. J.V. Shaik

Contents

Preface

In this new book, Dr. Seyed Azmayesh poses a very important question: what *really* happened at the crucifixion? Maybe this question can never be answered definitively and satisfactorily, but anyone who dares to make it the focus of his investigations deserves our deepest respect. Azmayesh' story is like one of a detective, scrutinizing all the available and well-known data and delivering a brand-new composition. And, as is the case with every brilliant detective, we can only be convinced by the probability of what he proposes: what if it really happened that way, what if this reconstruction is right? Then we shall have to change all our views, beginning with the images we hold of Jesus and Judas. And whether we are able to accept his challenging vision also depends on our ability and willingness to change our beliefs.

I met Dr. Azmayesh for the first time in April 2008, when we were both invited as key speakers at a spiritual festival in Zutphen, the Netherlands. The conference focused on four religions meeting each other. Dr Azmayesh represented Sufism, the mystical way of the Islam, as I represented Gnosticism, the inner way of Christianity. We only had one hour during dinner time to well and truly meet each other. In that hour we became brothers, recognizing each other's path as our own, knowing that Sufism and Gnosticism share the same source. And we discovered that both of us agree in our divergent opinion about the relationship between Jesus and Judas, and Judas' role. We both believe Judas to be a high initiate and absolute confidant of Jesus. And to us, the whole idea of 'betrayal' seems highly illogical and utterly impossible: ridiculous, to say the least. The newly-found Gospel of Judas supports us in this position.

To me, Judas was a close relative of Jesus, helping him with his mission wherever he could. He belonged to the inner circle of Jesus' disciples, and he was one of the very few people, like Thomas and Mary Magdalene, with whom Jesus shared his secret knowledge. It is no coincidence that in our time the Gospels of precisely those people that the Christian tradition called 'traitor', 'unbeliever' and 'whore' were unearthed again, in order to restore these apostles to their proper status as initiates. In this sense, I think an agreement existed between Jesus and Judas about what Judas' role should be. It was, so to speak, an accord between two souls. Whatever the reason may have been for Jesus to think that his mission in Palestine had to come to a close, we can be quite sure that Judas knew all about it and was helping him to complete it - even to the extent that his fellow disciples and future generations would think of him as a betrayer. And moreover, this idea of 'betrayal' is mainly based on a guilt-ridden translation of the Greek *paradidonai*, which simply means: to transfer, or to hand over.

In the Gnostic scriptures, found in Nag Hammadi in 1945, and dating back to the first centuries of our era, we can meet a Jesus who differs greatly from the traditional one. But he has equally old papers. We find a Jesus who is a teacher trying to awaken us to our true nature, our pearl, our light. There is no trace of a Jesus suffering and dying for the redemption of our sins; it is quite the contrary. We find him laughing at the whole scene of the crucifixion. Here, I will present a few remarkable quotations taken from three different treatises.

> 'James, do not be concerned for me or for these people. I am He-who-was-within-me. Never have I suffered in any way, nor have I been distressed. And these people have done me no harm.'[1]

So Jesus, here talking to James - who was disturbed by his supposed suffering - explains that there was no suffering at all. And when there is no victim suffering pain; then there cannot be a guilty offender, or a betrayer. For when there is no effect, there is no cause. Here, Jesus teaches us a lesson in forgiveness: he has removed all the guilt from the scene. And at the same time he points at his true nature: He-who-is-

---

[1] *Apocalypse of James, NHC V.3*, codex p. 31.

within-me, the Christ. And Christ, by virtue of his nature, cannot suffer at all. He is above pain and death.

> 'And I did not die in reality, but in appearance. (...) And I suffered (only) according to their sight and thought. (...) For my death which they think happened, (happened only) to them in their error and blindness. (...) He who drank the gall and the vinegar, it was not I. They struck me with the reed, it was another. Who bore the cross on his shoulder, it was Simon. It was another upon whom they placed the crown of thorns. But I was rejoicing in the height (...) and I was laughing at their ignorance.'2

This is a firm statement Jesus made. He says: it only looked as if I died, but in reality I did not die at all. It can only seem that way, when you are in error and blind, when you believe in the illusion of death; when you look solely at the body and the outer appearances. Again, Christ cannot die or suffer any pain. So when you think that I, Jesus, drank the gall, was struck with the reed, bore the cross and wore the crown of thorns, please look again. And when you have unclouded your vision, rejoice with me, for nothing happened in reality.

> 'He whom you saw above the cross, happy and laughing, this is the living Jesus. But the one into whose hands and feet they drive the nails is his fleshly part, which is the substitute. They put to shame the one who came into being in his likeness. But look at him and (look) at me. (...) Therefore he laughs at their lack of perception, knowing that they are born blind. So then the one susceptible to suffering shall remain behind, since the body is the substitute. But what they released was my incorporeal body. I am the intellectual Spirit filled with radiant light.'3

---

2 *The Second Treatise of the Great Seth, NHC VII.2,* codex pp. 55-56.

3 *The Apocalypse of Peter, NHC VII.3,* codex pp. 81+83

Again, there is this challenging invitation: look at him who is suffering in the flesh, or look at me who am the living Jesus. Choose between the body and the Christ. And the crucifixion seen in this perspective in essence is liberation: they released the Spirit, the light body. And when we look now at the Gospel of Judas, we find the same, where Jesus is saying to Judas:

> 'But you will exceed all of them. For you will sacrifice the man that clothes me.'[4]

So Judas, as an initiate, willingly sacrifices the body of Jesus, which is the garment of Christ. The beauty of it is that Judas becomes the vehicle by which the Christ is liberated from the flesh that is bearing him, a common Gnostic theme as we saw. At the same time, it all points out the way to real resurrection for all of us: to know that what we really are cannot suffer or die, and that our true nature is imperishable divine light.

This is one way to interpret these quotations. But they are open to other interpretations as well, which you will find after reading Azmayesh' book. So you are invited to read these quotations again in the light of what he is telling you.

In conclusion, I would like to state that essentially there are four ways to interpret the crucifixion:

1. The traditional version: Jesus died on the cross to atone for our sins.

2. The Docetist version (from the Greek *dokein*: to seem): Jesus seems to die at the cross, but in reality the Christ was liberated.

---

[4] **Codex** p. 56

3. The stand-in version: it was not Jesus hanging on the cross but somebody else, be it Simon of Cyrene, Judas or some other person.

4. The survival version: Jesus survived the crucifixion, continuing to live in Syria or India, or returning as the Apostle Paul.

(And of course there is a fifth: there never was a crucifixion, because it cannot be proven historically. This particular interpretation is not considered here.)

Good detectives never give away their plots. Thus, you will have to find out for yourself to which of these four versions Azmayesh' pioneering book belongs.

Dr. Willem Glaudemans[5]

---

[5] Dr. Willem Glaudemans is the Dutch co-translator of *the Nag Hammadi Scriptures.*

It was John the Baptist who started the process of Jesus being identified as Christ. It was not Jesus' wish. It was imposed on him. All of a sudden Jesus was involved in a process that had been started at the will of John the Baptist. John the Baptist gave his life for this, by not evaluating all the dangers caused by this action. But Jesus wanted to be in control of everything. Therefore, he wanted the process of his identification as Christ to end quickly, so that he could start another process: one of his own will and under his own control. Thus, his crucifixion served as the end of the initial process.

Introduction

A delicate subject in a wider perspective

We are currently living in a time of great discoveries and great changes. These discoveries not only concern the present and the future; they often they challenge us to look at the past again and to re-evaluate certain historical events on the basis of new evidence. Although the subject of this book, historically speaking, is almost 2000 years old, the opinions expressed by a majority of people concerning the event of the crucifixion have been of major importance to the world throughout the centuries. It is right here where our exploration starts.

This book aims to examine the general opinion about the event of the crucifixion. By 'general opinion' we mean the assumption that a disciple of Jesus named Judas betrayed him and sold him to the Romans, who crucified him in accordance with the will of the then-leading Jewish authorities. Jesus died on the cross and was resurrected after three days. This is, in general, what can be derived from the four canonical Gospels (by Mark, John, Luke and Matthew) and it generally represents the explanation given by the official church. This is, roughly, what most people believe concerning the crucifixion. It is one of the cornerstones of the Christian faith. For centuries this opinion has been propagated by the church and it has had a profound influence in history, up to the present day.

The book traces the sequence of events before and after the crucifixion with the help of old manuscripts as well as recently discovered documents. The book approaches its subject on the basis of the traditionally accepted manuscripts, as well as scriptures that were rejected in the past. It looks at the subject from the angle of Christianity as well as from the angle presented by the texts of the Qur'an. The book looks into the structure of the group of disciples around Jesus, their mutual relations and the relation to their master. Additional details are also provided about the way Jesus used to teach his disciples in a Gnostic manner. In doing so, the book draws a radically different conclusion compared to the usual opinions about what happened during those days and why things happened the way they did.

It is not for the first time in history that this generally accepted vision is doubted. The Qur'an contains a number of verses about the event of the crucifixion. These verses do not accept *"Jesus, son of Mary"* as the crucified person. The Qur'an states that Jesus, during the event of the crucifixion, was taken to "'a high place'"[6] and that 'a mistake' was made. Simultaneously, the Qur'an describes another opinion on the crucifixion.

> "After Jesus' death early Christians shared accounts of his life and teachings. Dozens were written down, but the church fathers in the end chose only four to be included in the New Testament. During the past century, many rejected Gospels have been rediscovered. A few, such as the *Gospel of Peter*, are parallel to the chosen four. Others, such as the Gospel of Judas, are strikingly different, emphasizing gnosis (...). Some examples: *Gospel of Mary*, written in the early 100s, reveals secrets Jesus gave to Mary Magdalene alone and not his male disciples. The *Gospel of Thomas*, ca.110, includes the unique saying of Jesus: "If you bring forth what is within you, what you have will save you ... What you do not have within you will kill you". The *Gospel of Truth*, ca.150: in this account Jesus' teachings liberate the soul from a flawed

---

[6] ***Qur'an. IV.*** Verse 157: They killed him not, they crucified him not. They committed a mistake about him [his identity], they don't have the exact knowledge about him [the crucified person], and they follow only their supposition. They killed him not for sure. "VI. 158: "But Allah brought him up to Him ". 19. 57:" We brought him up to a high place."

physical world: "You are the perfect day, and in you dwells the light that does not fail". The *Secret Book of John,* ca.150, denounces the Old Testament God for trying to hide the truth from humanity. It claims that Adam and Eve received the divine spirit from the true God.[7]

Many old scriptures have been found over the past decades. Some of these scriptures, too, express a different view on the event of the crucifixion. For example, the *Second Discourse of Great Seth,* 200s, says that the true Christ was *never crucified."*[8]

These scientific discoveries force us to take another look at the event of the crucifixion because many of them do not support the generally accepted version of the historical events. In the past, governmental and religious institutions often tried to propagate certain opinions at the cost of others. Falsifying facts, destroying manuscripts and persecuting people who held dissenting opinions are only a few of the tools that were used in the past. However, the voice of those with a different opinion could never be silenced completely. Today, we live in a time in which more research can be done. More and more of the original sources are becoming available but nobody knows what is still hidden from our eyes. As often happens with dramatic discoveries in other fields of scientific research, we notice certain reluctance on the part of the general public to accept and assimilate new insights and opinions when they concern some of the roots of their own beliefs.

We are well aware that this study touches a delicate subject. In fact, we investigate the validity of one of the central dogmas of official Christianity. It is for this reason that we ask the reader to study the text of the book carefully and to consider its contents. At the same time,

---

[7] **National Geographic.** May 2006, p. 89.

[8] Ibid.

the reader is invited to remain aware of his (often hidden) pre-suppositions and sentiments regarding this subject.

It may be the case that certain old opinions will have to be sacrificed. Maybe a feeling of fear and emptiness will arise, and maybe an impression will be left that the spiritual element is lost by dissecting and examining the texts in this way. Nevertheless, we think that a considerable part of the true intention and the true message of Jesus are restored by this investigation. In order to clarify this statement it is necessary to elaborate on our angle of approach and the wider perspective in which the event of the crucifixion has to be understood.

We approach our subject from the Gnostic angle. This has many implications. The Gnostics regard the presence of a human being on Earth as a possibility for their souls to be re-united with God. The souls are 'sown' in human bodies by the Creator.[9] The 'education' of the soul needs a master, just as a developing seed needs a gardener in order to grow.

The Gnostics believe that the soul continues its travels and its spiritual search after the death of the physical body. The physical body is regarded as an important vehicle and an important possibility to learn during life on earth. But it functions only for a short period of time. **So, a Gnostic is not attached to his body at all. On the other hand, the prophet needs his physical body in order to accomplish his mission in the material world.** In his fight with the Pharaoh, Moses was not concerned about his physical body at all: he was totally focused on his mission to save the Jews and take them to the Promised Land. We see this aspect in many prophets. Although they have great spiritual capacities, they accomplish their mission through their physical bodies. In doing so they are well and truly put to the test.

---

[9] *St. Matthew, XIII.* See also the **Gospel of Judas** about the corruptible seeds.

According to the Gnostics, the tradition of Gnosticism started with Adam and his third son "Seth", and is transferred from master to master by the pact of initiation. Only a master who is connected to the chain of initiations is authorised to accept and to educate students. Also the canonical Gospels describe the initiation of Jesus by John the Baptist. It is regarded as a major event in the life of Jesus[10]. After being initiated by John the Baptist, Jesus started his mission as a person dedicated to his objective. The Gnostics regard Jesus as the source of the eternal light and the divine guide: an important spiritual master (educator, instructor) and also a prophet. He wanted to educate his disciples and to spread his discipline and teachings all around the world. For Jesus, his mission was the most important. According to certain signs it can be supposed that after the event of the crucifixion Jesus continued his mission for a while in Ephesus[11] before his death, when he was old, in Jerusalem[12].

These elements may grant the reader an entirely new perspective. Gradually, a new vision emerges. We feel that the scientific discoveries

---

[10] There is a considerable body of evidence indicating that the line of initiation to which Jesus belongs continues in the Prophet Mohammad. Dr. John van Schaik and Dr. Azmayesh published their views about this subject in *Een ontmoeting met Jezus in Christendom en Islam (A meeting with Jesus in Christianity and Islam).* Ten Have, 2008.

[11] The Greeks-land, is in present-day Turkey. In this region there is a place named "Zan-Jaan", harbouring a tomb attributed to Saint John the apostle, and a small temple attributed to Saint Mary.

[12] The *Qur'an* version certifies that Jesus kept preaching until the end of his life when he was at an old age (Surat.III, verse 46). A familial tomb, 2000 years old, was recently found in Jerusalem bearing the names of Jesus, Mary, and Judas, (father, mother and son). According to an old ritual common in the East, when somebody sacrificed his life for another person, that person named his son after the sacrificed person, in order to relate their astral bodies and to let both souls grow up at the same time. The Judas of this familial tomb is assumed to be the son of Jesus and Mary. (Here, we refer the reader to our conclusion "Whose is this tomb?")

made so far in combination with research on historical documents offer increasing support for the Gnostic point of view.

We try to approach the plan of Jesus through rational reasoning and by investigating the written reports.

When St. John the Baptist introduced Jesus as the eschatological saviour; he suddenly created a very difficult situation for Jesus. Through this announcement and by his appearance, Jesus drew the attention of many people and the governing authorities feared the possibility of a revolution. Jesus wanted to control this unexpected situation in order to successfully accomplish his mission. Many things happened in a very short period of time. Many of the seemingly random events that took place are today explained in a rational manner and can be grasped as pieces of a bigger whole.

With this book we challenge the reader to think about the event of the crucifixion. But what is more, we hope that the reader will acquire a deeper and better understanding of the message presented by Jesus and its implications for our lives.

Global view

"Yahuda, Anta rafi' kollohom

Yahouda, Atit bakh hadday bakrah

Da Anashdamo kasiho"

'Judas! You're higher than all of them. Judas! For you will sacrifice the man that clothes me.'

This is what Jesus says to Judas in the Aramean language[13] according to the recently published Gospel of Judas, attributed to a person at whom considerable blame and many accusations have been directed for hundreds of centuries: Judas Iscariot, a man believed to have betrayed his master Jesus for 30 silver coins.

It is officially stated that this Gospel of Judas was found in an Egyptian cave, written on papyrus in the Coptic language. Only 12 out of 32 pages were in a condition and order that they could be recovered and translated into the languages of the western world. The above-mentioned sentences are the English translation of a highly central statement made by Jesus Christ. In these sentences we find the Coptic word *"Kasiho"*, which has been translated by 'to

---

[13] After the discovery of the scriptures of the Dead Sea scrolls (1947) it became clear that the common language spoken by the Jewish community in the region of Palestine during the period of Jesus was Aramaic. One manuscript in six was edited in that language, and later on – in the time of Jesus - writing an Evengelium in the Aramean language was absolutely possible. This discovery changed people's beliefs before the first half of the 20th century: witness *"The original language of the Gospel"* by Edgar Goodspeed (published by Thomas Kepler. N.Y. 1944. cited by *"Les manuscrits de la mer Morte"*. M.Wise; M. Abegg; E. Cook. Published by Tempus. 2003, France p.20).

clothe'. "Kasiho" (from "*kesvat*" or *lebass* is cover) can be translated in the same way: 'to clothe', 'envelope' and 'to cover'. Thus, the translation from Coptic into English seems to be accurate. But the meaning of this sentence is very obscure and leaves room for different interpretations.

A version proposed by National Geographic interprets this statement as follows: "the man that clothes me" is the physical body of Jesus that bears Christ, the eternal soul, and in order to liberate this eternal soul, the body must be sacrificed.[14]

According to this interpretation, "Judas' Gospel says Jesus asked Judas to betray him, thereby freeing his soul from his body"[15]. So Jesus would have asked Judas to deliver Jesus to his murderers.

If we follow this interpretation, we find that Judas acts as an instrument for a sophisticated plan of **suicide on Jesus' part** - if we suppose that the act of **Jesus' suicide** achieved through **Judas' complicity** was carried out in order to liberate his soul from his body! Why would Jesus do that and then come back a few days later in his body, expose himself to his disciples and ask them to touch his body to realise that it was made of flesh and blood? This apparent contradiction is not acceptable to us and therefore we would like to present our own interpretation.

"The man that clothes me" is a specific person resembling Jesus. We derive this from the word "Kasiho", which we interpret to mean a cover, a double of Jesus, i.e. a person that resembles Jesus. This shows that we agree with the interpretation formulated by National Geographic that adjudicates to Judas as performing a secret mission

---

[14] This subject is debated on the DVD of the **Gospel of Judas**, a documentary made by National Geographic, 2006. NGHT.

[15] **National Geographic Magazine**. May 2006, p.86.

for Jesus. But it also implies a complete new interpretation of the events surrounding the crucifixion and it sheds a different light on the picture of Judas Iscariot and the mission of Jesus Christ.

The main statements of our book are:

1. We claim that Judas Iscariot was by no means a traitor, but instead a very close and advanced disciple of Jesus Christ with a very specific and delicate mission.

2. Jesus Christ's main message aimed to teach people not to be attached to their body, but to develop their "real self" and to nurture the hidden capacities of the "*Sofia*" (real self/soul): love, peace, and faith. It is the famous 'Die before you die' and learning to liberate your soul while you are in the body. We think Jesus needed time to write his "*Enjil*" (ensemble of his teachings), to educate a number of disciples, and finally to send them to different corners of the world - with the copies of his book to sow the seeds of real spirituality and to show humanity the path of substantial evolution.

3. Jesus Christ needed his body to accomplish his mission until the end, so he had to thwart the plans of the Pharisees to kill him and yet make them firmly believe he had died.

We will first present the reader with a new version of the events of the crucifixion and later show on the basis of officially approved documents – as far as we were able to collect them - how our version can be detected in them in a step by step manner.

The secret story of the crucifixion

When John the Baptist initiated his cousin Jesus in the Jordan River he could see a 'white dove' sitting on Jesus' head. From his master and father Zacharias he had learned that this would be the sign by which to recognise the expected Messiah. Henceforward, he announced everywhere he travelled in the region that Jesus from Nazareth was the Messiah, and Jesus' name became well known.

This was during the time when the Roman Empire controlled the land of the Jews, and many Jews were waiting for the Messiah to liberate them from the foreign reign. They were waiting for a leader who would liberate the country. Many religious sects were spread throughout the region cherishing their own interpretation of the prophecy of a Messiah[16]. All this created a very particular atmosphere, that today we might even call it a hysterical or psychotic atmosphere.

The high priests and the Pharisees were responsible for leading their people under the Roman reign. They were thus, afraid of agitation and a possible disturbance affecting their people because of the appearance of a Messiah. On the one hand, they were afraid to lose their power as a religious and worldly authority, and on the other

---

[16] *"L'attente du Messie en Palestine a la veille et au debut de l'ere Chretienne"*, Ernest Marie Laperrousaz, edition A. et J. Picard, 1982. Part of the Dead Sea texts (written next to the time of St. John and Jesus) talks about an "Eschatological prophet" or a "Master of Justice". The image of this saviour-personage existed in the minds of many people in the region of Palestine, before Christianity and its founder, Jesus son of Mary. The "Master of Justice" is mentioned 3 times in the writing of Damas, 2 times in the commentary of Psaume 37 times, once in Michee, 8 times in Habacuc. These texts [talking about the "Master of Justice"] are the part of the Dead Sea scrolls closest to the time of Jesus. There are considerable resemblances between those descriptions and the image of Jesus introduced in the Gospels. The reader is also referred to other research carried out by Ernest Marie Laperrousaz: *"Quomran et ses manuscrits de la Mer Morte"*, edition Mon lieu 2006, France; *"Les Esseniens selon leur temoignage direct"*, edition Desclee.1982; *"Qoumran. L'etablissement essenien des bords de la mer Morte. Histoire et archeologie du site"*, 1979, edition A. et J. Picard; **"Les manuscrits de la Mer Morte"**. Edition P.U.F. (Que sais-je), Paris, 2003.

hand they were afraid their people would be extinguished by the Romans should an uprising against their reign take place.[17]

That is why they decided to orchestrate a plan to put an end to the hysteria concerning the Messiah. Jesus knew about their plans because he had some disciples among the leaders of the Jewish community, for instance Nicodemus (John 3:1) and Joseph of Arimathea (John 19:38), who informed him about the discussions and decisions made between the leaders.

As it appeared to be very difficult task to catch Jesus in the streets, the Pharisees decided to get hold of one his disciples, one who would betray his master and show them the way to Jesus of Nazareth.

In response Jesus started to make up his own plan to achieve two goals:

1. To give the impression to everybody that the Messiah had reached his end, so that any expectations concerning the liberation of the country would no longer be connected to Jesus.

---

[17] In the Dead Sea scrolls the revelation about the events runs parallel with the time of Herod the Great. The Essenien community was formed by a group of people dedicated to fierce spiritual practice, spread in Palestine, similar to another esoteric community staying in Damascus under the name of Tsadokites. Cf. *Le Bible a la l'archeologie* J.A. Thompson. Edition L.L.B. 1988; *Les manuscrits de la mer Morte* F. Mebarki/ E. Puech. **Edition du Rovergue**. 2002. It is not considered a fact that the community of Qumran were Essenes, nor that the Dead Sea scrolls were solely Essenian in origin. Read for instance: *Who wrote the Dead Sea Scrolls?* Norman Golb. New York, 1995, Chapter 4, where he presents the Qumran-Essene theory as a myth. It is more likely to have been a library, consisting of texts from different Jewish groups and sects.

2. The fulfilment of his true mission, teaching people how to liberate their souls through his (spiritual) teachings.

Jesus entrusted Judas Iscariot with the task of fetching and leading the Pharisees' guards and the Roman soldiers to the house where Jesus would be during the night. So, Judas went on a mission to the Pharisees, a task assigned especially to him by Jesus, and offered to betray his master for 30 silver coins. In the middle of the night - together with the guards and the soldiers - he moved to the garden of Cedron[18], where Jesus had told him he would be with his disciples. There, the crowd met Peter, who Jesus had asked to keep a lonely watch with his sword while the others slept in the house. Peter went towards the incoming crowd and asked them what they wanted. The head of the Roman soldiers asked for Jesus of Nazareth, and he answered them: "I am Jesus",

"And Judas - the person who did hand over him to them - was also standing up with them." [19]

But the soldiers did not pay attention to his answer.[20] Judas told the soldiers he would go into the house to fetch Jesus. Then he went inside the house in the garden of Cedron, the place in which Jesus' disciples were in deep sleep.[21] In the house, without the apostles'

---

[18] Cedron, Kedron, Quedron, Kidron. In this form, the **N.T.** gives the name of the brook Kidron in the ravine below the eastern wall of Jerusalem (***Gospel of St. John XVIII.1***, only) [mentioned in the Gospel of St. Barnabas as well]. Beyond it was the garden of Gethsemane, ***Smith's Bible Dictionary***, edition Pyramid Books. N.Y. 1967. P.100. The Brook, a torrent or valley, lay between the city of Jerusalem and the Mount of Olives: now commonly known as the "Valley of Jehoshaphat".

[19] ***St. Johns Gospel***. Ch.18. 5. (Persian language. p. 179).

[20] Ibid. Ch.18.6. They turned their heads and fell down on the ground (Persian language p. 179).

[21] ***St. Barnabas' Gospel***. 215. 3 [See: "Toward the original sources".]

knowledge, he was changed, so the looks and manner of Jesus were enacted perfectly on him.[22] A few minutes later, the soldiers saw "'a son of man'" coming out, asking them for whom they were looking.[23] **This second time, the name of Judas is no longer mentioned in** *St. John's Gospel.* And as the guards said once again they were looking for Jesus of Nazareth, he answered: "I am Jesus. Deal with me and let all the others go."[24] So the guards tied "'the son of man" who claimed to be "'Jesus'"[25] and immediately went to Kaiphas, the high priest of the time, to challenge him with the accusations of those who wanted to get rid of Jesus. The true Jesus, meanwhile, rested in a hidden cave behind the house for a period of seclusion. Later, the very moment the guards untied the captured person, who gave the impression of being Jesus, something highly peculiar happened.[26] In a situation of chaos and disorder, a group of people took him out of the hands of the Roman soldiers. He escaped.[27] The guards, angry and hysterical, shouted very loudly and nervously: "Don't let Jesus evade", "Arrest

---

[22] *St. Barnabas' Gospel* 216-5 [See: "Toward the original sources".]

[23] *St. John's Gospel.* Ch.18. 7.

[24] *St. John's Gospel.* Ch.18. 8

[25] *St. Barnabas' Gospel* 217 - 1

[26] This version is in agreement with the explanation presented in one Muslim book in the Arabic language *"Tarikh e Tabari"*, and two Persian books *"Tarikh Bal'ami"* and *"Majmal at-Tawarikh wal- Qesas.* The book of *Majmal at-Tawarikh wal-Qesas* [Ensemble of the histories and tales] was written in 520 h/1126 A.D. By an unknown author/ or by Ibn Shady Asad Abadi. First editor Mohammad Taghi Bahar- Tehran 1939. New edition Tehran- Donyaye ketab, 1996, Ali Ashar Abdollahi.

[27] *Tarikh Bal'mi.*352/ 973 AD Translation of *Tarikh Tabari* [ibn Jarir tabari 310/ 931 A.D.] Tabari, whose book was translated by Bal'ami, was not only famous as a Muslim historian, but also a Qur'an-interpreter. His version of the event of crucifixion regards the verses of the *Qur'an* in this matter. See: "Toward the original sources".

him! Arrest him!", "Arrest Jesus", "Arrest Jesus", "Where is Jesus?"
The crowd moved left and right in order to find an "evading Jesus".
After a while, among the crowd, the guards got hold of a Jew called
"'Jesus'", a man whose manner and looks resembled those of the
escaped person, and who must have been a cover of Jesus.[28] Thus,
we now have a "double of Jesus", a person who is willing to
sacrifice his life. He is not there by accident, but as a part of a
complex plan that required enormous preparations. Through his
actions, he establishes a new balance between Jesus and his enemies,
to the advantage of Jesus. He goes through all the pain before being
put on the cross, and, some time later, on the cross itself. But Jesus'
plan was to save his life at the same time. This is why only Jesus'
secret disciples ((in the adversary's camp)) like Joseph of Arimathea
and Nikodemus were very closely involved in the event of the
crucifixion ((not the apostles and not Jesus' relatives)). The latter
should hold the illusion of his death. But Joseph and Nikodemus
made sure that the person on the cross was put into a cataleptic
coma after that person gave the secret sign: *Eloi, eloi, lema sabagthani!*
They let him smell a very powerful narcotic solution (composed of
nutgall and vinegar[29]) which made him appear to be dead, so Joseph
could ask Pilate to take down the body from the cross very quickly,
keep him away from all the relatives and treat him with another
substance, so the person who was on the cross could recover and
leave the tomb empty, after everybody had departed and the
situation had calmed down. In this framework, it is important to
take into account that Golgotha – the place of crucifixion - was
right next to the garden of Joseph of Arimathea, where a cave had
been prepared: initially for burying Joseph himself. The Sabbath was
drawing near, and this meant that it was not allowed to have anyone

---

[28] The word "Jesus" was pronounced "Yassou", Issou", "Ishu", Yashu", "Isa",
"Isaiah".

[29] *The Gospel of St. Matthew.* 27- 34 Persian version. p.50.

on the cross as this was considered to be unclean. All these circumstances helped to accomplish this subtle plan.

Time was a very critical factor and through all these facts, the risk of losing the man of the cross was minimized. Jesus, during the period of his seclusion, had an extraordinary experience – of ascending to the sky,[30] something which reminds us of the event involving the prophet Ely (Elijah), who was picked up to be taken to the sky[31]. After an absence of three days, when Jesus came back and presented himself to his disciples, he was very hungry. His disciples were shocked to see him and they would not believe that it was him. They touched him all over, especially his hands and feet. They thought he might have been only a ghost, or a type of hallucination, but what they felt was in fact his complete body in flesh and blood.

Thus, Judas' mission was to hand over Jesus' double: "The man that clothes me". Still, we do not have any exact information about these two people (that is (Judas and the second 'Jesus')) after the event of crucifixion. And Jesus could carry on his mission of teaching the people how to free their souls during their life on earth. – Until the end of his life when he was old ((*The Qur'an*. III. 46)).

Bodily Ascension

The Christian official Gospels and the Muslim texts (including the Qur'an) share a brilliant common point about Jesus: Jesus went up bodily to the sky. They differ about the moment of his celestial travel: before (The Qur'an and Muslims texts) or after crucifixion (the Gospels). There is also a certain resemblance with the case of

---

[30] *The Gospel of St. Barnabas*, 215.5-6.

[31] *The Encyclopedia Britannica*, the encyclopedia **Wikipedia**. See appendix and http://www.britannica.com/biography/Elijah-Hebrew-prophet.

Elijah, who was picked up into the sky from the top of the mountain by a fiery whirling stream of a celestial vehicle. In the case of Jesus, the Gospels report strange clouds above the mountain[32] and audible voices thundering in the Sky.[33]

---

[32] ***The Gospel of St. Mark.*** Ch.9-7: And there was a cloud that overshadowed them and a voice came out of the cloud, saying: "This is my beloved son. Hear him". [And while coming down from the mountain, Jesus ordered his three disciples –witnesses of the event- to be silent about that experience.] ***The Gospel of St. Matthew,*** Ch.17: 1-9 "A bright cloud overshadowed them"…

[33] ***The Gospel of St. John.*** Ch.12. 29-30: "Then came there a voice from Sky, saying "I have both glorified it, and will glorify it again." The people, that stood by, and heard it, said that it thundered. Others said "An angel spoke to him"

An investigation of the original sources

One of the most important events in the history of mankind is the crucifixion. It is one of the central dogmas in official Christianity. For centuries there has been a difference of opinion about the case of the crucifixion, not only between Muslims and Christian communities, but also within the Christian community itself.

In order to better understand this problem we must go back to the original sources. In the following chapters we shall try to investigate, as a neutral observer, the oldest Christian documents as they are accepted by the majority of Christians throughout the world. To understand these texts better we shall also use other Christian documents, such as the Apocryphal and Gnostic Gospels. In addition, we investigate the sources of the Muslim texts, including the Qur'an, on the subject of the crucifixion. We need to differentiate between two categories of sources: Muslim and Christian:

A) Muslim texts

The Qur'an

The first Muslim document that discusses Jesus' life and times is the holy Qur'an. A complete report concerning Jesus' life is given in different Qur'an verses and Sourats[34], but here we are only interested in the case of the crucifixion.

"And when Jesus perceived unbelief on their part, He said, who will be my helpers with God? The apostles said we will be God's helpers! We believe

---

[34] See: S.M. Azmayesh & J. V. Shaik: *Een ontmoeting met Jezus in Christendom en Islam.* Ten Have 2008.

in God, and bear thou witness that we are Muslims (submitted to God). O Lord! We believe in what thou have sent down, and we follow the messenger; write us up, then, with those who bear witness to him. And they (Pharisees) plotted, and God plotted; but of those who plot God is the best. Remember when God said "O Jesus! Verily I will take you out of the world and bring you up to myself and deliver thee from those who believe not, and I will place those who follow thee above those who believe not, until the day of resurrection (the Last Day, the day of the last judgement). Then to me is your return and wherein ye differ will I decide between you"[35]

In the commentary described in the Qur'an entitled "Tafsir ol Jalalayn"[36] these verses are commented on as follows:

When Jesus perceived/ *knew*/ unbelief on their part/ *and the fact that they decided to kill him*/ told who is my helper/ *my assistant*/ toward God/ *to help the God's religion*? The apostles replied "we are the God's helpers"/ *your assistance for his religion*. **And they were first-rank disciples of Jesus, who believed on him before anybody else and they were 12 men with the white mantle (HOUR).** We believe on God and O Jesus be our witness that we are Muslims. O Lord we trust in what you sent/ *Enjil*/ and follow your messenger Jesus write down our name with other witnesses that you are the only one, and Jesus is your messenger. They / *the no-believers Jews people*/ plotted against Jesus/ *to send an agent to kill him by surprise*/ **and God plotted in front of them**/ *to impose the figure of Jesus*

---

[35] ***Qur'an.*** S.3. verses 52-55.

[36] This book of commentaries of *the Qur'an* was written by two commentators. From the beginning to the end of Surat "Al- Esra" it was written by Imam Jalal od Din Soyouti, and from the Sourat of 'Kahf'/'Cave' to the end of *the Qur'an* by Al-Imam Jalal od Din Mohammad ol Mahalli. Because of this fact it is famous under the name of Commentary of Two Jalal (od Din): *Tafsir ol Jalalayn.* Ed. in Beirut.

to the man who wanted to kill him. Finally they killed that person in place of Jesus and Jesus was brought to the sky/ **and God is the best of the plotters. Remember when God told O Jesus! I'm your "Motevaffi"/** *abductor (Gabez)/* **and I'm your picker up to myself/** *from the world, without dying/* **and I'm your purifier/** *separator/* **from the non-believers …"**[37]

"And for their saying: "Verily we have slain the Messiah, Jesus the son of Mary, the messenger of God. Yet they slew him not, and they crucified him not, but they had only his likeness. And they differed about his case (of crucifixion), were in doubt concerning him: no sure knowledge had they about him, but followed only an imagination (illusion), and they did not really slay him, but God took him up to Himself. And God is Mighty, Wise."[38]

"They told proudly/ we killed Messiah, Jesus, son of Mary the messenger of God, in their opinion! They killed him not, they crucified him not, but they fell down in an illusion that the crucified and killed person was Jesus, but in reality God imposed the figure of Jesus to that person and they thought he is truly Jesus! And people - who differed about that person or Jesus, were in doubt concerning his murder - were in two groups: when certain of them said to other ones- after seeing the crucified person- that his face looked like the Jesus' face, but his body was different than the Jesus' body. And other ones told truly He was Him (and not anybody else). But (even in the moment of the crucifixion) they differed about the event and did not have the real knowledge about his murder. They only

---

[37] *Tafsir Jalalayn.* p.73.

[38] *The Qur'an.* s.4:.157-158.

followed their imagination and doubt (*laken yatabe'ouna fihe az-zan alazy takhaylouh*) and they killed him not for sure. But God took him (Jesus) to Him-self."[39]

So, according to the Qur'an's version and its interpretation, each of the 12 apostles, one by one, was the example of honesty and sincerity. *And they were the Jesus' apostles of the first rank, who believed on him before anybody else and they were 12 men with the white mantle hour).*

Six Books

From the third and fourth centuries of Hegira ((Abbassid period)) four historically important books remain:

1. The book of history famous under the title of *"Tarikh e Ya'ghoubi"*, written by Aby Vazeh Ahmad ibn Abi Ya'goub Eshag ibn Ja'far ibn Vazeh Kateb Akhbari Abbasi Esfahani Ya'ghobi, who died 279 of Hegira/ 900 AD.[40]

2. The book of history famous under the title *"Akhbar ot Teval"*, written by Abou Hanifeh Ahmad ibn Davoud Dinvary, who died about 290 of Hegira/ 911 A.D.

---

[39] *Tafsir Jalalayn.* pp.130-131.

[40] Ya'ghoubi mentions the name of Judas in his book according to the content of the official Gospel, as we will see in the following lines. He writes the following sentences from *the Gospel of St. John*. "Jesus went to a place where he used to gather with his companions. Judas had known that place for some time, and as he saw the agents tracing Jesus, he led them and the servants of the Pharisees to him. Jesus went out and asked them "what is your purpose?" They stated "we would like to arrest Jesus". He replied: "I am Jesus of Nazareth". They went and came back again. Jesus told them: "I am Jesus of Nazareth. If you want, take me...." *Tarikh Ya'ghobi.* Vol.1. Persian translation by Dr Ebrahim Ayati, Elmi, 6th edition, Tehran 1366. p. 95.

3. The history book, named *Tarikh Tabari* written by Abou Ja'far Mohammad ibn Jarir Tabari, who died in 310 of Hegira/ 931 A.D.

4. The books of a famous writer named Abou Zeyd Ahmad ibn Sahl Balkhi, who died in 322 of Hegira/ 943.

5. The book of history known under the name of *Tarikh Bal'ami*, 352/ 973 A.D.

6. The book of history named *"Remaining traces from the lost centuries"* (*Asar ol baghieh anel goroun el khalieh*), written by El-Birouni 360 – 440/ 1061 A.D. that we introduced in the preceding lines as well.

The Muslims historians and writers knew the official canonical version of the crucifixion of Jesus, as written in the four Gospels, perfectly well[41]. By reporting this version in their books, they kept reminding their readers of its non-concordance with the Qur'anic version[42].

In his book of history, Ya'ghobi presents a complete explanation of the four canonical Gospels about the life of Jesus, his crucifixion, his reappearance to his apostles, and he adds certain paragraphs from the Book of the Acts ((B-2/ B-6, I-5)).[43] After introducing the

---

[41] *The Holy Book/ Old and New Testaments*. Persian version/ translated from Hebrew, Kaldean and Greek. Photographic reproduction from the Edition 1904, Iran, 1982.

[42] The books of el-Birouni and Ya'ghobi only have a scientific-historical nature. As such, they mention the content of the official Canonical Gospels about the crucifixion. They constrict their writing to showing the difference between the contents of 4 Gospels.

[43] *Ya'ghoubi*. Ibid: p.83-100.

entire contents of the Gospels, including the death of Jesus on the cross and the subsequent events, he mentions:

"... It was entirely the content of the sayings of the authors of the Evangeliums (four Gospels), and they differ with each other about every detail. God the highest told (in the Qur'an)" They killed him not, they crucified him not. They misunderstood. And the persons who differ about this case are in doubt about him, they don't have any knowledge in this matter, and they follow their suppositions. They killed him certainly not, but Allah brought him up"[44]

In his book *"Asar ol Baghieh"*, El-Birouni also writes and explains a detailed résumé of the life and the crucifixion of Jesus **according to the four Gospels, and he compares their contents - showing the contradiction between them.[45]**

Al Birouni's source of knowledge - and that of many other serious researchers and historians involved with Christianity that followed him ((from different branches and differing in their world views, their books and manuscripts, their social and clerical hierarchies and such)) was based on three points:

1. .A detailed study of the written Christian texts ((official Gospels and other sources)).

---

[44] *Qur'an:*/ Sura Nessa'- v 157, cited by Ya'ghobi / ibid. p. 98 .The translator of the book of Ya'ghoubi, Dr Ayati, here adds the following in a footnote:" refer to *the Gospel of Barnabas*, Ch. 217".

[45] *Asarol Baghieh An el Ghoroun el Khalieh* [The remaining traces from the lost centuries]. This is on the books written by El-Birouni (940-1020 A.D.) 360-440 H. in Gazneh in Arabic language. This book is translated in Persian by Akbar Dana Seresht and published by Amir-Kabir, Tehran 1363.

2. The Book of **Ma'ref or Roum**, written by Abol-hassan
   Ahmad ibn Hossein Ahwazi e Kateb.[46] This book was an
   ensemble of a ten-year in-depth study, written by a Muslim
   researcher in the days of the Byzantine Empire. We have
   found no trace of this book yet, but it is frequently quoted in
   the works of the serious historians such El-Birouni. Also,
   the unknown author of the important book: **Majmal ot
   Tavarikh** shows its importance.

3. Field work investigations carried out by different groups of
   knowledgeable Muslim researchers in Byzantine and other
   Christian territories. These groups were sent to Rome
   (Byzantine Empire) by the Caliphs of the Abbasid dynasty in
   order to spread to different parts of the empire and carry
   out in-depth scientific research. One of these groups was led
   by a researcher named Mehdi Moussa Shaker. He was sent
   to the region of Ephesus upon the authority of the
   Byzantine Emperor and in collaboration with Muslim
   embassy in Constantinople.[47]

---

[46] "Abol hassan Ahmad ibn Hossein Ahwazi Kateb reports what he had seen by his
own eyes during his stay in Constantinople and other cities and towns of the
Byzantine empire" **Asar ol bagieh** p. 44, the content of the book of El-Byrouni
concerning the religion, the traditions, and the costumes of the Romans {Christian of
the Byzantine Empire} is reportage of the book of Al-Ahwazi, as he mentions his
names in different paragraphs.

[47] El-birouni, ibid- 450-452. Mehdi Moussa Shaker went to Roum in the company of
the ambassador of Almo'tassam, the Abbassid kalif. He was the brother of Ma'moun,
and the third son of Haroun or Rashid. It seems that this type of research into
Christianity interested many people. El Birouni writes that it was said by the
Christians that the cousin of Haroun or Rashid, the important kalif of Abbasid
dynasty, was converted to Christianity, and was killed because of this crime!!. He had
changed his name to Antonious Abou-Rouh. Ibid, p. 453.

El-Birouni divides the Christian community into three different main branches: the Maleka'ieh ((Constantinists), living in the Byzantine Empire, (and worshipping the wooden cross and adhering to the Trinity of God); Jacobin communities, and finally Nestorian communities (also in other Muslim sources this ideology is extensively debated and discussed).

The reason for the extensive interest in Christianity as expressed by the Muslims lay in the old challenge concerning the final destiny of Jesus. The official canonical Gospels and the Qur'an introduced a contradictory view about the crucifixion of Jesus. Both religions accept the event of crucifixion, but they differ in their understanding of who was the crucified person. So, the study of the case of the crucifixion in essence reveals an existential competition between two religions and communities concerning the legitimacy of their beliefs.

In his book, El-Birouni reports the contents of the canonical Gospels related to the event of the crucifixion and mentions the name of Judas as the betrayer of his master. Here is El-Birouni's text:

> *"Judas Iscariot, one of his students, went to the Pharisees and the leaders of that tribe (Jews) and gossiped about Jesus and received 30 Bouma (Dinar or coins) from them, and he showed to them the secret house of Jesus"... They captured Jesus, tortured him, put on his head a thorny crown, beat him, and in the third hour of Friday, according to the writings of Matthew and Mark and Luke, they hanged him on the wood. But according to John they hanged him on the wood at 6 o'clock."[48]*

Some centuries later, Afzalod din Badil ibn Ali Khaghani Shervani (6th century of Hegira), born to a Nestorian mother and a Muslim

---

[48] El-Birouni, ibid-p. 487

father, talks in one of the long poems contained in his book - entitled *"The poetry of Christianity"* - about the world view held by the Iranian-Nestorians and mentions the name of Judas (Yahouda in Persian).[49] The name and the story and the sayings of Jesus are mentioned throughout Muslim Arabic/Iranian culture, and more specifically in the texts of the Sufi masters. A summary is omitted here as it would go beyond the scope of the present work. But in the following lines we would like to expose two new texts from the old manuscripts written in the 9th and 12th centuries A.D.

1- **Majmal al-Tawarikh wa al-Qasas** (Ensemble of the histories and tales)[50]:

"... The Jews made a conspiracy to kill him (Jesus), and the governor of Jerusalem gave them a hand.

Jesus told his apostles: "Keep protecting me tonight", but all of them slept! Jesus told them: "One of you will sell me at a cheap price, and will lead the enemies to me and will become a non-believer".

Jesus said to another one: "You will let me down and will hate me before the cock crows".

The Jews arrested an apostle who left the group on another day and asked him to lead them to Jesus.

---

[49] *The poetry of Khaghani explained By Minoresky.* Translated in Persian by Abdol hossein Zarin koub- Farhang Iran Zamin. 1332, Khagani and Andronikus

[50] *Majmal al-Tawarikh wa al-Qasas* (مجمل التواريخ و القصص) Malek o Sho'ar Mohamad Taghi bahar. Tehran, 1318/ 1939- pp:216-219.

Majmal al-Tawarikh wa al-Qasas was written by an unknown author in Persian in 1126 A.D. [Some authors have claimed the name of the author to be *Ibn Shadi Asad abadi* (ابن شادی اسدآبادی).]. The title means *"The Collection of Histories and Tales"*. The book mostly chronicles Persian Kings and is often cited as a source of reference for historical events of the 12th century and earlier.

He replied: "I hate Jesus", and he became a non-believer.

They captured another one.

He told them: "Give me some presents to bring you to him".

They did pay him 30 coins and he showed the secret corner of Jesus.

The Jews made a crowd around him (Jesus) and attached his feet and hands, and all of the apostles evaded and left him alone.

The Jews brought the wood of the cross and told him: "Help yourself if you can, as you pretended to be able to give back life to the dead!"

Finally, they opened the cords from his feet and hands to hang him on the cross. In that moment God let him disappear from their eyes, and brought him on the 4th sky in the place of Beytolma'mour.

They looked everywhere, and did not find any trace of him.

They told: "He did something magical, and within one hour the effect of the magic will be vanished".

God the highest imposed the figure of Jesus on the face of Ishou' who was the leader of the Jews.

They arrested their own leader in place of Jesus, and did not pay any attention to his explanations. They brought and hanged him on the cross, and they, as well as the apostle and St Mary, thought it was Jesus.

... in the night of the 7th day after the crucifixion, God sent back Jesus on the earth, he met his mother and his apostles .... asked them to go to different countries,... talked with them as he would like, and about the early morning he went back to Beyt ol ma'mour in order to keep praying God till the end of the time, and the period of Dajjal (Anti-Christ). He

will come back in that time, in order to refresh the religion of the prophet of Islam (peace be upon him).

And I studied in a book named Ma'aref [51] *that the Tarsa/Christians are named Nasrany because of the birth place of Jesus in (Naserieh) Nazareth".*

In this book, the name of Simon Kifa Peter, who denied Jesus three times, and the name of Judas Iscariot are not mentioned at all. But it is obvious that **the betrayer of Jesus is not the same person** who was arrested and crucified in place of Jesus. He was named Jesus, and he looked like Jesus. **He was victimized due to his resemblance to Jesus. Not only did he have a physical resemblance to Jesus, but also a similar name.**

The same story, with certain differences, was also written in the Book of Bal'ami before the publication of this book. [52]

2- In the version of Bal'ami, there is no mention of the name of Judas at all. The betrayer of Jesus is Sham'oun (Simon). It could be "Ibn Sham'oun" (the son of Sham'oun)/ Judas himself was actually the son of Sham'oun as well.

The canonical Gospels mention two people called Shamoun (Simon). One is Peter (who denies Jesus three times), whose name is Simon. And there is another one: the father of Judas (the betrayer of Jesus).

---

[51] It means the book already cited and written by al-Ahwazi is mentioned multiple times by El-Birouni.

[52] *Tarikh e Bal'ami* Abou Ali Mohammad Ibn Mohammad Bal'ami. The translation and commentary of *Tarikh e Tabari* by Malek Osho'ar Bahar Mohammad Parvin Gonabadi, Tehran-1341- pp.230-244. This Persian digest of the work of At Tabari, was made in 963 A.D. by the Samanid scholar Bal'ami

In the book of Bal'ami, the denier of Jesus and his betrayer for 30 coins are both introduced under the name of Simon (Shamoun). The person who was hanged is neither of them, but instead a second 'Jesus'.

It is written in the book of Bal'ami (as well as in the Book of Majmal) that when Shamoun walked out of the house in which Jesus had been living in secret for a period of one week, he was accidentally arrested by the enemies, who forced him to show them the place where Jesus was hiding himself. Thus, the betrayer of Jesus was not a real traitor acting according to a specific plan in conspiracy and complicity with the enemies.

> *"They brought him to hang him on the cross. The Jews who crowded around Jesus had a chief whose name was Ishou'.*
>
> *When they opened the cords from the hands and feet of Jesus, God let him disappear from their eyes and imposed the figure of Jesus onto the face of Ishou' ...*
>
> *After one hour of waiting, they arrested their leader who looked just like Jesus because of his absolute resemblance to Jesus and his explanations proved to be useless. They hanged him on the cross, and God brought Jesus to the sky.*

Where is my betrayer?

> *... in the seventh night God the Highest sent down Jesus towards Mary. He gathered 12 apostles, and he found seven of them.*
>
> *He asked: "Where is my betrayer?"*

They told him, "He felt so shameful, and he hanged himself"[53]

Jesus replied: "It was not necessary. He should only have asked for the forgiveness of God. If he asked, God would accept to forgive him. In the world, under the clemency of God, the unforgivable sin does not exist".

... In the early morning Jesus prayed and asked God to bring him back to the sky. And the Christians cheered so much and celebrated the memory of that night ..."

As mentioned, the book of Bal'ami is the Persian translation of an older document named **Tabari's Akhbar al-rusul wa al-muluk**, or **Tarikh e Tabari**. The author was a Mazandarani historian, theologian and commentator of the Qur'an who died in 310 of Hegira (the first half of the 9th century A.D).[54] This book is a historical chronicle written from the Creation of the universe to 915 A.D. and is renowned for its detail and accuracy concerning Muslim and Middle Eastern history.[55]

The importance of the books of Tabari – Bal'ami

The story of Jesus in the texts of Tabari and in Bal'ami is edited as the commentaries of the verses in the Qur'an with respect to the story of Jesus' life. Through this, we see related historical tales incorporated into a theological – ideological framework. They explain how the Qur'an introduces somebody else taking the place

---

[53] Here the text of Bal'ami corresponds with *the Gospel of St Matthew,* Ch.27- 5. Only this Gospel mentions the suicide of Judas.

[54] Abu Jafar Muhammad ibn Jarir ibn Yazid ibn Kathir al-Tabari (838-923).

[55] *Tarjomeh tafsir Tabari* [The translation of the commentary of Tabari] habib Yaghmai, edition university of Tehran, 1339.

of Jesus on the cross.[56] In their books of the Qur'an commentary, they want to show another aspect of the event of the crucifixion, one in which Jesus was neither crucified nor killed.[57] In their interpretations they reach the conclusion as expressed in the Qur'an where it says that:

a) 'Jesus was taken up to the highest level of the sky'[58];

b) "all of the companions of Jesus, without exception, were the examples of sincerity and honesty[59] and nobody between them was a wrongdoer";

c) Jesus escaped because of the generosity of his companions, who would like to be "Ansar e Allah" (the help for Jesus in the way of God).[60]

In their commentaries, they introduced more verses of the Qur'an concerning Jesus' life, his mission and his writings.[61] Tabari – Bal'mi must have used the old Christian texts as the source of their commentaries of the verses of the Qur'an. We found citations of the "Prophet" in the texts of the Qur'an commentaries the sources of which were completely unknown until the discovery of the Gospel of Judas. This is of vital importance. It means that the

---

[56] *The Qur'an,* s. 4: 157. In the Qur'an, the event of the crucifixion is accepted but it says that the people fell in the trap of a big illusion concerning the person who was crucified, and that he was not Jesus.

[57] *The Qur'an,* s. 4: 157.

[58] *The Qur'an,* s. 19: 57- s. 158.

[59] *The Qur'an,* s. 61: 14.

[60] *The Qur'an,* s. 3: 52.

[61] *The Qur'an,* s. 57: 27. 'We sent after the Prophets, Jesus- the son of Mary- and we gave him the Evangelium'.

Muslim world had somehow had access to the forgotten Christian apocryphal-Gnostic texts for centuries.[62]

In this case we have to investigate a pre-Islamic book talking about Jesus with different characteristics than the four canonical Gospels. It is a book, used by at least some parts of the Christian community, based on the unity of the Creator and the duality of creation, rejecting the trinity of God and the crucifixion of Jesus,[63] a book named *Enjil*. What we deduce from the Qur'an verses, the book of Jesus named **Enjil**[64] was not a narrative book about the Jesus life from the birth to crucifixion, but a collection of wise advice and teachings, something comparable to *the Gospel of St. Thomas*[65] or to the book of Mani, the Iranian claimer of Farghelitus (*Paracletous*).

"In the 4th century, Cyril of Jerusalem mentioned a "Gospel of Thomas" in his **Cathechesis** *V.* "Let none read the Gospel

---

[62] Look at the second volume of this study.

[63] "And when Jesus perceived unbelief on their part [Jews] He said "Who will be my helper with Allah [Ansar Allah]? The Apostles replied "We are the Ansar Allah. We believe in Allah and bear thou witness that we are Muslims. O our Lord! We believe in what you have sent down and we follow the messenger! Write us up, then, with those who bear witness to him." And they [Jews] plotted, and Allah plotted. But of those who plot Allah is the best. Remember when Allah said "O Jesus verily I will take you up and bring you high to myself and deliver thee from those who believe not until the day of resurrection. Then to me is your return and wherein ye differ will I decide between you [people]". *The Qur'an* s. 3 Al Emran: 47 to 49.

[64] *The Qur'an*, s. 5, Maedeh: 46.

[65] *The Gospel of St. Thomas* is a collection of teachings that some attribute to Jesus of Nazareth. Parts of Greek versions of the text were found at Oxyrhynchus, Egypt, in the late 1800's. A complete version in Coptic (an Egyptian language derived from the Greek alphabet) was found at Nag Hammadi, Egypt, in 1945. The complete text has been dated to about 340 A.D, while some of the Greek fragments have been dated as far back as 140 A.D.

http://www.allaboutjesuschrist.org/gospel-of-st-thomas.htm

according to Thomas, for it is the work, not of one of the twelve apostles, but of one of Mani's three wicked disciples."[66]

Mani son of Pathak

Mani ibn Patak (third century A.D.)[67] had a book named *Enjil-zindag* (adviser Enjil). He introduced his book as the true Enjil of the Shining Jesus Christ revealed to him by Gabriel.[68] Mani

---

[66] Very few traces of Manichaean dualism can be detected in this "sayings" Gospel, *the Gospel of Thomas*, which is agreed to be simpler and less legend-filled than one would expect from a Manichaean text.

The Gospel of St. Thomas declares that the Kingdom of God exists upon the earth today if people just open their eyes. There is "divine light" within all of us, which allows us to see the Kingdom of God in our physical surroundings. The Image of God at the beginning of creation (Genesis 1) still exists today. We can assume that Image still, which is different than the image of fallen man (Adam) in Genesis 2. *The Gospel of St. Thomas* reveals that mankind can and should restore their identities to the image of God now, and see the Kingdom of God on earth now. http://www.allaboutjesuschrist.org/gospel-of-st-thomas.htm

[67] The books and the life of Mani are presented by Mohammad ibn Abou Ya'ghoub Ishaq ibn Mohammad ibn Ishaq Varraq "Ibn Nadim" [b. 297- d.385 h] in his book *Al-Fehrest* [written in 377- 4th century of hegira, 10 th A.D]. Edition Asatir, Tehran 1381. The author himself seems to be an open-minded Muslim with respect to other religions, including the religion of Mani. He collected very useful information from first-hand sources, and the very old manuscripts in writing the 10 chapters of his book Al Fehrest. The book of Ibn Nadim is absolutely unique and it contains information and reports that cannot be found elsewhere. In the study about Mani's religion Ibn Nadim's book is one of the most important sources of research.

The substance of this book was extracted and translated into German by G. Flugel. *Mani, Seine Lehre und seine Schriften.* 1862. Here, we the writings of Abou Reyhan El-Birouni, *Asarol baghieh*, already cited.

[68] This *evangelium of Mani* was written in Syrian [Soryani]. Upon completion, he decorated it with many illustrations and miniatures for the illiterate. He named this illustrated book *Arjang*. He was inspired by the ensemble of poetries by the prophet David and so, in the same manner, he compiled a book of hymns and poetry named *Zabour*, like the book of David, also in the Syriac language.

introduced himself as the follower of Jesus, and the rejuvenator of his true religion.

The book of Mani was based on the unity of the Creator and the duality of creation. Even if the name of Mani is not mentioned in the Qur'an, his teachings may have reached to the period of the prophet Mohammad. In any case, the Enjil of St Thomas, supposed to be written under the influence of Mani, or Mani's own books like the *Enjil Zindagh, Zabour, the book of Hymns*[69] are the texts concerning Jesus, coming from a pre-Islamic period with similar descriptions and with the picture of the *Enjil* in the Qur'an (see appendix: the **Iranian Christianity**).

Mani's opinion about Jesus

Next, we will explore a brief extract from different texts written by Mani in the framework of the hymns, concerning Jesus. In all of these hymns Mani, son of Pathak, gives this picture:

> *"Jesus, shiny being, is the alive light, the help of humble, poor people, and breaker of the proudness of the oppressors. He was never on the cross and was never killed. He is bodily immortal, but the enemies crucified a double of Jesus. The plan of the enemies was to bring Jesus in their trap, but they fell in the trap of Iscariot (Judas) and they finished to be ruined all. Later on, the city of Jerusalem had also been several times occupied and destroyed due to the different historical streams."*

---

[69] Look at *The Manichean Hymncycles Huyadagman & Angad Roshnan in Parthian and Sogdian.* Sundermann, London. 1990; *The disintegration of the Avestic Studies.* W.B. Henning. Acta Iranica 15, Leiden 1977, "*A Pahlavi Poem* Acta Iranica15. Selected Papers. Leiden. 1977; *The Manichean Hymn cycles in Parthian.* M. Boyce. London, 1954, *& A reader in Manichean Middle Persian and Parthian.* Leiden. 1975 & *A word-list of Manichean middle Persian and Parthian.* Leiden 1975 & *Parthian writings and literature.* Cambridge History of Iran. Vol 3, part II. Cambridge. 1983.

Mani says:

a) Hymn, written in the middle Persian language[70]

    1. They appeal to "the son of Mary";

    2. If He is Lord of everyone

    3. Who (could) crucify his son?!

    4. The evil ones will reach hell by justice

    5. Because they did wrong, and by their deeds

    6. They caused the elimination of the wrongdoers

    7. And they captured a "similar (to) Jesus"

    8. And killed him

b) Dialogue between Jesus and student. Hymn in the Parthian language[71]

Son:

For a second time, Jesus brought his forgiveness to me

And sent four streams to my support

Related to 3 other streams

He ruined Jerusalem

With the angry towers

---

[70] ***The poetries of light***. (The Hymns of Mani) Edition Ostoureh. Tehran, 2007, gathered by A. Esmailpour. p.335.

[71] Ibid. 331.

Jesus:

The cup of poison, death, and hate became fulfilled for you

By the hand of Iscariot and Pharisees (children of Israel)

And several more weaknesses

c) Hymn from **Zabour**[72]

Admired and alive

Aware and immortal, You are!

O my Lord! Shiny Jesus

You are sign, soul, and body

Of the dearest light-beings

O! King Jesus

You are a life healer (doctor in medicine)

You are God

You are saviour and liberator

You are God

O King, God, life-giver

d) Hymn in the middle Persian language[73]

We worship you, O shiny Jesus

O! You, new paradise

We appeal you,

For you are

---

[72] Ibid. p. 255.

[73] Ibid. p. 256.

Only LIFE

You! You are Master of Justice

You are free-healer

Dearest son

Dearest soul

Come in, liberated King

Come in, to help, O Soul!

O! Messenger of the highest happiness

Help of the humble, breaker of oppressors

We target our wish on you

For You are

Only LOVE

B) The Christian texts

The complementary writings of the Gnostic and Apocryphal Books

We should be aware that the case of the crucifixion is pivotal to the place that Judas has in the world of Christianity. Recently, a book named the Gospel of Judas[74] was discovered and published by the National Geographic. Even though it does not discuss the case of the crucifixion directly, it contains considerable important and interesting information offering the reader a better understanding of the circumstances in the time of Jesus, and of the relationship between the

---

[74] Saint Jude (or Judas) is a Christian saint based on the characters of Jude of James and Thaddeus in **the New Testament**. He is also called Lebbaeus, Thaddaeus, or Judas Thaddaeus. He should not be confused with **Judas Iscariot**, another apostle and later considered by the four official Gospels to be the betrayer of Jesus.

Apostles and Jesus. In our examination of the crucifixion we have also used this book as one of the complementary documents.[75]

One of our other documents is the Gospel of Thomas, which was found in 1945 during the discoveries of Nag Hammadi.[76] Often, in the margin of our study, we also refer to a book named "the Gospel of St. Barnabas".[77] The reason for this lies in the fact that there is no general agreement of opinion concerning this book. The official church, adhering to St. Paul's theology, is of the opinion that St. Barnabas separated from St. Paul and sailed to his native land (Cyprus). Here, the scripture ceases to mention him. In addition, the epistle attributed to him is believed (by the Church) to have been written early in second century.[78] Ascribed by tradition to St. Barnabas the apostle, the writing possibly dates back to as late as AD130.[79] Therefore, it would seem

---

[75] *The Gospel of Judas.* Translated by Rodolphe Kasser, Marvin Meyer, and Gregor Wurst, in collaboration with François Gaudard. From **The Gospel of Judas**, 2006 by The National Geographic Society.

[76] Scholars Version translation of *the Gospel of Thomas* taken from *The Complete Gospels.* Annotated Scholars Version.* Copyright 1992, 1994 by Polebridge Press. *The Gnostic wisdom of Jesus,* J.Y. Leloup, Amazon.com.

[77] *Irenaeus and the Four-Gospel Canon,* T. C. Skeat. Novum Testamentum, Vol. 34, Fasc. 2 (April 1992), pp. 194-199, doi:10.2307/1561042

Iranaeus (130-200) wrote in support of pure monotheism and opposed Paul for injecting into Christianity certain doctrines of the pagan Roman religion and Platonic philosophy. He quoted extensively from **the Gospel of Barnabas** in support of his views. This shows that the Gospel of Barnabas circulated in the first and second centuries of Christianity. In 383 A.D. the Pope secured a copy of **the Gospel of Barnabas** and kept it in his private library. Barnabas.net – www.barnabas.net.com

[78] *Smith's Bible dictionary.* William Smith. Pyramid edition. p.72.

[79] *Encyclopedia Britannica.* The **letter of Barnabas** was essentially a treatise on the use of the *Old Testament* by Christians… Barnabas' alleged martyrdom and burial in Cyprus are described in the *Apocryphal Journeys and Martyrdom off Barnabas,* a 5th century forgery.

that under a very powerful clerical authority every trace of the writings attributed to this Apostle was annihilated for centuries.[80] Evidently regarded as scriptural in Egypt, the letter of Barnabas was included in **the Codex Sinaiticus,** a 4th century Greek manuscript of the Bible, and it was also quoted by the presbyter of Alexandria (d.c.215).[81] On the other hand, we know that the pope Gelasius 1[st][82], in the year 492, forbade the reading and studying of the writings of Barnabas. But subsequently, following absolute religious interdiction in 5th century, every trace of Barnabas was banned from the history of Christianity to such an extent that now it is very hard to find any trace at all of this book and of the name of Barnabas. In the Christian world, only a small minority of people know anything about Barnabas[83]. In Cyprus, his

---

[80] The book attributed Barnabas was also unknown in the Arabic and the Muslim world for centuries. In 1974 this book was translated from Latin into French and it was the subject of a doctoral study under the direction of the professor Henri Corbin, (1903-1978), the French director of Religious Studies at the old Sorbonne of Paris. After this study, the book became very well known in the Muslim world.

[81]. http://www.britannica.com/biography/Saint-Clement-of-Alexandria

[82]"Gelasius' election, March 1, 492, was a gesture for continuity: Gelasius inherited Felix's struggles with the Eastern Roman Emperor Anastasius I and the patriarch of Constantinople and exacerbated them by insisting on the removal of the name of the late Acacius, patriarch of Constantinople, from the diptychs, in spite of every ecumenical gesture by the current, otherwise quite orthodox patriarch Euphemius (q.v. for details of the Acacian schism). The split with the emperor and the patriarch of Constantinople was inevitable, from the western point of view, because they had embraced a view of a single, divine ('Monophysite') nature of Christ, which the papal party viewed as heresy. Gelasius' book 'De duabus in Christo naturis' ('on the dual nature of Christ') delineated the western view. Thus Gelasius, for all the conservative Latinity of his writing style, stood on the cusp of Late Antiquity and the Early Middle Ages". Free Electronic Encyclopedia **Wikipedia.**

[83] The reader should note that this author has travelled the world extensively, in order to collect any valuable information that could shed greater light on the true story and important events of Jesus' life. He has travelled to Cyprus a number of times: to the birthplace of Barnabas and the place where he died. However, during his travels he did not meet many people with extensive knowledge of Barnabas.

country of birth, it is said that when his tomb was discovered, a copy of his book was found resting on his corpse. But no trace of this book currently exists, as it seems to have been sent to the Vatican some time during the 6th Century. Of course, in very old Christian documents, such as those of Irenaeus[84] of Lyon, the name of Barnabas is indeed mentioned and it shows that certain writings of this apostle actually existed.

Figure 1- Saint Barnabas tomb in Cyprus

---

[84] Some say that *The Gospel of Barnabas* was accepted as a Canonical Gospel in the Churches of Alexandria till 325 A.D. In 325 A.D, the Nicene Council was held, where it was ordered that all original Gospels in Hebrew script should be destroyed. An Edict was issued that anyone in possession of these Gospels had to be put to death - **Barnabas.net**

A book named the *Gospel of Barnabas* is listed in two early catalogues of apocryphal texts. Another book with the same title, Gospel of Barnabas, survives in two post-medieval manuscripts in Italian and Spanish. Although the book is ascribed to Barnabas, close examination of its text suggests that the book was written either by a 14th century Italian or a 16th century Spaniard. However, we also know that two copies of this book attributed to St. Barnabas were also found in Spain and in Italy and were later translated into Latin and Arabic. But unfortunately, we have now lost every trace of the manuscript found in Spain. Nevertheless, the Latin version of the book is now accessible and has been translated into many different languages.

Contrary to the canonical Christian Gospels, and in accordance with the Islamic view of Jesus, this later Gospel of Barnabas states that Jesus was not the son of God, but a prophet, and it calls Paul "the deceived." The book also says Jesus rose up to heaven alive without having been crucified, and that Judas Iscariot was crucified in his place[85] as punishment for his wrong deeds.[86] But this version of the book has been the subject of numerous discussions and contrary opinions. The specialists of Christianity do not wish to give any weight to this book. So, the trace of Barnabas is removed from the world of Christianity. In the Muslim world and in Pre- and Post-Islamic Arabic culture we do not find any mention either of an Apostle of Jesus named Barnabas.

---

[85] This entry incorporates text from the public domain *Easton's Bible Dictionary*, originally published in 1897. This article includes content derived from the *Schaff-Herzog Encyclopedia* of Religious Knowledge, 1914, which is in the public domain.

[86] *St. Barnabas Gospel.* Ch. 217-67.

The Gospel of St. John[87]

We base our research on the four Canonical Gospels and mainly on the Gospel according to Apostle St. John. "No doubt has been entertained at any time in the Church, either of the Canonical authority of this Gospel, or of its being written by St. John."[88] St. John[89] (Youhanna Gheddis), the son of Zabadaeus and Salome and brother of Jacob, was one of the closest and perhaps one of the dearest Apostles to Jesus. After joining Jesus, he followed him like a shadow. He did not want to be separated from him for a moment. One of the four canonical Gospels accepted by the official church is attributed to him, and its name is the 'Gospel according to the Apostle St. John'. It is known that St. John met a mighty angel during a dream or during deep meditation. Afterwards, he started to write different books through direct inspiration granted by this angel.

The other writings of St. John, such as the Apocrypha by St. John and the Book of Secrets, are important documents among the Gnostics of the Christian world. The Canonical Gospels, such as the Gospels according to St Mark, St Luke or St Matthew, describe similar events and circumstances. However, each shows considerable variability in the way they describe the same events. Thus, the reader cannot fully understand which represents the best

---

[87] *New Testaments.* Translated from the Original Greek and with the former translations diligently compared and revised by his Majesty's special Command/ authorizing King James Version, with explanatory notes and cross references to the standard works of the Church of Jesus Christ of Latter-day Saints. *New Testament.* Persian translation from Greek, Latin, and Hebraic, 1982.

[88] *Smith's Bible Dictionary.* William Smith. Ed Pyramid inspiration. p.306.

[89] **St. John the Apostle** (Greek Ἰωάννης, see names of John) was one of the Twelve Apostles of Jesus. Several New Testament works, including the Gospel of John, are attributed to him in the Christian tradition.

and most precise version of the events as described in these books. Still, in our investigation we aim to use these three Gospels as a form of complementary evidence for the Gospel according to St. John (because of its well-established place in the church, "either of the canonical authority of this Gospel, or of its being written by St. John the apostle").[90]

The content of the Gospel according to St. John

After the destruction of Jerusalem (A.D. 69), Ephesus likely became the active centre of life for Eastern Christendom. The Gospel of St. John is supposed to have been written either in Ephesus or in Patmos in about A.D. 78 (approximately 30-35 years after the event of the crucifixion).[91] The Gospel states that St. John is a student of Jesus who witnessed all these events and who wrote his report in this book to tell that Jesus did in fact achieve and perform so much, that the whole world cannot contain it.

> 24 This is the disciple who testified these things, and wrote these things: and we know that his testimony is true. 25 And there are also many other things which Jesus did, which, if they should be written every one, I suppose that even the world itself could not contain the books that should be written.[92]

So, from this statement we can conclude that the author wants to explain to us that in his book he only extracted a few samples of what Jesus did during his life. In order to gain a better

---

[90] *Smith's Bible dictionary.* p. 306.

[91] *Smith's Bible dictionary,* p. 306. Probably, Jesus was alive until that time, and after his death St. John immediately edited this Gospel himself, or with the help of one of his students.

[92] *Gospel of Saint John,* last chapter. Ch.21 v. 24-25. Persian version p.186

understanding of the contents of the Gospel of St. John we must make a partition here and include the following three sections:

Section A: A report on the sayings of Jesus

In this section, we indicate the parts in which the author reports on what Jesus said; directly during his speeches or indirectly as lessons, teachings or as directives. Part A consists of three subdivisions:

i.   The general teachings. With these we mean sayings and teachings of Jesus which he used to communicate with the crowd in general during open gatherings.

ii. The teachings which Jesus exclusively revealed to his own disciples only.

iii. The personal teachings and advice that Jesus exclusively offered to St. John - and not to any other disciples - and which John could not reveal to the crowd without Jesus' authorisation. It is certain that what Jesus revealed to St. John, but did not authorise him to repeat to others, cannot be found in his book. Looking at this from another angle, it is certain that Jesus also offered his other students many personal and private teachings. This is also revealed, for instance, in the Gospels of Thomas, Judas and Mary. So, St. John was also not aware of these personal teachings that Jesus' other disciples had received from their master. As a result, St. John's book also lacks any private and personal teachings which other disciples of Jesus received from their master. Consequently, the author only mentions in his book what St. John was supposed to have heard from Jesus. But because he was not always with Jesus he could not hear everything, and because he was also not allowed (by Jesus) to report everything, there were many things he could not mention - through this lack of permission.

Section B: A report of events - not the sayings

This section is subdivided into two parts:

i.   The events that actually occurred while St. John was present.

ii.   The events mentioned by St. John but to which he was not a direct witness. Thus, he must have heard them from others and then mentioned them to others. So, events such as the first meeting of Jesus with John the Baptist, the initiation of Jesus by the hand of John the Baptist, what John the Baptist said concerning Jesus, the meeting between Jesus and a Samaritan woman, the dialogue between them, the journey of that woman to the city in order to bring others to Jesus, the gathering of the Pharisees in order to take a decision to solve the problem that the presence of Jesus in their community had caused them; all of these cases are reported in the book of St. John, and yet St. John was not a direct observer of any of these events.

Section C: The personal commentaries

Often, when the author of the Gospel according to St. John quotes Jesus, he tries to give an interpretation of Jesus' sayings; but this interpretation is his own personal opinion and the reader must remain alert not to consider the interpretation of the author of the Gospel of St. John to be the commentary of Jesus himself.

For this reason, the book of St. John partly contains reports on Jesus' commentaries and partly the personal opinion of the author related to the events, sayings, and information based on his own personal deductions, which may have nothing to do with the thoughts, explanations and the actual words expressed by Jesus.

A few examples

In order to clarify more clearly what we mean by looking at the text this way, let us examine the following examples - to be found in the chapters of the book of St. John. The 6th chapter of St. John's Gospel, verses 64–71 contain a collection of sayings, interpretations and reports.[93]

The saying of Jesus:

"Jesus says: there are people among you who do not accept to believe."

The personal opinion of the author of the St. John's Gospel about Jesus' words:

"It means from the very beginning Jesus knew who were the people who would not believe in him and thus were likely to help his enemies."

Report:

"In that moment a large number of Jesus' students left Jesus alone and parted company."

---

[93] 64. But there are some of you that believe not. For Jesus knew from the beginning who they were that believed not, and who should [a]betray him. 65 And he said, Therefore say I unto you, that no man can come unto me, [a]except it were given unto him of my Father. 66 From that time many of his [a]disciples went back, and [b]walked no more with him. 67 Then said Jesus unto the twelve: "Will ye also go away?" 68 Then Simon Peter answered him: "Lord, to whom shall we go? Thou hast the [a]words of eternal life. 69 And [a]we believe and are sure that thou art that Christ, the [b]Son of the living God." 70 Jesus answered them: "Have not I [a]chosen you twelve, and one of you is a devil?" 71 He spake of Judas Iscariot the *son* of Simon: for he it was that should betray him, being one of the twelve. The *Gospel of St. John* - King James Version, *Gospel of St. John- New Testament, Persian version*, p. 156.

Another example is a dialogue between Jesus and the Apostles.

Dialogue between Jesus and St Peter:

> Jesus said to the twelve Apostles: "Would you also like to leave me?" St Peter answered. "Where can we go? Your words are the source of eternal life. We believe and we know you and we know that you are Christ, the son of the existing God."

Saying of Jesus:

> Jesus answered to them: "I selected among you, twelve Apostles, and one of you is a devil".

The commentary of the Gospel of St. John:

> "He was talking about Judas, the son of Shamun Iscariot, because it was him who brought the others to Jesus, and in order to arrest him, and he was one of the twelve Apostles.

Here one can observe that the author of the Gospel of St. John would like to influence the mind of the reader by his own interpretation of the words of Jesus.

Another example can be seen in the 7th chapter of the Gospel of St. John1-37 verses.[94]

---

[94] 1 After these things Jesus walked in Galilee: for he would not walk in Judea because the Jews sought to kill him. 2 Now the Jews' feast of tabernacles was at hand. 3 His brethren therefore said unto him: "Depart hence, and go into Judaea, that thy disciples also may see the works that thou doest. 4 For there is no man that doeth anything in secret, and he himself seeketh to be known openly. If thou dost these things, shew thyself to the world." 5 For neither did his brethren believe in him. 6 Then Jesus said unto them: "My time is not yet come: but your time is always ready. 7 The world cannot hate you; but me it hateth, because I testify of it, that the

Report:

Jesus was walking in Galilee because he was unwilling to walk in Jerusalem where the high priests wanted to kill him.

The saying of the brothers of Jesus:

"Why don't you want to go to Jerusalem? You pretend to be Christ, so you cannot work in hiding. You must go and show yourself to the world."

---

works thereof are evil. 8 Go ye up unto this feast: I go not up yet unto this feast; for my time is not yet fully come." 9 When he had said these words unto them, he abode still in Galilee. 10 But when his brethren were gone up, then went he also up unto the feast, not openly, but as it were in secret. 11 Then the Jews sought him at the feast, and said: 'Where is he?" 12 And there was much murmuring among the people concerning him: for some said: "He is a good man: others said, Nay; but he deceiveth the people. 13 How be it no man spake openly of him for fear of the Jews. 14 Now about the midst of the feast Jesus went up into the temple, and taught. 15 And the Jews marvelled, saying, How knoweth this man letters, having never learned?" 16 Jesus answered them, and said: "My doctrine is not mine, but his that sent me. 17 If any man will do his will, he shall know of the doctrine, whether it be of God, or whether I speak of myself. 18 He that speaketh of himself seeketh his own glory: but he that seeketh his glory that sent him, the same is true, and no unrighteousness is in him. 19 Did not Moses give you the law, and *yet* none of you keepeth the law? Why go ye about to kill me? 20 The people answered and said: Thou hast a devil: who goeth about to kill thee? 25 Then said some of them of Jerusalem, Is not this he, whom they seek to kill? 26 But, lo, he speaketh boldly, and they say nothing unto him. Do the rulers know indeed that this is the very Christ? 27 Howbeit we know this man whence he is: but when Christ cometh, no man knoweth whence he is." 28 Then cried Jesus in the temple as he taught, saying Ye both know me, and ye know whence I am: and I am not come of myself, but he that sent me is true, whom ye know not. 29 But I know him: for I am from him, and he hath sent me. 30 Then they sought to take him: but no man laid hands on him, because his hour was not yet come. 31 And many of the people believed on him,

The ***Gospel of St. John***, King James Version. ***Gospel of St. John, New Testament***, Persian version, p. 156-157.

<u>The commentary of the Gospel:</u>

"It means that the brothers of Jesus didn't believe in him."

<u>Saying of Jesus:</u>

Jesus replied: "The world takes me for his enemy. You can go, but I don't want to join you in Jerusalem."

<u>Report:</u>

"After his brothers left him, Jesus went to Jerusalem as well, but in a secret manner in order not to be discovered by his enemies; because the High Priests were looking for him, in order to arrest him and were enquiring about Jesus' whereabouts.

There were many discussions about Jesus in the crowd. Jesus was among them but in a hidden manner and during the middle of the feast Jesus revealed himself saying: "I am Jesus. And I would like to present you my teachings." The Jews were very astonished and they said to each other: "But this person was never part of our lessons, how can he now give lessons to others?"

<u>Saying of Jesus:</u>

Jesus replied: "The teaching that I give you does not come from me. It comes from the person who sent me to you. Moses gave you the Old Testament, but nobody among you applies the teaching of Moses. Why would you like to kill me? "

Report:

> Certain people from Jerusalem said: "Is it not the same person that the Jewish people would like to kill? Why is he there? Why is he talking to the people, and why does nobody arrest him?" The heads of the community were certain that he truly was Christ. They knew this because they knew where he came from. They knew, from the scriptures, that Christ comes from nowhere.

Saying of Jesus:

> And when Jesus was giving the lesson in the Temple of Jerusalem, he said: "You know who I am, and where I come from. I didn't come to you for myself. I am among you because my Sender sent me to you and He is God. You don't know him, but I know him because I come from him and He sent me to you."

Report:

> They decided to arrest him, but nobody could touch him because it was not the right moment. Many people started to trust him, and were attracted to his mission.

What the reader cannot find in the Gospel of St. John.

As we explained, the *Gospel of St. John* contains reports concerning Jesus and those who had some form of relationship to Jesus.

The things that Jesus had said to other people - other disciples - or that were in fact part of his personal teachings to his other students could not be reported in the Gospel according to St. John. Even if the reader cannot find these kinds of commentaries in this Gospel, it does not mean that this type of teachings or discussions did not occur or that they do not exist in other books such as the Gospels of Thomas, Mary, Judas, etc. Moreover, the fact that these types of teachings and commentaries are not reported in the Gospel according to St. John does not invalidate their existence or their importance.

From the above discussion it follows that the readers of the Gospel according to St. John should realise clearly and carefully that they should not let the interpretations and the personal commentaries of that book take the place of the reality behind the events. Readers should be aware that the content of the book according to St. John is not the revelation of God. Therefore, they should use a rational framework in order to examine the contents of St. John's Gospel, to look at this book from an angle of serious investigation and to study it so that they can appreciate the reality of the events.

Jesus' transfiguration on the Mount of Olives is not reported in the Gospel of St. John, even though St. John was one of the three eye witnesses of that event. On the contrary, the event of bringing down the body of the "crucified "Jesus" is reported in the Gospel of St. John[95], even though he was in his own house taking care of the women!

---

[95] "Scholars are at last convinced that none of the Gospels can possibly be eye-witness accounts. In this regard, their work is consistent with the traditions of their predecessors, in that Gospels are a series of meditations and sermons, linked by narrative. They are all based on oral traditions and were composed to point out, as the eventual editors saw it, the role Christ played in the continuing development of the Hebrew Saga. The works were compiled in accordance with traditions that had become associated with the following persons: Mark (between 65-70); Matthew (during 70); Luke (70-85); John (90-100). Paul is now thought to have been written by a disciple early in the second century AD..." Edmund Hartley: *Simple guide to the Hebrew Bible*. pp.121-122.

The event of the crucifixion

The announcement about Christ

"1 NOW in the fifteenth year of the reign of Tiberius Caesar, Pontius Pilate being governor of Judea, and Herod being tetrarch of Galilee, and his brother Philip, tetrarch of Ituraea and of the region of Trachonitis, and Lysanias, the tetrarch of Abilene, 2 Annas and Caiaphas being the high priests (of the Jewish community), the word of God came unto John the son of Zacharias in the wilderness. 3 And he came into all the country about Jordan, preaching the baptism of repentance for the remission of sins"[96]

Jesus, son of Mary, was born in the year 304 of the Alexandrian calendar, and the sudden announcement about his reality to be the "awaited Christ" occurred in 335, which corresponds to the ancient prediction formulated in the Old Testament.[97]

John the Baptist was the spiritual successor of Zacharias and took Zacharias' place, after his death.

---

[96] *The Gospel of St Luke*. Ch. 3: 1-3. The Christians take as evidence a secret sentence of Daniel to define the date of the appearance of Christ. This is the following sentence: "Yashou' Masshiha Phoro Ghareba" meaning Jesus is the greatest saviour, and the mathematical value of this sentence gives the number of 1335. This date was revealed first time to Daniel in a vision during his prayer in the third year of the reign of Cyrus of Persia." Al-Birouni, *Asar ol Baghieh an el Ghoroun el khalieh* written between 360-440 of hegira in Khorassan. p. 23 This book contains the extract of the personal researches of Aboul Hossein Ahmad ibn Hossein Ahvazi Katib. The author Ahvazi spent some years in Byzanthium and travelled to different towns and cities and collected a great deal of information which he wrote down in his book *the knowledge about Rome* Ibid. p.449.

[97] "**Ashry Mahky va ki' layamim alf va shaloush miouth va shaloushim va hamtha**" is written in the *Book of Daniel,* meaning Lucky is the man waiting until the year 1335. *Asar ol Baghieh An el Goroun el Khalieh,* Al-Birouny, Persian version by Akbar Dana Seresht, published 1363, Tehran, Amir Kabir al-Birouni p. 22.

"And the same John had his garment of camel's hair, and a leathern girdle about his loins; and his meal was locusts and wild honey".[98]

In accordance with their old tradition[99], the newcomers and the ancient disciples of Zacharias went to John to renew their pact of initiation and to be initiated by his hand.[100] One of them was Jesus of Nazareth. He went from Galilee to Jordan to meet John the Baptist."

Figure 2- Initiation – Lisbon, Portugal.

After Jesus' baptism, whenever John initiated anybody, he directed them to Jesus by telling them that Jesus was the promised Messiah

---

[98] *The Gospel of Matthew,* Ch. 3. v. 4. Persian version, p.3, 1982. *The Gospel of Marc,* chapter 1:6.

[99] The Sethian tradition of initiation and wearing the "suf" (long white hairy dress), see the second volume of this study published by the author.

[100] *The Gospel of Matthew,* Ch. 3. - v.11. Persian version, p.4 "John answered them, saying, "I baptize with water: but there standeth one among you, whom ye know not"- *the Gospel of St. John,* first chapter 26, Persian version p.144.

predicted by the Holy Books. John the Baptist did this because of the revelation he had received which had told him: "That whenever you are initiating somebody and you see at the same time a white dove coming from the sky and resting down on this person's head, you should know that this person is Christ, the promised person from the Holy Books".

It is clear that even though Jesus was the cousin of St. John the Baptist, and both of them were the children of the same family, living, growing up together under the affectionate attention of their respective mothers and spiritual educator, Zackary, he did not know that Jesus was the promised Messiah. This fact is made clear in the Gospel according to St. John, the apostle:

> John said: *"And I knew him not; but he that sent me to baptize with water, the same said unto me, upon whom thou shall see the Spirit descending, and remaining on him, the same is he which baptizeth with the Holy Ghost."*[101]

And since that moment, St. John the Baptist gave witness to his discovered experience about Jesus, saying:

> "I saw the Spirit descending from heaven like a dove, and it abode upon him".[102]

---

[101] *The Gospel of St. John*, Ch. 1:33. This part is in contradiction with the Gospel of Matthew, Ch. 3:13-14: "St. John the Baptist said to Jesus: 'Don't ask me to baptize you, because I need to be baptized by you". As John did not acknowledge the Messiah in the being of Jesus before the ceremony of Baptizing - as he said: "I knew him not" -, how could he tell such a significant sentence? Both Jesus and St. John saw the dove after the moment of baptizing, not before. This fact is stated precisely in the Gospel of Luke : "Now when all the people were baptized, it came to pass, that Jesus also being baptized, and praying, the heaven was opened, and the Holy Ghost descended in a bodily shape like a dove upon him" *The Gospel of St Luke*, Ch. 3: 21-22.

[102] *The Gospel of St. John*, Ch. 1: 32.

Hence, in the very moment of baptising, St. John discovered that his cousin Jesus was in fact the announced Christ. According to St Matthew, Jesus also discovered this fact himself during the same ceremony.

> "And Jesus, when he was baptized, went up straightway out of the water and, lo, the heavens were opened unto him, and he saw the Spirit of God descending like a dove, and lighting upon him."[103]

At that time, Jerusalem was under the rule of the Romans and the Jewish community was awaiting and expecting the coming of Christ, the king of the Israelites. They were counting the hours and expecting his arrival.[104]

In the past, the Jewish community had been dominated by the Pharaohs in Egypt. Then Moses led them back to freedom. After that, they were enslaved by the Babylonian kings whose domination[105] was terminated by the intervention made by Cyrus of Persia. It was because of this that the Jewish community was expecting a new Saviour, a new Christ who would come and give them back their freedom and remove the rule of the Roman Empire from their territory.[106] For the majority of people, their expectation of a saviour had a political colour and they

---

[103] *The Gospel of St Matthew*, Ch. 3: 16, The Gospel of Marc, chapter 1: 10.

[104] The writers of the different parts of the old Qumran manuscripts announced that the time of the apparition of the Saviour of God was close. The people expected the coming of the Saviour and just at that moment John the Baptist announced that Christ had already appeared and that his name was Jesus of Nazareth.

[105] *The book of Daniel*, first chapter, 1 *Old Testaments*. Persian version. p.1284.

[106] "Know and understand that it takes 7 weeks and 62 weeks since the moment that the order is given to repair and build again the temple of Jerusalem to the coming of Christ the leader" *The book of Daniel*, chapter 9: 35. *Old Testament Persian version* pp. 1303-1304.

envisaged[107]: "a powerful mighty king like David and Salomon, founder of a new independent Israelite kingdom governed by a central state". This majority of the Jewish community never expected a saviour coming to preach to them that "The kingdom of my Lord is in heaven!" However, a certain number of people in the Jewish community expected the arrival of a saviour of the soul, a divine guide, a prophet, a teacher to open the gates of heaven to the seekers of perfection and substantial evolution.[108]

---

[107] *La veritable histoire de Jesus,* James Tabor, French version published by Robert Laffont, Paris 2007. The author of this book believes that the main mission of Jesus had in reality a political nature, and that he (Jesus) really had the intention to create a new Jewish independent state. This rededication is in obvious contradiction to the story of Jesus in all the known Gospels.

[108] An example of this group of people is given in the *Gospel according to St Luke.* Chapter 2: 25-38.

25 And, behold, there was a man in Jerusalem, whose name was Simeon; and the same man *was* just and devout, waiting for the consolation of Israel: and the Holy Ghost was upon him. 26 And it was revealed unto him by the Holy Ghost, that he should not see death, before he had seen the Lord's Christ. 27 And he came by the Spirit into the temple: and when the parents brought in the **child Jesus,** to do for him after the custom of the law, 28 Then took he him up in his arms, and blessed God, and said, 29 Lord, now lettest thou thy servant depart in peace, according to thy word: 30 For mine eyes have seen thy salvation, 31 Which thou hast prepared before the face of all people; 32 A light to lighten the Gentiles, and the glory of thy people Israel. 33 And Joseph and his mother marvelled at those things which were spoken of him. 34 And Simeon blessed them, and said unto Mary his mother, Behold, this child is set for the fall and rising again of many in Israel; and for a sign which shall be spoken against; 35 (Yea, a sword shall pierce through thy own soul also,) that the thoughts of many hearts may be revealed. 36 And there was one Anna, a prophetess, the daughter of Phanuel, of the tribe of Aser: she was of a great age, and had lived with an husband seven years from her virginity; 37 And she was a widow of about fourscore and four years, which departed not from the temple, but served God with fastings and prayers night and day. 38 And she coming in that instant gave thanks likewise unto the Lord, and spake of him to all them that looked for redemption in Jerusalem.

After John baptized Jesus, he sent him to spend a period of 40 days of fasting in seclusion.[109] After this period, he gave him the authorisation to accept the hands of the people and to initiate them to the chain of the initiation by means of baptizing them with water.[110] According to St Luke at that time he was about 30 years old.[111]

---

[109] *The Gospel of Mark*, Ch. 1:13, *The Gospel of Matthew*, Ch. 4:2.

"As it is written in the Evangeline, after being baptized in the river of Jordan he fasted for a period of 40 days to the day of Friday... and in the end of this quarantine, on the 41st day he resurrected a dead from the tomb in the region of the Olives mountain next to Jerusalem" *Asar ol Baghieh An el Goroun el Khalieh*, Al-Birouny, Persian version by Akbar Dana Seresht, published 1363- Tehran, Amir Kabir, p. 486.

[110] *The Gospel of St. John*, Ch. 3: 22- Persian version p. 147.

[111] "23 And Jesus himself began to be about thirty years of age, being (as was supposed) the son of Joseph, which was the son of Heli, 24 Which was the son of Matthat, which was the son of Levi, which was the son of Melchi, which was the son of Janna, which was the son of Joseph, 25 Which was the son of Mattathias, which was the son of Amos, which was the son of Naum, which was the son of Esli, which was the son of Nagge, 26 Which was the son of Maath, which was the son of Mattathias, which was the son of Semei, which was the son of Joseph, which was the son of Juda, 27 Which was the son of Joanna, which was the son of Rhesa, which was the son of Zorobabel, which was the son of Salathiel, which was the son of Neri, 28 Which was the son of Melchi, which was the son of Addi, which was the son of Cosam, which was the son of Elmodam, which was the son of Er, 29 Which was the son of Jose, which was the son of Eliezer, which was the son of Jorim, which was the son of Matthat, which was the son of Levi, 30 Which was the son of Simeon, which was the son of Juda, which was the son of Joseph, which was the son of Jonan, which was the son of Eliakim, 31 Which was the son of Melea, which was the son of Menan, which was the son of Mattatha, which was the son of Nathan, which was the son of David, 32 Which was the son of Jesse, which was the son of Obed, which was the son of Booz, which was the son of Salmon, which was the son of Naasson, 33 Which was the son of Aminadab, which was the son of Aram, which was the son of Esrom, which was the son of Phares, which was the son of Juda, 34 Which was the son of Jacob, which was the son of Isaac, which was the son of Abraham, which was the son of Thara, which was the son of Nachor, 35 Which was the son of Saruch, which was the son of Ragau, which was the son of Phalec, which was the son of

So, both Jesus and St. John the Baptist at the same time started to accept the hands of the people and to connect them to the chain of initiation. Also at the same time, Jesus started to introduce himself to the people as Christ. From that moment onwards a great number of ordinary people, knights, Gnostics and members of the Jewish community, started to join his circle. The majority of these people were fishermen.

"18 And Jesus, walking by the sea of Galilee, saw two brethren, Simon called Peter, and Andrew his brother, casting a net into the sea: for they were fishers. 19 And he saith unto them, Follow me, and I will make you fishers of men. 20 And they straightway left their nets, and followed him. 21 And going on from thence, he saw two other brethren, James the son of Zebedee, and John his brother, in a ship with Zebedee their father, mending their nets; and he called them. 22 And they immediately left the ship and their father, and followed him."[112]

Each day, more and more people joined the circle of Jesus and his name became well known.

"24 And his fame went throughout all Syria: and they brought unto him all sick people that were taken with diverse diseases and torments, and those which were possessed with devils, and those who were lunatic, and those that had epilepsy; and he healed them. 25 And there followed him great multitudes

---

Heber, which was the son of Sala, 36 Which was the son of Cainan, which was the son of Arphaxad, which was the son of Sem, which was the son of Noe, which was the son of Lamech, 37 Which was the son of Mathusala, which was the son of Enoch, which was the son of Jared, which was the son of Maleleel, which was the son of Cainan, 38 Which was the son of Enos, which was the son of Seth, which was the son of Adam, which was the son of God". *The Gospel of St. Luke*, Chapter 3: 23-38.

[112] *The Gospel of St Matthew*, Ch.4: 18-22. The names of some other disciples of Jesus are cited in *the Gospel of St. John*, Ch. 1: 35-51, Persian version p.144-145.

of people from Galilee, Decapolis, Jerusalem, Judea, and from beyond Jordan."[113]

Because the feast of the Jews was approaching, Jesus went to Jerusalem and entered the Temple. There, he found the merchants who sold cows and pigeons. He became very angry with them and pushed them away from the temple and told them: "Here is the house of my father, which you have changed into a market."

> *"13 And the Jews' Passover was at hand, and Jesus went up to Jerusalem, 14 And found in the temple those that sold oxen and sheep and doves, and the changers of money sitting: 15 And when he had made a scourge of small cords, he drove them all out of the temple, and the sheep, and the oxen; and poured out the changers' money, and overthrew the tables; 16 And said unto them that sold doves, Take these things hence; make not my Father's house a house of merchandise."*[114]

Jesus direct manner made the Pharisees and the High Priests of the Jewish community furious. They were forced to encounter a young man, who was little older than 30, and who was setting about fixing the rules for the whole community. This enraged them, because this was against the tradition of the community. Consequently, they decided to arrest him and put him into prison.

This forced Jesus to change his method of carrying out his actions. He even stopped initiating people and he passed these responsibilities to

---

[113] *The Gospel of St. Matthew*, Ch. 4: 24-25, Persian version p.5.

[114] *The Gospel of St. John*, Ch. 2: 3-16, Persian version p. 146, "15 And they came to Jerusalem: and Jesus went into the temple, and began to cast out them that sold and bought in the temple, and overthrew the tables of the moneychangers, and the seats of them who sold doves; 16 And would not suffer that any man should carry any vessel through the temple. 17 And he taught, saying unto them, Is it not written, My house shall be called of all nations the house of prayer? But ye have made it a den of thieves." *The Gospel of St. Mark*, Ch. 11: 15-17, Persian version p.74.

his Apostles.[115] He stopped showing himself directly and openly to the people. He changed his appearance and the way he appeared in public. By doing this, his enemies were no longer able to recognise him in the crowd as they did not know what he looked like. So, he went about his duties in a covert way, appearing among the people suddenly and then vanishing before his enemies could reach him. He would appear suddenly and say: "I am Jesus. I am Christ"; and he would preach to the people about righteous and non-righteous acts. Then, all of a sudden he would leave the crowd talking and arguing about him among themselves, while he moved on to a different place. Several times the Pharisees and the High Priests wanted to arrest him, but they could not reach him.[116]

Meanwhile', John the Baptist, his students and Jesus students continued initiating newcomers to the chain of initiation and introducing them to the Christ.

> *"23 And John also was baptizing in Aenon near to Salim, as there was much water there: and they came, and were baptized. 24 For John was not yet cast into prison. 25 Then there arose a question between some of John's disciples and the Jews about purifying. 26 And they came unto John, and said unto him, Rabbi, he that was with thee beyond Jordan, to whom thou barest witness, behold, the same baptizeth, and all men come to him. 27 John answered and said, A man can receive nothing, except it be given him from heaven. 28 Ye yourselves bear me witness, that I said, I am not the Christ, but that I am sent before him"* [117]

---

[115] **The Gospel of St. John.** Ch. 4:2, Persian version p.148.

[116] **The Gospel of St. John**, Ch. 7:1 Persian version p.156.

[117] **The Gospel of St. John**, Ch. 3: 23-28.

Jesus, Master of clandestine actions

The Pharisees were convinced that Jesus would appear among the crowds during the Passover feast, so they made preparations to arrest him. But Jesus let everybody know (even his brothers, Mary and Joseph the Carpenter) that he would not participate in that great feast.[118] His brothers said: "But you pretend to be Christ and Christ must show himself to the people. You cannot be Christ and hide yourself at the same time." Jesus answered: "I don't want to be with you and I don't want to come with you because the High Priests would like to arrest me. You can all go, there is no danger for you, but for me it is different".[119] When everybody (except Jesus) had arrived in Jerusalem, the Pharisees were certain that Jesus had changed his mind and that he did not want to come and join them. So, they started with their own traditional customs and affairs. All of a sudden, in the middle of the feast, Jesus appeared among the crowd. Initially, nobody recognised him because he had changed his clothes, his style, and his manner[120].

> "10 But when his brethren were gone up, then went he also up unto the feast, **not openly, but as it were in secret**."[121]

---

[118] *The Gospel of St. John*, Ch. 7:5, Persian version, p.156.

[119] *The Gospel of St. John*, Ch. 7:2-4, Persian version, p.156.

[120] This report reminds us exactly of the different passages of the book *Samak e Ayyar*. According to this book, the Ayyars [the members of a clandestine community based on brotherhood] used to change their figure and clothes constantly during their actions and missions. They always carried with them a bag containing the necessary elements to make up their faces and change their looks and appearance. They used certain water-soluble powders to wash their faces and change the colour of their skin, and certain oils to make spots on their facial skin. *The Samak's city* P.N. Khanlary, Tehran. 1988. Agah, p.79-81. See appendix: **Bihoushaneh & the path of Ayyari**

[121] *The Gospel of St. John*, Ch. 7:10, Persian version, p.157.

This shows how he was able to change his style and hide himself. He was a master of disguise in concealing his identity.

All of sudden, he introduced himself to the people and he told them: "I am Jesus of Nazareth. I am the promised Christ who you are expecting." People abandoned their priests and gathered around him[122] and he started to give them many lessons and teachings. The Pharisees and the High Priests tried to catch Jesus, but their hands could not once again reach him.[123] The friends of Jesus who had encircled him enabled him to escape the gathering safely. After this gathering, Jesus kept going to other gatherings, in the same covered style and then suddenly appearing among the people, talking with them.

> *"58 Jesus said unto them, Verily, verily, I say unto you, Before Abraham was, I am. 59 Then they took up stones to cast at him: but* **Jesus hid himself,** *and went out of the temple,* **going through the midst of them,** *and so passed by."*[124]

Usually Jesus appeared and disappeared among the crowd - to spread his message to everybody - as he was able to materialize and dematerialize himself. **The secret of the subtle manner of hiding** was known by the community of the "clandestine knights" (Ayyar)[125], as is mentioned in the following quotation taken from the old Persian book *Samak e Ayyar.*

---

[122] *The Gospel of St. John*, Ch. 7:14, Persian version p. 157.

[123] *The Gospel of St. John*, Ch. 7:30. It is written in the *Qur'an* that God reminds Jesus "When I have forbidden the hands of the people of Israel from you" Surat 5: verse 110.

[124] *The Gospel of St. John*, Ch. 8:58-59, Persian version, 161.

[125] *Samak Ayyar.* Abdollah kateb Arjani. **Edited and published by** P.N. Khanlary. Tehran. 1988. Agah. See appendix: **Bihoushaneh & the path of Ayyari**

"When "Alam-Forouz" wanted to leave the clandestine corner of his friends for the city, his companions avoided him and told: "Do not go! Because everybody knows you, a bad event could happen". He replied: "Don't bother your mind for me. I know very well how to do. I have the knowledge about this action (self- camouflage). Even if I appear a hundred times among them and talk with them, they don't recognize my identity". So he brought out from his belt the "bag of hilat/ (tricks). He took out something and solved it in his hand, and used it to mask his face. So within a few minutes he changed his face; and with a white-red skin he looked like the people of Farang (Western face)".[126]

To gain a deeper understanding of the "community of the clandestine knights" (Ayyar) can help us to understand certain passages of the Gospels about Jesus better.

Jesus strove to cause chaotic situations, but at the same time he remained in control of events. His style was to appear suddenly among the crowds where he was least expected, and then hide before the enemy was able to react. What is interesting is that he was still able, among the chaos, to maintain a very strong connection with the crowd. The enemies of Jesus could not know about his decisions in advance, so he was always one step ahead of his adversaries. They never knew what Jesus would do next, nor did they know where he would or would not appear. Jesus devised his own plan and subsequently imposed it on others. In order to understand the behaviour and the style of Jesus' actions and his covert manner, we need to be able to understand the deepest layers of his personality. He did not rest in a single place for long periods of time. He often changed his location. He moved from place to place frequently. He went from left to right, and from right to left. Wherever his adversaries went to arrest him: he could not be found. Where they least expected him, he would appear!

---

[126] *The Samak's city,* P.N. Khanlary. Tehran. 1988. Agah, p.80. See appendix: **Bihoushaneh & Ayyari**

These are very important points to be taken into consideration in order to understand the manner of Jesus' actions when he confronted his adversaries. If we do not take these facts into consideration, we will not be able to obtain a clear picture of the real events that occurred at the time.

John's most important deeds were his sudden remarks about Christ. With these he focused the attention of the people on Jesus. So, great numbers of people became unexpectedly interested in and attracted to Jesus, and went to him.[127]

Two events

"3 Is not this the carpenter, the son of Mary, the brother of James, and Joses, and of Juda, and Simon? and are not his sisters here with us? And they were offended at him. 4 But Jesus said unto them, A prophet is not without honour, but in his own country, and among his own kin, and in his own house".[128]

Some of the old scriptures of the Essenian and the Israelite manuscripts, (the book of the Prophets and the book of Daniel) contain certain prophesies about Christ, the Saviour, where the characteristics of this person are described in some detail[129] We

---

[127] *The Gospel of St. John*, Ch. 10: 39-42. Persian version p.165.

[128] *The Gospel of St. Mark*, Ch. 6: 3-4.

[129] *Les manuscripts de la mer morte*, E.M. Laperrousaz. Edition P.U.F. (Que sais je?). 2003; *L'attente du Messie en Palestine a la veille et au debut de l'ere Chretienne*. E.M. Laperrousaz. Edition A. et Picard. 1982; *The Gospel of St. John*, first Ch. 44-45 :" 44 Now Philip was of Bethsaida, the city of Andrew and Peter. 45 Philip findeth Nathanael, and saith unto him, We have found him, of whom Moses in the law, and the prophets, did write, Jesus of Nazareth, the son of Joseph". Persian version p.145.

presume that Jesus,[130] as well as John the Baptist, and many others knew all of these descriptions.[131] So, Jesus and John the Baptist knew the characteristics of a person who was prophesized to be Christ. Being Christ meant being the King of the Israelite community. Also, being King of the Israelite community meant ruling over the Clergy's authority (and eliminating the hegemony of foreign enemies, such as the Roman Empire).

One of the things said about the Christ and written in the old manuscripts is the fact that when he appeared, he would go to Jerusalem on the back of a donkey. One day, Jesus asked one of his companions to go and fetch a young donkey, and he went to Jerusalem on the back of the animal in order to fulfil this prediction. People in Jerusalem became very happy to see him: they were waiting for him with a great deal of enthusiasm and they covered his path with date tree leaves as was written in the Old Testament. And they exclaimed: "Welcome, oh king of Israel, Hushianah, Hushianah!"[132]

"1 AND when they came nigh to Jerusalem, unto Bethpage and Bethany, at the Mount of Olives, he sendeth forth **two of his disciples,** *2 And saith unto them, Go your way into the village over against you: and as soon as ye be entered into it, ye shall find a colt tied, whereon never man sat; loose him, and*

---

[130] **The Gospel of St. John**, Ch. 5: 45-46. Persian version p.153, "46 For had ye believed Moses, ye would have believed me: **for he wrote of me. 47 But if ye believe not his writings,** how shall ye believe my words?"

[131] **The Gospel of St. John**, Ch. 4: 25-30, "25 The woman saith unto him, **I know that Messias cometh, which is called Christ: when he is come, he will tell us all things**. 26 Jesus saith unto her, I that speak unto thee am *he*. 27 And upon this came his disciples, and marvelled that he talked with the woman: yet no man said, What seekest thou? or, Why talkest thou with her? 28 The woman then left her water pot, and went her way into the city, and saith to the men, 29 Come, see a man, which told me all things that ever I did: is not this the Christ? 30 Then they went out of the city, and came unto him".

[132] **The Gospel of St. John**, Ch. 12: 13. p. 169. It means 'welcome, welcome'.

bring him. 3 And if any man say unto you, Why do ye this? say ye that the Lord hath need of him; and straightway he will send him hither. 4 And they went their way, and found the colt tied by the door without in a place where two ways met; and they loose him. 5 And certain of them that stood there said unto them, What do ye, loosing the colt? 6 And they said unto them even as Jesus had commanded: and they let them go. 7 And they brought the **colt** *to Jesus, and cast their garments on him; and he sat upon it. 8 And many spread their garments in the way: and others cut down branches off the trees, and strawed them in the way. 9 And they that went before, and they that followed, cried, saying, Hosanna; Blessed is he that cometh in the name of the Lord: 10 Blessed be the kingdom of our father David, that cometh in the name of the Lord: Hosanna in the highest. 11 And Jesus entered into Jerusalem, and into the temple: and when he had looked round about upon all things, and now the eventide was come, he went out unto Bethany with the twelve.'*[133]

The second event was the case of Lazarus who died following an affliction similar to a heart attack. Jesus was asked by Martha, the sister of Lazarus, to come to the body of her brother. Jesus went to Lazarus and used his magnetic and spiritual powers in order to bring him back to life.[134] After that moment, Lazarus, his family, Maria and Martha, told the people about this event wherever they went. They told the people: "Jesus is able to give life to the dead. He is really Christ. He is able to bring back to life a person who has passed away. And it is only Christ who is able to do this. Therefore, Jesus of Nazareth is really the promised Christ."

These two events, the fact that Jesus went to Jerusalem on the back of a donkey and the resurrection of Lazarus proved to be the limit of Pharisees' patience and tolerance. They decided to arrest and kill Jesus

---

[133] *The Gospel of St Mark*, Ch. 11:1-11.

[134] *The Gospel of St. John*, Ch. 11: 1-46. P.v. p 167.

and to finish this matter once and for all. In their opinion, Jesus had crossed the forbidden red line. They heard that people were talking about him.

"31 And many of the people believed on him, and said, When Christ cometh, will he do more miracles than these which this man hath done? 32 The Pharisees heard that the people murmured such things concerning him; and the Pharisees and the chief priests sent officers to take him".[135]

Their fear was based on the thought that if people believed in Jesus as Christ and as the King of the Israelite community they would confront the Roman soldiers in an attempt to end the Roman suppression, something which in turn would result in a bloody confrontation in which the Pharisees and the High Priests would lose their place due to the people's reaction towards the Roman Authorities.

"47 Then gathered the chief priests and the Pharisees a council, and said, What do we? For this man doeth many miracles. 48 If we let him thus alone, all men will believe on him: and the Romans shall come and take away both our place and nation. 49 And one of them, named Caiaphas, being the high priest that same year, said unto them, Ye know nothing at all, 50 Nor consider that it is expedient for us, that one man should die for the people, and that the whole nation perish not. 51 And this spoke he not of himself: but being high priest that year, he prophesied that Jesus should die for that nation; 52 and not for that nation only, but that also he should gather together in one the children of God that were scattered abroad. 53 **Then from that day forth they took counsel together for to put him to death"**.[136]

[135] ***The Gospel of St. John***, Ch. 7: 32-33. Persian version. v.158.

[136] ***The Gospel of St. John***, Ch. 11: 47-53. p.v.166-167.

Thus, they decided to arrest Jesus[137] and to kill him. They not only decided to get rid of Jesus but also to eliminate both John the Baptist and Lazarus.[138] Their first step was to catch John the Baptist and to kill him, because for them he was the easiest target - as he was openly in contact with the people and accepted the hand of any person willing to be initiated. Therefore, he was quickly arrested, imprisoned and decapitated.[139]

When Jesus heard that they had arrested John the Baptist he left the area of Jerusalem and Jordan in order to return to Galilee.

"12 Now when Jesus had heard that John was cast into prison, he departed into Galilee; 13 and leaving Nazareth, he came and dwelt in Capernaum, which is upon the sea coast, in the borders of Zabulon and Nephthalim."[140]

The plan of the Pharisees

In the assembly of the Pharisees there was a man called Joseph of Arimathea.[141] He was very rich and a follower of Jesus, but nobody was aware of his relationship to Jesus. His task was to deliver to Jesus a summary of every meeting of the Assembly. Thus, Jesus knew every

---

[137] *The Gospel of St. John*, Ch. 7: 19. p.v.157: "Did not Moses give you the law, and *yet* none of you keepeth the law? Why go ye about to kill me? "

[138] *The Gospel of St. John*, Ch. 12: 10-11. p.v-.168, Lazarus constantly invited people to believe in Jesus and introduced him as the Christ/ Messiah able to resurrect the dead.

[139] About the martyrdom of St. John the Baptist *the Gospel of St. John* apostle is silent. But in the *Gospel according to St Mark*, chapter 6: 21-29 the event of his arrest and assassination is clarified. P.v- p.63. His sacred head is a in a tomb in the Omaiid Mosque in Damascus in Syria.

[140] *The Gospel of St Matthew*, Ch. 4: 12-13. Persian version. v-5.

[141] El-Birouny names this person "Yousef –e- Ramie", Yousef-e- Ramshani, and Yousef –e- Boulatani, *Asar-ol-bagieh*, p.486.

plan and every programme that the High Priests devised against him. When he discovered their plan to kill him, he, changed his appearance and left the city. He went to a ruin in the desert near the city of Ephraim, where he also gathered his students.

> *"54 Jesus therefore walked no more openly among the Jews; but went thence unto a country near to the wilderness, into a city called Ephraim, and there continued with his disciples".[142]*

As we can see, he is constantly changing his location;[143]he moves between Jerusalem, Galilee, Nazareth, Ghedroun, Ephraim, the river Jordan, the region of Gethsemane, the mountain of Zita, Delmonita, Sur, Sidon, Bethesda, Gennesaret, Bethsaida, Tyre, Decapolis and finally the Sea of Galilee.[144] He commanded his twelve disciples to move two by two[145], and to follow the footsteps of their master. Sometimes Jesus travelled to the top of a mountain in order to pray and to meditate[146], and at other times he walked and gathered in the desert ruins[147] with his disciples. Furthermore, from time to time he would suddenly appear at the houses of his followers[148], knocking at their doors, entering, and spending the night at their house.

---

[142] *The Gospel of St. John*, Ch. 11: 54. Persian version. 167.

[143] *The Gospel of St. Mark*, Ch. 7:24. Persian version. p.66, "And from thence he arose, and went into the borders of Tyre and Sidon, and entered into n house, ªand would have no man know it: but he could not be hid".

[144] *The Gospel of St. Mark*, Ch. 6 & 7 & 8: "And straightway he entered into a ship with his disciples, and came into the parts of Dalmanutha", Chapter 8:10.

[145] *The Gospel of St. Mark*, Ch 6: 7. Persian version. p.62.

[146] *The Gospel of St. Mark*, Ch 6: 45. Persian version. p.64.

[147] *The Gospel of St. Mark*, Ch. 6:31. Persian version. p. 63.

[148] *The Gospel of St. Mark*, Ch. 6:10. Persian version. p. 62.

*"7 And he called unto him the **twelve**, and began **to send them forth by *two* and two;** and gave them power over unclean spirits; 8 And commanded them that they should take nothing for their journey, save a staff only; no scrip, no bread, no money in their purse: 9 But be shod with sandals; and not put on two coats. 10 And he said unto them, in what place so ever ye enter into a house, there abide till ye depart from that place. 11 And whosoever shall not receive you, nor hear you, when ye depart thence, shake off the dust under your feet for a testimony against them. Verily I say unto you, It shall be more tolerable for Sodom and Gomorrah in the day of judgment, than for that city. 12 And they went out, and preached that men should repent. 13 And they cast out many devils, and anointed with oil many that were sick, and healed them.[149]*

30 And the apostles gathered themselves together unto Jesus, and told him all things, both what they had done, and what they had taught. 31 And he said unto them, Come ye yourselves apart into a desert place, and rest a while: 32 And they departed into a *desert* place by ship privately. 33 And the people saw them departing, and many knew him, and ran afoot thither out of all cities, and out went them, and came together unto him. 34 And Jesus, when he came out, saw much people, and was moved with *compassion* toward them, because they were as sheep not having a *shepherd*: and he began to *teach* them many things. 35 And when the day was now far spent, his disciples came unto him, and said, *This* is a desert place, and now the time is far passed: 36 Send them away, that they may go into the country round about, and into the villages, and buy themselves bread: for they have nothing to eat."[150]

While moving, Jesus was certainly aware of the plan and the program devised by his enemies and he named them the children of Iblis

---

[149] *The Gospel of St Mark*, Ch. 6:7-13. Persian version. p. 62.

[150] *The Gospel of St. Mark*, Ch. 6: 30-36. Persian version. p. 63.

(Satan), who would like to follow their father because their father was a murderer from the beginning.[151]

Roman Involvement

The Pharisees and the high priests tried hard to gather information about Jesus' plan of action, his movements and his whereabouts; but they were unsuccessful. So, they changed their plan. They said: "We cannot achieve our plan by ourselves. It is better to go to Pontius Pilate, the Roman governor and ask for his assistance. We will tell him that all of us are the admirers of Caesar in Rome. But this person who[152] is named Jesus of Nazareth pretends to be Christ, and he pretends to be the King of the Israelites. He gathers people to be included in his circle and he wishes to deny the validity of the Roman rule over Israelite land. Therefore, you should arrest him and bring him to court and put an end to his life because we do not want to be associated with and pay for his treacherous activities."

In this way, they wanted to involve the Roman governor in their plans[153] in order to rely on his assistance to achieve the ultimate goal of their strategy. They were certain that when the Roman governor gave the order to arrest Jesus everybody in the land would be under

---

[151] *The Gospel of St. John*, Ch. 8: 44. Persian version. p. 161.

[152] *The Gospel of St. John*, Ch. 19:12-14-15-19. Persian version. p. 181 "12 And from thenceforth Pilate sought to release him: but the Jews cried out, saying, If thou let this man go, thou art not Caesar's friend: whosoever maketh himself a king speaketh against Caesar. 14 and he saith unto the Jews, Behold your King! 15 saith unto them, Shall I crucify your King? The chief priests answered, We have no king but Caesar. 19 And Pilate wrote a title, and put it on the cross. And the writing was, JESUS OF NAZARETH THE KING OF THE JEWS".

[153] *The Gospel of St. Matthew*, Ch. 26: 3-4, Persian version. p.45, *The Qur'an*, Surat 3: v.54. in the Gospel of Matthew the plan of the Pharisees is cited as a "trick". In the Qur'an their plan is named "makr": plan/strategy. In the Qur'an Jesus applies only the "strategy of Allah", which is the best strategy and plan.

pressure to denounce Jesus and to surrender him to his enemies. Once a governmental order was given it became necessary for everyone to adhere to it.

Next, the leader of the Pharisees gave the order that whoever knew the location of Jesus should immediately provide this information to the authorities so that Jesus could be apprehended.

> *"57 Now both the chief priests and the Pharisees had given a commandment, that, if any man knew where he were, he should show it, that they might take him".*[154]

Once this new plan had been implemented, it became extremely risky for Jesus to stay in one particular place for long. The Pharisees were very hopeful that through this new plan they would finally be able to arrest Jesus and put him on the cross so that the threat he presented to them would be eliminated as quickly as possible.

Jesus' reaction

Jesus was aware of the plan that the Pharisees had devised for capturing and eliminating him. Until then he had been very successful in remaining in contact with the people through his own covert style. But when the Pharisees went to involve the Romans he decided to alter his plan and to design a more subtle strategy in order to evade the Pharisees' plan.

The secret plan of Jesus

In reality, the Roman governor was not at all interested in the Jewish community's inner conflicts. The Romans did not know Jesus and they

---

[154] *The Gospel of St. John.* Ch. 11: 57. Persian version. p 181.

were not interested in arresting and killing him. The elimination of Jesus was not the will of the Romans, but the will of the priests.

> 1 After these things Jesus walked in Galilee: for he would not walk in Jewry, **because the Jews sought to kill him.**[155]

The Pharisees and the High Priests' plan focused entirely on the elimination of Jesus and it did not go beyond his removal from the scene. As long as the priests were convinced that Jesus was eliminated they would be satisfied. The Romans would also be happy, once they were convinced that he was eliminated.

Thus, once we take this into consideration, we can see that it was merely enough for Jesus to hide himself for a short while away from the eyes of the people, and to provide the Pharisees with the illusion that he was no longer alive. In that way he could solve his problem forever. He could reappear somewhere else and restart his mission in another way, and not be bothered by anybody. Therefore, it was necessary for Jesus to create for his adversaries the illusion that he was eliminated, so that he would no longer be bothered by them.

When the Pharisees went to Pontius Pilate they asked him to arrest Jesus on Sunday in order for them to have a whole week of torturing and prosecuting him, and finally to fulfil their plans. They insisted that the arrest of Jesus should occur in the coming week starting on Sunday. They wanted to keep Jesus on the cross for one whole week so that everybody could see Jesus on the cross and so that his fate would act as an example to others who intended to confront the High Priests.

However, if Jesus was arrested between on Thursday night and Friday, then the Priests would be forced to complete their plan by Friday, as

---

[155] *The Gospel of St. John.* Ch. 7: 1. Persian version. p 156.

the following day was the Sabbath. It was also necessary for them to arrest Jesus soon and not delay his arrest - as they did not want to risk losing him again. Furthermore, the High Priests were under the illusion that their plan was still secret, as they did not know about the disciple of Jesus who was in their midst and who kept Jesus constantly informed.

They were planning to arrest Jesus on Sunday. It was this that they asked from the Romans. But Jesus was informed about all of these conspiracies and he knew that they would not be satisfied until he was dead.[156]

So, in order to give them the illusion that they had killed him, before he could leave Palestine forever; he made a new plan in response to the High Priests' plan. **He managed to impose on the enemies his own timeframe for his arrest.** Jesus' plan would be realised at a very high price because its fulfilment required someone to sacrifice his life in order for the plan to be accomplished. In fact, Jesus wanted to escape the trap which was suddenly set for him, and to make a new start with his mission. For this, it was necessary to give his adversaries the impression that they had succeeded in their aim and had in fact eliminated him.

The qualities of a spiritual actor

To maintain this illusion, someone was needed who would sacrifice his life for Jesus, and who would introduce himself as Jesus to be arrested in his place. So this person would need to answer the question posed by Jesus' enemies when they asked "Who is Jesus among you?" He

---

[156] *The Gospel of St. John*. Ch. 7:19 & 30. Persian version. p. 157: "19 Why go ye about to kill me? 30 Then they sought to take him: but no man laid hands on him, because his hour was not yet come".

would have to answer: "I am". After this, he would be arrested and would be escorted to his own execution by his enemies.

This person had to be a volunteer and act as a replacement for Jesus on the cross. A person with a pure heart was needed, who would die for his master. This person needed to have certain qualities: he had to live like Jesus, he needed to have a deep heart connection to Jesus, he had to be able to keep this secret in his heart forever and never discuss it with anybody else. He had to be the type of person of whom nobody expected to carry out such a sacrifice. It had to be a deep secret that this person should never tell anyone and which he would have to take with him into the grave. By eliciting information from various texts we have tried to collect different pieces of this mysterious puzzle, in an attempt to put them together again. Furthermore, it is not only the case of the sacrifice which is important in this affair. In addition to the actual sacrifice, this person had to be ready *to be blamed* by all coming generations. He had to perform an act as the result of a secret only known to him and his master.[157]

Collecting and re-assembling the mysterious puzzle

Ordinary people tend to take superficial glances only and do not delve into the deeper layer of important events. Thus, their judgements tend to be superficial, too. They look at the surface and judge on the basis of what they see and not on the basis of what lies beneath the façade. People's superficial judgements make them very quick in attributing blame. People often blame others without looking at all the facts, while a knight is a person who does the right thing only for his

---

[157] There are several new proposals about the event of the crucifixion. The last one is proposed by the **National Geographic,** in a video documentary-cum-reconstruction. It is concluded that Judas was not a traitor but a missionary of Jesus to betray him and to prepare his assassination!! In the Qur'an, the idea of Jesus' crucifixion is rejected, and there is a discussion about the complicated plan of Jesus.

beloved. Moreover, a knight is ready to keep secrets in his heart and he is willing to accept the blame which people may thoughtlessly attribute to him. The only thing that is important in a knight's eyes is the satisfaction of his Beloved. For Jesus' plan to be successful, a man was needed who possessed all these qualities.

This plan had to be composed of series of steps, each of which had to be carried out by different people who were only connected to Jesus. So, in a way Jesus' plan can be viewed as series of different pieces which then made up one big puzzle. The puzzle was formed by Jesus' thought processes, but each person was responsible for his/her own pieces, remaining unaware of the connection between each of the different pieces. Each person had no prior knowledge about the exact time that the other pieces were going to be involved. Earlier, we spoke about the fact that Jesus used to teach in public, in small groups and individually.

It was an ingenious plan. Once we approach the event of the crucifixion from this angle, we can understand how this plan was accomplished. And if we consider the event from this perspective, we discover a new reality within the actions of Jesus. Jesus used a secret language between himself and each of his companions. This language consisted of a series of secret codes which were only understood by Jesus and by the specific disciple who was responsible for his individual piece of the plan.

Jesus was used to using coded symbols, for example when he was talking in the crowd, and during his discussions he would use certain coded language.[158] That way, only a person who was aware of this language was able to understand these words and know what Jesus was

---

[158] *The Gospel of St. John*, Ch. 16: 18. Persian version. p.176.

talking about.[159] Others who were present heard the words and thought that they understood what Jesus wanted to teach them. But in reality, Jesus' words contained a hidden layer that was only meant for certain students and his companions.

"25 And there are also many other things which Jesus did, the which, if they should be written every one, I suppose that even the world itself could not contain the books that should be written."[160]

Gathering twelve people (apostles)

As was mentioned earlier, Jesus selected twelve people from all of his followers.[161] He concluded a particular pact with them. These people had already been initiated by his hand and had been connected to the chain of initiation. But when he compiled this new group, he concluded a new pact with them. All of them, one by one, were ready to sacrifice their lives for Jesus. When Jesus selected these individuals the first question he asked was: "Would you like to go or would you like to stay? The door is open. So will you stay or will you go?"[162] One by one they answered: "Where can we go? Our life is due to the source of your teachings. So where can we go without you?"[163] Thus, these twelve individuals became the central part of the organisation which played a crucial role in the most important activities.

---

[159] No pearl for the swines, but everyone is thought on his own level. *The Gospel of Philip*, NHC II.3, codex page 81, Robinson p.157.

[160] *The Gospel of St. John*, Ch. 21: 25 Persian version. p.186.

[161] *The Gospel of St. John*, Ch. 6: 66.

[162] *The Gospel of St. John*, Ch. 6: 67.

[163] *The Gospel of St. John*, Ch. 6: 68-70.

"Jesus answered them, Have not I chosen you twelve, and one of you is a devil?"[164]

Who was the disloyal/evil member?

Who is this evil one? The first thought that comes to mind is Judas. Of course, but why? Is it not because St. John pointed his finger at him in his Gospel?[165] However, in reality. Jesus himself, according to all of the canonical Gospels, did not describe Judas as a devil. The only time when Jesus describes one of the twelve apostles as a devil or Satan occurred in the case of St. Simon-Peter.

> "33 But when he had turned about and looked on his disciples, **he rebuked Peter, saying, Get thee behind me, Satan**: for thou savour not the things that be of God, but the things that be of men".[166]

The twelve apostles knew each other, and they had all joined their master for the Last Supper. It seems that Jesus chose special codes to communicate with each one of them.

From the very beginning, when Jesus created the group of twelve apostles, he set them certain rules. One of these rules was that no member of this organisation should travel alone. For each task and activity that needed to be carried out, Jesus insisted that they be performed by at least two members of the group and never alone.[167] Two by two the apostles were sent to perform different tasks and to realise different missions. Hence, the apostles were either on a mission

---

[164] *The Gospel of St. John*, Ch. 6:70.

[165] "71 He spake of Judas Iscariot *the son* of Simon: for he it was that should betray him, being one of the twelve. *The Gospel of St. John*, Ch. 6: 71.

[166] *The Gospel of St. Mark*, Ch. 8: 33- Persian version. p.33.

[167] *The Gospel of St. Mark*, Ch. 6: 7. Persian version. p.62.

as a pair, or in the circle of twelve around their master, in the corner of a ruin, reporting about their activities.[168] It is clear that Jesus was very careful about this aspect of security and safety. He did not leave anybody on his own because it was all too easy for a single person to fall into the trap prepared by the enemy and to become an enemy informer or a double agent. When they operated as duos and one of them would come under the influence of the enemy, the other one could go to Jesus immediately and inform him. This was one aspect of the safety, solidarity and security measures in this organisation which occupied a central place in Jesus' activities.

It is certain that when the Pharisees and the Romans wanted to arrest Jesus, the easiest way to approach Jesus was through one of the apostles, or one of the friends who was a member of Jesus' inner circle. Certainly a great risk existed for each one of them to fall into enemy traps. However, when they always moved in pairs, and when they were in contact with the people should a problem arise or some accident happen, then the whole organisation could be informed about it immediately. This was the best way to protect the organisation against infiltration and to prevent enemy access to the group. It shows the importance of the security details in the eyes of Jesus[169].

It is true that some of Jesus' faithful disciples were among the members of the high priests of the supreme hierarchy of the Jewish clergy[170], but on the on the other hand none of the twelve apostles were supposed to be under the influence of the enemy, or to conspire against Jesus in secret. This was not easily possible, because everybody

---

[168] *The Gospel of St. Mark*, Ch. 6: 30-31. Persian version. p.63.

[169] The reader may have the impression here of a Jesus who is scared to lose his body. We therefore wish to stress and remind the reader that it was his *mission* which was of paramount importance to Jesus. The teachings to the disciples had just begun in this period.

[170] The technical term "infiltrated agents".

was watched by his companion. The only way for one of the group members to be sent on a mission alone would be if that person was sent by Jesus himself; aware of certain details that nobody else knew. For this reason, if Jesus wanted to send off a certain member on his own, he first had to separate this member from the rest of the group under a certain pretext (for instance to instruct him), after which he could send him on a certain mission whilst it would appear to others that this person was still in his company.

Therefore, the separation of a sole member from the group was only possible under the direct order and the guidance of Jesus himself. This type of mission, (i.e. to send somebody alone on Jesus' own command) happened at least twice: it happened to Judas.[171]

Other parallel organisations

The twelve apostles were not the only organisation working for Jesus and carrying out a variety of tasks. There were other organisations as well, running parallel to the twelve apostles.

One must also note that the only reason we know so much about the activities of the twelve apostles is because St. John, who was also an apostle, in his writings provides us with detailed accounts of their activities. However, since the other apostles presumably were not members of other organisations, we are unable to gather substantial information about their activities through the canonical Gospels.

---

[171] *The Gospel of St. John*, Ch. 13: 27-30. Persian version. p.172: Then said Jesus unto him (Judas), That thou doest, do quickly. Now no man at the table knew for what intent he spake this unto him. For some of them thought, because Judas had the bag, that Jesus had said unto him, Buy those things that we have need of against the feast; or, that he should give something to the poor. He then having received the sop went immediately out: and it was night.

Jesus had devised a complex plan in response to his enemies' strategy. He had a number of undercover agents who had managed to infiltrate the group of Pharisees[172], and amongst the Roman government and soldiers.[173] All of these agents worked in parallel, without knowing about one another's existence.

For example, one of the groups had the important responsibility to prepare a particular narcotic type of anaesthetic solution. Another responsibility was to take this liquid/narcotic composition one way or another to the cross during the act of crucifixion, and to exchange it with the water jar.[174] However, it is clear that it was not water at all, but

---

[172] One of these secret contacts with the heads of the hierarchy of the Pharisees is explained in the *Gospel of St. John*, Ch. 3: 1-5. "1 There was a man of the Pharisees, named **Nicodemus, a ruler of the Jews**: 2 The same came to Jesus by night, and said unto him, Rabbi, we know that thou art a teacher come from God: for no man can do these miracles that thou doest, except God be with him. 3 Jesus answered and said unto him, Verily, verily, I say unto thee, except a man be born again, he cannot see the kingdom of God. 4 Nicodemus saith unto him, how can a man be born when he is old? Can he enter the second time into his mother's womb, and be born? 5 Jesus answered..."

[173]. the *Gospel of St. John*, Ch. 19: 38 Persian verson.182 " And after this Joseph of Arimathaea, being a disciple of Jesus, but secretly for fear of the Jews, besought Pilate", *The Gospel of Luke*, Ch. 23: 50-52. Persian version. p.139 " 50 And, behold, there was a man named Joseph, a counsellor; and he was a good man, and a just: 51 (The same had not consented to the counsel and deed of them ;) he was of Arimathaea, a city of the Jews: who also himself waited for the kingdom of God. 52 This man went unto Pilate"

[174] *The Gospel of St. John*, Ch. 19: 29 Persian version.182 *The Gospel of Mark*, chapter 15: 36. Persian version. p. 84, *the Gospel of St. Luke*, ch.24. 35; *the Gospel of Matthew*. Ch. 27: 34 & 48, Persian version. p. 50-51. This passage reminds us of *The city of Samak*, p.78: The vapour of the medicine mixed in the wine penetrated in the brain of "Magogar", he lost his awareness, and the cup fell down from his hand ...His head turned, and without any control he fell down in a coma [bi-houshi]". *The Samak's city"* P.N. Khanlary. Tehran. 1988. Agah, p.77-78. See appendix: Bihoushaneh and the path of Ayyari.

"wine/ vinegar mingled with myrrh/gall".[175]   Its effect was that of a powerful anaesthetic. This powerful liquid was used to cause a person to fall into a cataleptic coma. Simply smelling a small dose of it was enough to put a person into a deep cataleptic coma, with the body becoming as rigid as a corpse.

At the same time there was another liquid, similar to a perfume composition extracted from a particular flower and combined with another solution named 'morr'.

> *"39 And there came also* **Nicodemus,** *who at the first came to Jesus by night, and brought a mixture of myrrh and aloes, about a hundred pound weight."*[176]

This second solution was used to annihilate the effects of the narcotic liquid. Thus, the first liquid was used to put a person into a cataleptic coma, whilst the second solution was used to annihilate the effect of the first and to bring him back to consciousness.

The narcotic and anti-narcotic compositions were prepared by a group of Jewish women leaded by Mary Magdalene. Jesus named them the **"daughters of Jerusalem".**[177]   Many questions spring to mind here. How did they bring these two compositions to the centre stage of the crucifixion? How did they bring them near the mouth and the nose of

---

[175] They wanted to give him to drink "the wine **mingled with gall".** *The Gospel of St Matthew.* Ch. 27.34. "The New testament. Edited by The Gideons International. 1967. p 28 & 46. In The Persian version of *The New Testament* it is written: "mingled with[175] They wanted to give him to drink "**the wine mingled with myrrh**", *Gospel of St. Mark.* Ch.15. 23; "They wanted to give him to drink the "**vinegar** *The* Morr".

[176] *The Gospel of St. John,* Ch. 19: 39 Persian version .182.

[177] Robert B. Greenblatt, M.D. *Search the Scriptures. Illustrated Modern Medicine and Biblical Personages.* The Parthenon Press. 1985. pp 107-109. See the appendix.

the person on the cross? How did they bring down the person from the cross in order to use the anti-narcotic for him to regain consciousness?

> *"40 Then took they the body of Jesus, and wound it in linen clothes with the spices, as the manner of the Jews is to bury."*[178]

All of these steps go to show that a highly sophisticated organisation, charged with various different responsibilities and missions, was needed to accomplish Jesus' plan. To achieve such a complex plan required many people to work in parallel. This can be seen from the following sections.

> *"59 **Joseph** took the body and covered it with pure cotton, 60 and buried him in a new carved stony tomb that he had done before for him-self, and put on it a big stone"*[179]

It was not easy to use the narcotic solution. They needed to use this narcotic composition when the person on the cross gave them a secret message or signal:

> *"34 And at the ninth hour Jesus cried with a loud voice, saying, Eloi, Eloi, lama sabachthani?"*[180]

---

[178] ***The Gospel of St. John***, Ch. 19: 40 Persian version .183.

[179] ***The Gospel of St. Matthew***, Ch. 27: 49-50 Persian version. p.51.

[180] ***The Gospel of St. Mark***, Ch. 15: 34. What does it mean? This sentence is not translated in any of the Gospels. It is unclear what the exact sentence was that the man on the cross pronounced. If Jesus spoke in Aramean, it should be similar to Arabic. In the Arabic language, this sentence is meaningful and perfectly grammatical: "My God, My God, for you wrote before in my destiny." But when the person on the cross uttered this sentence in a loud voice, people interpreted it to mean that he was thirsty, And they brought him the liquid! In the Gospel of St Mark this sentence is interpreted as follows: "My God, my God, why hast thou forsaken me?" ***The Gospel of St. Mark***, Ch.15: 34. In the Gospel of Matthew the sentence is

By hearing this secret sentence, people began to talk to each other: "What is this man saying and what does he mean?"

> *"35 And some of them that stood by, when they heard it, said, Behold, he calleth Elias."*[181]

At that moment, an unknown person leaves the crowd and brings the liquid near the nose of the person on the cross.

> *"29 Now there was set a vessel full of vinegar*[182] *36 And* **one** *ran and filled a sponge full of vinegar, and put it on a reed, and gave him to drink, saying, Let alone; let us see* **whether Elias will come to take him down.**[183] *30 When Jesus therefore had received the vinegar, he said, It is finished: and he bowed his head*[184] *37 And Jesus cried with a loud voice, and gave up the ghost."*[185]

So, it is quite clear that with the help of the mysterious liquid (vinegar) the person on the cross fell into a state of deep unconsciousness. His loss of consciousness cannot be the effect of the crucifixion. It cannot have been anything else but a very powerful narcotic composition.

---

cited by this manner: Ili, Ili, **lama sabachthani**? And interpreted like this:" My God, my God, why hast thou forsaken me?" *The Gospel of St. Matthew,* Ch.27: 46. In the Gospel of St Luke this secret language is not mentioned, it only states: " 46 And when Jesus had cried with a loud voice, he said, Father, into thy hands I commend my spirit: and having said thus, he gave up the ghost". *The Gospel of St. Luke,* Ch.23: 46. In *the Gospel of St. John* it is written that Jesus said "I am thirsty": "28 After this, Jesus knowing that all things were now accomplished, that the scripture might be fulfilled, saith, I thirst". Ch.19: 28.

[181] *The Gospel of St. Mark.* Ch.15:35.

[182] *The Gospel of St. John.* Ch. 19.

[183] *The Gospel of St. Mark.* Ch. 19.

[184] *The Gospel of St. John.* Ch. 19:30.

[185] *The Gospel of St. Mark.* Ch. 15:37.

Still, the question remains how to achieve this effect and be certain that the right quantity is given to the person on the cross - so that he is not killed? This requires a great deal of care and knowledge about the way to act and to prevent the person on the cross staying there for too long.

It took an ordinary person on the cross an average eleven hours to die. But when they administered this narcotic type of anaesthetic to the person crucified, he had only spent three hours on the cross.[186] After he was exposed to this anaesthetic, he immediately fell into a cataleptic coma. After this, he had to be taken down from the cross quickly in order not to risk his life. So, part of the plan was to put this person on the cross and then to render him unconscious before finally taking him down from the cross.

After putting the man on the cross into a deeply unconscious state, the secret students of Jesus[187] who were in the hierarchy of the Jewish clergy (for instance Joseph and Nicodemous) convinced the others not to let the bodies of all those that had been crucified together stay on the cross - since the Sabbath was drawing near.

> *"31 The Jews therefore, because it was the preparation, that the bodies should not remain upon the cross on the Sabbath day, (for that Sabbath day was a high day,) besought Pilate ... that they might be taken away".[188]*

So, the members of clergy decided to send someone to Pilate to ask him to allow the bodies to be brought down from their crosses.

---

[186] ***The Gospel of St. Mark***, Ch. 15: 33-34.

[187] ***The Gospel of St. John***. Ch.19: 38-39: "38 And after this Joseph of Arimathaea, being a disciple of Jesus, but secretly for fear of the Jews, besought Pilate that he might take away the body of Jesus: and Pilate gave him leave. He came therefore, and took the body of Jesus. 39 And there came also Nicodemus"

[188] ***The Gospel of St. John***. Ch.19: 31-33.

"43 Joseph of Arimathaea ... came, and went in boldly unto Pilate, and craved the body of Jesus. 44 And Pilate marvelled if he were already dead: and calling unto him the centurion, he asked him whether he had been any while dead. 45 And when he knew it of the centurion, he gave the body to Joseph".[189]

To accomplish this complicated plan, it was necessary that different people in different positions were ready to do their tasks and take on their responsibilities. So, each task had to be performed one after the other in chronological order. Therefore, considerable discipline and awareness were required in performing these actions: everything had to run like clockwork.

After bringing the body down from the cross they immediately covered it from head to toe. They covered the body in order to prevent anybody from discovering his true identity. All the Gospels attest to the fact that they brought the complete body down from the cross.

"50 Joseph, (…) 51 of Arimathaea, a city of the Jews 52 (...) went unto Pilate, and begged the body of Jesus. 53 And he took it down, and wrapped it in linen, and laid it in a sepulchre that was hewn in stone, wherein never man before was laid".[190]

Before the actual crucifixion took place, every precaution was taken for each member of Jesus' family to be sent to their respective houses so that they were not involved in the event of crucifixion.

---

[189] ***The Gospel of Mark***, Ch.15: 43-45. It is written in ***the Gospel of St. John*** that they broke the legs of two other crucified persons, because they were still alive, and risked to escape, but they did not break the leg of the third crucified person, because they supposed him "gone". ***The Gospel of St. John***, Ch. 19: 32-33: "32 Then came the soldiers, and brake the legs of the first, and of the other who was crucified with him. 33 But when they came to Jesus, and saw that he was dead already, they break not his legs".

[190] ***The Gospel of St. Luke***, Ch. 23: 50-53.

"25 Now there stood by the cross of Jesus his mother, and his mother's sister, Mary the wife of Cleophas, and Mary Magdalene. 26 When Jesus therefore saw his mother, and the disciple standing by, whom he loved, he saith unto his mother, Woman, behold thy son! 27 Then saith he to the disciple, Behold thy mother! And from that hour that disciple took her unto his own home."[191]

The other part of the plan was to prepare a particular type of tomb, close to the place of the crucifixion. The tomb had been prepared in Joseph's private garden next to Golgota. In accordance with a secret plan, Joseph had previously prepared a deep tomb for this purpose.

*"41 Now in the place where he was crucified there was a garden; and in the garden a new sepulchre, wherein was never man yet laid. 42 There they laid Jesus therefore because of the Jews' preparation day; **for the sepulchre was nigh at hand.**"*[192]

It is written in the Gospel of St Matthew that Joseph buried him in a new tomb, a tomb he himself had carved out in the stone some time before.[193] They had chosen this particular garden for the tomb because of its close proximity to the crucifixion place and in order to avoid a

---

[191] ***The Gospel of St. John***, Ch.19: 50-25-27. Saint John wrote that immediately after Jesus was crucified he himself took the hand of Saint Mary and brought her to his own house. So they were absent when the event of the crucifixion happened. The reports we have after this point stem from others: Saint John was absent. When he writes in his book: "When they wanted to bring him down a Roman soldier touched his ribs with his spear" the matter remains uncertain. This fact is not reported in any other Gospels other than the Gospel of Saint John, and Saint John was not an eyewitness at the time. In ***The Gospel of St. John***, chapter 19: 35 it is written that the author reports the event from the eyewitness reports presented by somebody else: "35 And he that saw it bare record, and his record is true: and he knoweth that he saith true, that ye might believe".

[192] ***The Gospel of St. John***, Ch.19: 41, ***The Gospel of St. Luke***, ch 23: 53, ***The Gospel of St. Mark***. Ch 15: 46.

[193] ***The Gospel of St. Matthew***. Ch. 27: 60.

funeral. The plan was to remove the crucified person quickly, away from the eyes of the public, and to send the crowd back home. Then, Joseph asked some of the Roman centurions to watch the tomb.[194]

They did not use an old tomb but a new one, especially prepared for the case. The tomb was deeper than an ordinary tomb. How do we know the tomb was deeper than usual? Because Peter went into this tomb to see if it was empty. This shows that it was indeed a deep tomb[195]. They made it such a deep tomb because it was necessary for to retain enough air after they had laid the body in it and closed it with a heavy stone.[196] After this event, the people had to be sent home and time was needed for the stone to be removed in order to give the person in the tomb the anti-narcotic. During this period, the comatose person would still be in need of fresh air in order to be able to breathe. All of these steps were calculated ahead of time when the custom-made tomb was built for this purpose.

It is also clear that the group of undercover agents including Joseph, Nicodemus and other Jewish secret followers of Jesus were afraid that other disciples and students would come in the night and try to steal the body, and thus thwart their secret plan. This is specifically mentioned in the Gospel of St. Matthew:

> Joseph said to Pilate: "64 Command therefore that the sepulchre be made sure until the third day, lest his disciples come by night, and steal him away, and say unto the people, He is risen from the dead: so the last error shall be worse than the first. 65 Pilate said unto them, Ye have a watch: go your way, make it as sure as ye

---

[194] Pilate told him: "take some soldiers to take care of the tomb as you wish. So they went and sealed the tomb and it was watched by the guards." *The Gospel of St. Matthew,* Ch. 27: 65-66.

[195] *The Gospel of St. John,* chapter 20: 5.

[196] *The Gospel of Matthew,* ch.27: 60.

can. 66 So they went, and made the sepulchre sure, sealing the stone, and setting a watch."[197]

They told Jesus' other followers and the women: "To come back Sunday because tomorrow is Saturday, and it's the Sabbath".

"56 And they returned, and prepared spices and ointments; and rested the Sabbath day according to the commandment."[198]

All of this was part of an intricate plan carried out by different people, step by step and in proper chronological order. The person who brought the narcotic liquid near the nose of the person on the cross must have been absolutely unknown to the majority of Jesus' companions (including the twelve apostles and the women who were friends of Jesus). This person then disappeared from the crowd, fetched the liquid and carried out his task. He completed this act when the person on the cross said that he was thirsty. This was the signal he wanted. People thought that water was given, but it was no water.

Thus, a number of people collaborated in order to give the impression that Jesus was crucified and died on the cross. This illusion was not only for the benefit of Pharisees and the Romans, but for everybody. Each person who had performed a piece of this plan also believed that Jesus had died on the cross. Even the eleven disciples thought that Jesus had died on the cross. Only the person on the cross, Jesus himself, Joseph, Judas, and Nicodemus knew the depths and the layers of this plan. Such depth of illusion was needed in order to make the plan effective and convincing.

Jesus needed the purest and sincerest of people. From the number of people around him he selected several and created different

[197] *The Gospel of Matthew.* Ch. 27: 64-66.

[198] *The Gospel of St. Luke*, Ch. 23: 56.

organisations with various positions for his people in order for them to carry out different missions. One by one, the twelve apostles resembled Jesus: it seemed as if there were twelve versions of Jesus.[199] Jesus selected them one by one and educated them according to the method of substantial evolution.

Love & Blame

Each of Jesus' disciples felt a deep love for his master and was ready and willing to sacrifice his life for him. But none of them were ready to sacrifice his position and place for another disciple. Each one of them strove to be the best and the closest disciple of Jesus. Jesus formed different organisations in order to let his disciples work with each other, in an atmosphere of brotherhood and loving cooperation, rather than competition.

The inner connection of this group sprung from their love for Jesus. During the last night he spent with them, Jesus explained and stressed the importance of love. He told them that the sign of a good seeker is to be in love. "The person who is in love with me is a person who respects my orders, guidance and applies what I am telling him. Whoever loves me is also cared for by my father and I will reveal myself to him".[200] Jesus was a very kind teacher but at the same time he was also a very strict disciplinarian, closely watching his students. He told them that the gate was always open if anyone would want to leave.[201] But those who would like to stay with Jesus needed to be in a state of ceaseless love and to think about nothing else but love. Jesus told them that it was necessary not only to sacrifice your life for others

---

[199] **Gospel of Thomas** Logion 23: 'I shall choose you, one out of a thousand, and two out of ten thousand, and they shall stand as a single one.' Logion 108: 'Whoever drinks from my mouth shall become as I am, and I myself will become he.'

[200] **The Gospel of St. John.** Ch 14: 21.

[201] **The Gospel of St. John.** Ch: 67.

but also to be ready to accept the blame for others without providing any explanation or showing any kind of reaction. A lover must be ready to accept blame.

Where are you from?

> *"41 The Jews then murmured at him. 42 And they said, Is not this Jesus, the son of Joseph, whose father and mother we know? how is it then that he saith, I came down from heaven? 43 Jesus therefore answered and said unto them, Murmur not among yourselves. 44 No man can come to me, except the Father which hath sent me draw him: and I will raise him up at the last day.* ‹[202]*

One of the subjects of great interest to the students of Jesus concerns the origin of their teacher. They asked him: "Where do you come from?" - because it was said that Christ was from unknown origins. Nobody knew his origins. And the priests talked to their communities and said: "We know from which family he is coming. We know his father, mother and his brothers and sisters. So Jesus is a known person and not an unknown person. Therefore, he is lying when he pretends to be Christ." For this reason Jesus left his own place of birth and said: "Nobody can be a Prophet in his own city." In the company of his students he was exposed to these types of questions: "What is your origin, where are you from?" In the next gatherings Jesus introduced himself to his companions and:

> *"14 Jesus answered and said unto them, Though I bear record of myself, yet my record is true: for I know whence I came, and whither I go; but ye cannot tell whence I come, and whither I go. 15 Ye judge after the flesh; I judge no man.* '[203]

---

[202] *The Gospel of St. John.* Ch. 6: 41-44.

[203] *The Gospel of St. John.* Ch. 8: 14-15.

"23 And he said unto them, Ye are from beneath; I am from above: ye are of this world; I am not of this world."

In the Gospel of Thomas (Logion 13) Jesus himself asks his disciples: 'Make a comparison to me, and tell me whom I am like.' Jesus explained to them: "When love takes possession of the student's soul he becomes very humble and he reaches to a point that nobody can reach." Jesus explained all of this, and many people believed in him. He also told them that "if you remain respectful to what I am saying, you will be the real disciples of mine and you will know God and God will give you back your freedom."

"31 Then said Jesus to those Jews who believed in him, If ye continue in my word, then are ye my disciples indeed; 32 And ye shall know the truth, and the truth shall make you free.'[204]

On the day before the Romans tried to arrest him, the students received more knowledge about their master.

"29 His disciples said unto him; Lo, now speakest thou plainly, and speakest no proverb. 30 Now are we sure that thou knowest all things, and needest not that any man should ask thee: by this we believe that thou camest forth from God.'[205]

---

[204] *The Gospel of St. John.* Ch. 8: 31-32.

[205] *The Gospel of St. John.* Ch.16: 29-30. "29 His disciples said unto him Lo, now speakest thou plainly, and speakest no proverb. 30 Now are we sure that thou knowest all things, and needest not that any man should ask thee: by this we believe that thou camest forth from God. "

Jesus' dialogue with Judas Iscariot

Once he asked his disciples to sit down in a circle.

> *"1 And it came to pass, when Jesus had finished all these sayings, he said unto his disciples, 2 Ye know that after two days is the feast of the Passover, and* **the Son of man** *is betrayed to be crucified."*[206]

> *Then he asked them: "Which one of you can tell me from where I come from?" All of them remained silent except Judas Iscariot."*

Obviously, during the gathering Jesus did not mention who was to be arrested and how. The secret was absolute. So, this was the beginning of the implementation of his plan. The Gospel of Judas confronts us with considerable important and valuable information which can lead us to the truth behind the events that occurred.

Jesus is among his apostles when he asks them: "Who knows where I come from?" Nobody seems to know, and everybody is silent until Judas asks permission to speak. He says:

> *"I know from where you come. You come from the world of Barbelo and I don't dare to introduce your sender."*[207]

Jesus then tells him to step away from the group and to accompany him.[208] He tells him that he would like to talk to him about the secrets of God's kingdom in a private discussion. No one else is present

---

[206] ***The Gospel of St. Matthew.*** Ch. 26: 1-2.

[207] ***The Gospel of Judas,*** the website of the National Geographic publication-internet; and the translation in French version p. 25, Flammarion, 2006.

[208] ***The Gospel of Judas,*** French publication, p. 26: "*Separe toi des autres et je te dirai les mysteres du Royaume de Dieu Supreme*". This is exactly what happened to Thomas in the aforementioned Logion 13, (***the Gospel of Thomas***) where Thomas is the one who gives the right answer and is given secret teachings. We find the same in **the Gospel of Mary**, so it is not exclusive to Judas.

during this discussion. Consequently, this dialogue is not mentioned in any other Gospel. There are many other personal dialogues and experiences which are not mentioned in other Gospels. Therefore, it is reasonable to conclude that if something is not mentioned in other Gospels it does not invalidate the stories reported there or make them insignificant.

Jesus calls Judas from the group and starts to explain the origin of the soul to him; its travels from its origin and the greatness of the invisible world. Judas asks Jesus questions about destiny, the stars and the predestination of everybody, differences between people in the moment of creation, the path of substantial evolution, the reality of Sofia, and the corruptible Sofia that can never reach a state of perfection.[209] Jesus answers all his questions one by one. The teachings of Jesus to Judas are priceless. There are very important lessons to be learned from them. It shows the difference in level exhibited by his students, and the different levels of his teachings according to their level of spiritual evolution.[210]

Sacrifice in love

What we can learn from his lessons is that Jesus was preparing the minds and souls of his disciples in order to realise a very important and exceptional mission. The mission for him entailed sacrificing a person who clad his master (covering him by resembling him) instead of his master.[211] Jesus told him: "Judas, you will pass every level and every

---

[209] *The Gospel of Judas,* French version, p. 25.

[210] In this respect, the reader is invited to read the last part of *the Gospel of Mary,* from the Berlin Codex, where the other disciples are astonished about the content and depth of Jesus' teachings to Mary of Magdalene (Berlin Codex I:16, page 1122) and: Robinson, p. 526-527and *The Nagh Hammadi Scriptures, Berlin Code I, The Gospel of Mary Magdalene* 16-17.

[211] *The Gospel of Judas,* French version, p. 49.

degree because you are willing to sacrifice the person who clothes me"[212] In the English version (as is stated in the French version) prepared by Kasser and Meyer we read: 'But you will exceed all of them. **For you will sacrifice the man that clothes me.**' And in the edition Pagels/King we find: 'As for you, you will surpass them all. For you will sacrifice the human being who bears me.'

Here, we express our doubts regarding the exactness of the interpretation of this text as rendered by National Geographic, Pagels/King and Kasser & Meyer, and we put forward our own proposal - as described in our Global View (pages 8 to 13 of this book). Their interpretation of the sentence of "labassani[213]" / concerning the "envelope charnelle" - i.e. "the material body" of Jesus himself - does not sound exact. Moreover, it does not fit in with Muslim texts (the Qur'an's version and Majmal ot-Tavarikh val Ghesas), and it is in contradiction with the text of *the Gospel of St. Luke.*[214]

The book of Judas is composed of 32 pages; 20 pages are lost. In the twelve pages that exist the sacrifice is mentioned and giving one's life for a certain cause. In other Gospels we can observe similar teachings.

> *"12 This is my commandment, That ye love one another, as I have loved you.*
> *13 **Greater love hath no man than this, that a man lays down his life for his friends**. 14 Ye are my friends, if ye do whatsoever I command you.* '[215]

---

[212] Jesus dit a Judas "*Mais tu les surpasseras tous! Car tu sacrifieras l'homme qui me sert d'habit (envelope charnelle)*" Ibid p.32.

[213] 'qui me sert d'habit' from the French version (p.32) and 'who clothes me' in the English

[214] See the conclusion of this book.

[215] *The Gospel of St. John.* Ch.15: 12-14.

Here, a mention is included of the ultimate sign of love, which refers to a person who is willing to sacrifice his life for his friends. "If you apply this, and realise my wish, you are my lovers and my friends". Here, Jesus provides clear instructions about the principle of sacrifice as the ultimate sign of love. But he also mentions that a lover who sacrifices his life for a beloved like Jesus never dies, but becomes eternal. When a person expresses such a degree of Divine love, in reality he reaches a state of true resurrection and eternal life.

> *"I am the resurrection, and the life: he that believeth in me, though he were dead, yet shall he live: 26 And whosoever liveth and believeth in me shall never die".*[216]

On another occasion, Jesus introduces himself as the door to eternal perfection and eternity. Therefore, whoever sacrifices his life for Jesus without asking anything in return, and whoever is willing to bear the blame of all the coming generations, is the real lover who will reach substantial evolution.

> *"9 I am the door: by me if any man enter in, he shall be saved, and shall go in and out, and find pasture".*[217]

The lessons about the sacrifice for the beloved explained by Jesus and his disciples' readiness for being sacrificed were both necessary in order for him to realise this complex mission. Every disciple was willing to give up his or her life in order to let their master escape alive.[218] Still, this was not the relevant question. The only relevant question in the minds of his disciples was whose offer for being

---

[216] *The Gospel of St. John.* Ch.11: 25-27.

[217] *The Gospel of St. John.* Ch.10: 9.

[218] *The Gospel of St. John.* Ch.13: 37-38. Peter mentions here that he is ready to dedicate his life to Jesus.

sacrificed would be accepted by Jesus. For this reason they were jealous of each other.

Finally, Jesus selected Judas in order to accomplish this complicated mission (namely to sacrifice the person who clad Jesus). In his discussion with Judas, Jesus explained that he was chosen to perform and realise an important mission that would bring him to the highest level of spiritual evolution, to a level that is higher than that reached by any other disciple. But he was warned to be aware that until the end of time he would be rejected and hated by coming generations. From that moment onwards, he clarifies that in this mission a great deal of blame, many accusations and judgements would follow. However, Jesus wished that if coming generations blamed Judas out of ignorance at least his fellow disciples would not do the same. Jesus asked all of them not just to understand the plan but to be kind and loving to each other as well. So he said: [219] "This is my command to you; be kind and generous to each other, as I am kind and generous to you. Therefore, treat each other as I treat you".

> *"9 As the Father hath loved me, so have I loved you:* **continue ye in my love.** *10 If ye keep my commandments, ye shall abide in my love; even as I have kept my Father's commandments, and abide in his love."*

The discussion between Jesus and Judas continued for a few hours. Judas also talked to his master about a very strange vision he had had in his dream, and learned from his master its spiritual meaning.

Jesus selected each one of his disciples to play a role in a particular part of his overall plan, very much like the different pieces of one big puzzle.

---

[219] *The Gospel of St. John*, Ch.15: 9-10.

16 Ye have not chosen me, but I have chosen you"[220]

I shall choose you, one out of thousand and two out of ten thousand; and **they shall stand as a single one** *"*[221]

Jesus did the same with Judas. This is what he explained himself, according to Saint John's reports. The mission that he set for Judas consisted of different stages that he had to perform step by step following the guidance and directions of his master. The first step was to quickly and secretly meet the Pharisees and the Romans in order to encourage them to come and arrest Jesus. Judas achieved this by closing a secret pact with them and telling them that he was ready to betray Jesus in exchange for money (30 silver coins). He then starts to carry out the first part of his mission while the apostles are sitting in the circle, awaiting Judas' return. They are under the impression that Judas has gone walking with his master to receive further teachings. But they do not know that he is in the city to make a separate pact with the Pharisees and the Romans.

"14 Then one of the twelve, called Judas Iscariot, went unto the chief priests, 15 And said unto them, What will ye give me, and I will deliver him unto you? And they covenanted with him for thirty pieces of silver. 16 And from that time he sought opportunity to betray him.'[222]

Important chronological details

The official Gospels list very important chronological details. First, Jesus explains to his disciples that "Within two days the son of man will be arrested by his enemies". It is after this that Judas goes to Jesus' enemies, and not before.

---

[220] *The Gospel of St. John*, Ch.15: 16.

[221] *The Gospel of St Thomas*, logion 23.

[222] *The Gospel of St. Matthew*, Ch. 26: 14-16.

It is not the case that Judas first goes to Jesus' enemies and then Jesus becomes informed about it, announcing it to others. Rather, he tells them first and then *after* this, Judas goes. This is a very important, often overlooked fact.

When the four canonical Gospels accuse Judas of being dominated by the devil, this can be seen as an insult to the exact and perfect management on Jesus' part concerning the chaotic situation he was facing. When we consider the chronological details of the events, Jesus in fact showed his ability to control and manage the chaotic situation.

> *"1 Now the feast of unleavened bread drew nigh, which is called the Passover. 2 And the chief priests and scribes sought how they might kill him; for they feared the people. Then entered Satan into Judas surnamed Iscariot, being of the number of the twelve."*[223]

In the Gospel according to St. Luke, the action of Judas is attributed to the fact he had become possessed by the Devil and is not due to the order of his Master - because, as we can see, neither St Luke nor any other member of the twelve apostles was aware of Jesus' secret plan.

Once we accept the capacity of Jesus to predict events then we must also be willing to accept his ability to control the events before they occurred, as well as his ability to control chaotic situations. For Jesus, this was a confrontation between light and darkness, as he explained to his disciples. Once we believe in his clairvoyant ability to predict events, then he also must have had the capacity to dominate the situation and to take control of it, leaving his enemies empty-handed.

There are many interesting details in this event. For example, Judas does not visit the Pharisees only, but also the Roman soldiers.

---

[223] *The Gospel of St. Luke*, Ch. 22: 1-2.

"And he went his way, and communed with the chief priests and captains, how he might betray him unto them."[224]

Why would this be so? **Because Jesus intended to impose on his adversaries his own time frame for events to occur.** The Roman soldiers did not have any preference for Friday, Saturday or Sunday. For the Pharisees, Sunday was the best day. Jesus sent Judas to the Romans so that they would fetch the Pharisees during the night of Thursday to Friday. In fact, Judas offers both groups to bring them to Jesus secretly, so that they would be able to get him in their grasp. This fact is formulated very precisely in the canonical Gospels - and it is very important.

"5 And they were glad, and covenanted to give him money. 6 And he promised, **and sought opportunity to betray him unto them in the absence of the multitude."**[225]

Why? Because on the one hand neither the Pharisees nor the Romans knew Jesus, and on the other hand there were twelve people who resembled their master, each of whom were ready to sacrifice his life for him. Jesus' habit of constantly changing his appearance and his constant movements made both Romans and Pharisees unsure of his true physical appearance.

"30 And they departed thence, and passed through Galilee; and he would not that any man should know about it."[226]

The enemy simply wanted to arrest a person known as Jesus of Nazareth, and it was enough for them just to bring somebody who would say: "I am Jesus"; and then to sacrifice this arrested person.

---

[224] *The Gospel of St Luke*, Ch. 22: 5.

[225] *The Gospel of St Luke*, Ch. 22: 1-7.

[226] *The Gospel of St. Luke* Ch. 22: 13.

They planned to arrest Jesus but they did not know what he looked like.

After agreeing the secret pact with both Pharisees and Romans, Judas returns to his master, and by his order he joins the circle of the twelve apostles as usual.

> *"14 And when the hour had come, he sat down, and the twelve apostles with him."*[227]

Jesus knew that the apostles were burning with jealousy because it appeared to them that he had spent two days in private discussions with Judas. The jealousy of the eleven disciples towards Judas is reminiscent of the jealousy of Jacob's eleven sons towards Joseph.

Jesus then immediately starts to talk to them, and he compares himself to the sun.

> *"12 Then spake Jesus again unto them, saying, I am the light of the world: he that followeth me shall not walk in darkness, but shall have the light of life."*[228]

Here, he reveals a very important fact by comparing all of the twelve members of the organisation to the twelve hours that make up a day.

> *"9 Jesus answered, Are there not twelve hours in the day? If any man walks in the day, he stumbleth not, because he seeth the light of this world. 10 But if a man walks in the night, he stumbleth, because there is no light in him."*[229]

Then he refers to the presupposition of a traitor living among the twelve apostles. Jesus says *"You, twelve people are like twelve hours of a day*

---

[227] *The Gospel of St. Luke*, Ch. 22: 14.

[228] *The Gospel of St. John*, Ch .8: 12.

[229] *The Gospel of St. John*, Ch.11: 9-10.

and the sun is running hour by hour during every hour. The people who are walking during the hours of the day will never lose sight of the right way. But if somebody walks in the darkness of the night he risks committing many mistakes".

Paraklitus, in connection with the Jesus' disciples

Figure 3 - Paracletous (Paraklitius), in connection with Jesus' disciples

Thus, he compares his disciples to the hours of the day, twelve hours. But we know that only *two* days of the year are composed of exactly twelve hours, namely the first day of spring and autumn. During these two days, the lengths of day and night are exactly equal. Then, Jesus explains to all of his disciples that at that moment they are all like the hours of the day. From the beginning of the day, there is light. So the whole day is full of light. He then says. "I am running within each one of you. You are all equal to each other".

He reveals this fact after predicting that "Within two days **the son of man** will be arrested". **Here, he would like to clarify for all his disciples that Judas is not a traitor. He is one of the hours of the day.**

"Whoever drinks from my mouth shall become as I am, and I myself will become he"[230]

Still, this important teaching is not enough to stop them from being jealous of each other. Each one of them is in love with his master, and each one of them would like to be the student closest to his master. Consequently, they start to struggle and fight among each other in order to discover which one of them is the greatest disciple.

"24 And there was also a strife among them, which of them should be accounted the greatest."[231]

Again, Jesus quietens them and talks again about the necessity to nourish love within their hearts and not to look to see who is higher than the others. A seeker should be like a soldier, ready to realise the mission for his beloved. Jesus tells them:

"25 And he said unto them, the kings of the Gentiles exercise lordship over them; and they that exercise authority upon them are called benefactors. 26 But ye shall not be so: but he that is greatest among you let him be as the younger; and he that is chief, as he that doth serve. 27 For whether is greater, he that sitteth at meat, or he that serveth? is not he that sitteth at meat? but I am among you as he that serveth."[232]

Here is the way of poverty. If you would like to become a king this is not the place for you. A king holds the highest station among the people. People look at the king as their lord and owner. If you would like to be with me, you should know that the highest place is for the most humble person. The most humble one has the highest place. Among all of you I am like a servant, so you should be servants, too.

---

[230] *The Gospel of Thomas*, logion 108.

[231] *The Gospel of St. Luke*, Ch. 22: 24.

[232] *The Gospel of St. Luke*, Ch. 22: 25-27.

"29 And he said unto them, This kind can come forth by nothing, but by prayer and fasting."[233]

A Paradoxical situation

For his own safety, Jesus had to hide himself, and for his mission he needed to be in contact with the people. Moreover, his enemies intended to eliminate him. Thus, he was forced to look for a third solution.

The third solution was to render the Pharisees helpless, so that they would stop searching for him. For this he had to provide them with an illusion that they had arrested and killed him, so that they would consider the matter dealt with.

In order to accomplish this, it was necessary for Jesus to go to a secret place for a short while, and to come back to his close disciples after three days and then continue his mission in different manner.

"31 For he taught his disciples, and said unto them, The Son of man is delivered into the hands of men, and they shall kill him; and after that he is killed, he shall rise the third day."[234]

You will start to cry, and people in the world will be very happy. But your sadness will soon turn to happiness. You are sad now because of what I tell you, but when you will see me return, you will once again be very happy. Nobody will be able to take this happiness from your heart.[235]

---

[233] *The Gospel of St. Mark*, Ch. 22: 9, 29.

[234] *The Gospel of St. Mark*, Ch. 22: 9, 31.

[235] *The Gospel of St. John*, Ch.16: 16 & 20 & 22.

But the apostles could not understand any part of Jesus' plan.[236]

> *"18 I will not leave you comfortless: I will come to you. 19 Yet a little while, and the world seeth me no more; but ye see me: because I live, ye shall live also.'*[237]

I don't leave you behind as orphans. I will come back after a short while. The world does not see me anymore but you will be seeing me. **Because whilst I am alive, you will continue your life with me.**

> *"22 Judas saith unto him, not Iscariot, Lord, how is it that thou wilt manifest thyself unto us, and not unto the world? 23 Jesus answered and said unto him,* **if a man loves me, he will keep my words: and my Father will love him, and we will come unto him,** *and make our abode with him.*[238]

The reports of Jesus' words are clear. But still the disciples could not understand what he had said and they did not dare ask him to clarify his comments further.[239]

One important section of Jesus' statement is where he says that the son of man will be handed over to the Pharisees and the priests, and that he will then return after three days.

> *"31 And he began to teach them, that* **the Son of man** *must suffer many things, and be rejected of the elders, and of the chief priests, and scribes, and be killed, and after three days rise again.'*[240]

---

[236] *The Gospel of St. John*, Ch.16: 17.

[237] *The Gospel of St. John*, Ch.14: 18-19.

[238] *The Gospel of St. John*, Ch. 14: 23-24.

[239] *The Gospel of St. Mark*, Ch. 9: 31.

Jesus was talking about a plan based on the crucifixion of **the son of man,** in order to give the impression to his enemies that Jesus was killed. When everybody believed in his death they would leave him alone, enabling him to return to his companions. It seems that Peter at that moment understood the plan of his master and became very worried, as it was a very risky undertaking.

"32 And he spake that saying openly. And Peter took him, and began to rebuke him. 33 But when he had turned about and looked on his disciples, he rebuked Peter, saying, Get thee behind me, Satan: **for thou savours not the things that be of God, but the things that be of men.**[241]

New competition among the apostles

When Jesus talked openly about his plan, Peter held his arm and said to him: "Don't do it, don't do it". Jesus turned his head towards his other disciples and shouted to Peter: "Go away, O Satan, you do not trust in the divine plan, you limit yourself to ordinary calculations." The apostles understood that Jesus was resolute in his plan and that certain apostles would be involved in it. Then Jacob and John asked their master for a place in this plan. Jesus answered: "I do what destiny decides for each one of you. I give the place to each one of you according to your destiny and stars."

"And he spoke again to the twelve, and began to tell them what things should happen unto him, 33 Saying, Behold, we go up to Jerusalem; and the **Son of man shall be delivered unto the chief priests,**_and unto the scribes; and they shall condemn him to death, and shall deliver him to the Gentiles: 34 And they shall mock him, and shall scourge him, and shall spit upon him, and shall kill him: and the third day he shall rise again. 35 And*

---

[240] **The Gospel of St. Mark,** Ch. 8: 31. **Be killed** should be understood to mean **"being supposed to be killed".**

[241] **The Gospel of St. Mark,** Ch. 8: 32-33.

James and John, the sons of Zebedee, come unto him, saying, Master, we would that thou shouldest do for us whatsoever we shall desire. 36 And he said unto them, What would ye that I should do for you? 37 They said unto him, Grant unto us that we may sit, one on thy right hand, and the other on thy left hand, in thy glory. 38 But Jesus said unto them, Ye know not what ye ask:...[242]

The anger of the other apostles

When Jacob and John came to Jesus to ask for a particular place for them so that they would sit to his left and right side, other disciples became very angry towards them. Again, Jesus advised them:

"40 But to sit on my right hand and on my left hand is not mine to give; but it shall be given to them for whom it is prepared. 41 And when the ten heard it, they began to be much displeased with Jacob and John. 42 But Jesus called them to him, and saith unto them, Ye know that they which are accounted to rule over the Gentiles exercise lordship over them; and their great ones exercise authority upon them. 43 But so shall it not be among you: but whosoever will be great among you, shall be your minister: 44 And whosoever of you will be the chiefest, shall be servant of all. 45 For even the Son of man came not to be ministered unto, but to minister, and to give his life a ransom for many."[243]

A necessary warning

In order to understand the truth about the facts behind the crucifixion and the real place of Judas in this event, we must pay close attention to the psychological state and mind-set of the apostles. One of the oldest manuscripts we have to investigate in the case of the crucifixion is the

---

[242] *The Gospel of St. Mark,* Ch. 10: 32-38.

[243] *The Gospel of St. Mark,* Ch. 10: 40-45.

Gospel according to Saint John.[244] Saint John was one of Jesus' closest apostles. But we observe in the Gospel of St. Mark that Saint John was not a neutral person among the apostles. He wanted to have the highest place among the apostles. Therefore, this has to be taken into account when we try to evaluate his commentary about Jesus and the apostles. It is certain that Saint John felt closely attached to Jesus and that he cared dearly for him. But he also did not like to lose his place to somebody else or see that someone else was dearer to Jesus than he was. In his book, the author of Saint John's Gospel time and time again repeats sentences that aim to persuade his readers that Judas was a traitor and wrongdoer. But when we take an in-depth look at the book of Judas, we realise that he was a very advanced seeker who had many important visions and that he was able to receive and understand the highest lessons of his master. Jesus promised him that he would reach a place that nobody else could reach. Jesus talked with Judas about a world which no eye had seen and no ear had heard and that there was no information about it. A world in which there would be no harm or danger for the heart of the seeker.[245]

Therefore, these statements are all contrary to those mentioned in the book of Saint John. The author of Saint John's Gospel, from the beginning until the end of his book, wished to focus the intention of his readers to the wrong intention and bad deeds on the part of Judas.

---

[244] *The Gospel of St. John* is not the oldest canonic Gospel, but its manuscript is the oldest Christian document ever found in the world. All of the Gospels are supposed to have been written during first Christian century - between 50 and 90 A.D.

[245] Jesus said to Judas: "Come, that I may teach you about secrets no person has ever seen. For there exists a great and boundless realm, whose extent no generation of angels has seen, (in which) there is (a) great invisible (Spirit), (hidden heaven), which no eye of an angel has ever seen, no thought of the heart has ever comprehended, and it was never called by any name" *The Gospel of Judas,* Electronic version of the National Geographic publication.

But as we have seen, Jesus tells Judas: "You must not be afraid to accept the blame of all generations until the end of time".

The practical teachings of courage

At that moment, Jesus decides to commit a very courageous and risky act in order to remove the fear from the minds of the disciples. He tells them: "I would like to go back to Jerusalem. And those who would like to come with me must bring their cross with themselves." The Gospel according to St Mark says: "Each one of you who would like to follow me must deny himself, take his cross and come with me".

If somebody would like to escape and save his own life he should be aware that he is killing his soul. A person who would like to free his soul must let go of his life. And a person who is willing to sacrifice his life for my path and my Evangelium is a person who brings his soul to the ultimate point of perfection. What is the point if somebody gains the whole material world and yet he loses himself?

> "34 And when he had called the people unto him with his disciples also, he said unto them, **Whosoever will come after me, let him deny himself, and take up his cross, and follow me.** 35 For whosoever will save his life shall lose it; **but whosoever shall lose his life for my sake and the Gospel's, the same shall save it.** 36 For what shall it profit a man, **if he shall gain the whole world, and lose his own soul?** 37 Or what shall a man give in exchange for his soul?"[246]

The apostles asked him: "Where are you going?" He answered: "I am going to Jerusalem". And he walked towards Jerusalem. He went ahead of the group. The apostles followed him and they were all overwhelmed by fear.

---

[246] *The Gospel of St Mark*, Ch. 8: 32-38.

"Behold, we go up to Jerusalem; and the Son of man shall be delivered unto the chief priests, and unto the scribes; and they shall condemn him to death, and shall deliver him to the Gentiles: 34 And they shall mock him, and shall scourge him, and shall spit upon him, and shall kill him."[247]

Jesus went to a corner and began to talk with them again.

We hope the reader is aware of the fact that Jesus' world view is one that is based on **the sacrifice for love**: to be annihilated in love, in the way a sugar crystal dissolves in hot water.

Jesus wanted to explain and to clarify for his companions - and for the history of humanity - that what would happen in the next few days would be done through his own decision, and that no one could impose anything on him. There were no bad intentions towards him among his companions. Many new things would happen, but not because of any bad intentions from his followers: everything would be of his own decision. **His enemies wanted to arrest him, but he refused to fall into his adversaries' trap and under their control with his hands tied**.

All of these teachings shed important new light on our investigation. When Jesus was walking around, somebody came running towards him and asked him: "What should I do to gain eternal life?" Jesus answered him: "Go, sell everything you have, give your money to the poor, take your cross and follow me".

"17 And when he was gone forth into the way, there came one running, and kneeled to him, and asked him, Good Master, what shall I do that I may inherit eternal life?

18 And Jesus said unto him, Why callest thou me good? There is none good but one, that is, God.

---

[247] ***The Gospel of St. Mark***, Ch. 10: 32-34.

19 Thou knowest the commandments, Do not commit adultery, Do not kill, Do not steal, Do not bear false witness, Defraud not, Honour thy father and mother.

20 And he answered and said unto him, Master, all these have I observed from my youth.

21 Then Jesus beholding him loved him, and said unto him, One thing thou lackest: **go thy way, sell whatsoever thou hast, and give to the poor, and thou shalt have treasure in heaven: and come, take up the cross, and follow me.**

22 And he was sad at that saying, and went away grieved: for he had great possessions.

23 And Jesus looked round about, and saith unto his disciples, How hardly shall they that have riches enter into the kingdom of God!

24 And the disciples were astonished at his words. But Jesus answereth again, and saith unto them, Children, how hard is it for them that trust in riches to enter into the kingdom of God!

25 It is easier for a camel to go through the eye of a needle, than for a rich man to enter into the kingdom of God.

26 And they were astonished out of measure, saying among themselves, Who then can be saved?'[248]

As we can observe, the picture is very clear. **There is no place for bad intentions, or for being a traitor: it is simply a case of sacrifice. Jesus had an extremely complex plan and he went all**

---

[248] ***The Gospel of St. Mark,*** Ch. 10: 17-26. We would like to remind the reader that the paragraph about the passage of the camel through the eye of the needle is reported in exactly the same fashion in the Qur'an as well.

the way to realise his plan. It is not so much a case of prediction but rather the management of the situation.

Jesus knows very well that going to Jerusalem means that he is going to be killed. Everyone who would like to stop his plan is firmly rejected by him. He is resolute about his plan. Jesus says: "Go away Satan". They talk to him from a perspective of love and care for their master, but they are all talking from sentiment. But Jesus views the affair from above. He has decided to realise something and that nobody is going to change his mind. Jesus talks about everything and explains every detail. And he explains that **everybody who would like to follow him must be ready to sacrifice his life.**

Application of the divine plan

When Jesus prepared his plan, he imposed his own timetable on his enemies for his capture. **The enemies did not want to capture him during the feast of Passover. Jesus imposed it on them.** The heads of the priests and the Pharisees gathered together in their central place. With their head Kayafas, they talked about the date and the way in which they would capture Jesus. They were adamant that it should not happen on the day of the feast. This was the weak element in their plan, and Jesus discovered this weak point when he became aware of their plans through his followers among the Pharisees.

> *"1 Now the feast of unleavened bread drew nigh, which is called the Passover. 2 And the chief priests and scribes sought how they might kill him; for they feared the people."*[249]

> *3 Then assembled together the chief priests, and the scribes, and the elders of the people, unto the palace of the high priest, who was called Caiaphas, 4 And consulted that they might take Jesus by subtlety, and kill him. 5 But they*

---

[249] ***The Gospel of Luke***, Ch. 22: 1-2.

said, **Not on the feast day, lest there be an uproar among the people.**[250]

So they did in fact want to arrest Jesus, but not on Thursday - as it was the festive day - or on Friday - because it was the preparation day - and especially not on the Shabbat, because this was a forbidden day. And Jesus said:

> *"1 And it came to pass, when Jesus had finished all these sayings, he said unto his disciples, 2 Ye know that after two days is the feast of the Passover, and the Son of man is betrayed to be crucified."*[251]

The reader can easily observe that these are two opposite plans, which are in a direct contrast with each other. From the moment Jesus received the information about the plan of his adversaries, he decided to hide himself even more from the public eye by changing his clothes and his appearance.

> *"47 Then gathered the chief priests and the Pharisees a council, and said, What do we? For this man doeth many miracles. 48 If we let him thus alone, all men will believe on him: and the Romans shall come and take away both our place and nation. 49 And one of them, named Caiaphas, being the high priest that same year, said unto them,* **Ye know nothing at all** *50 Nor consider that it is expedient for us, that one man should die for the people, and that the whole nation perish not. 51 And this spake he not of himself: but being high priest that year, he prophesied that Jesus should die for that nation; 52 And not for that nation only, but that also he should gather together in one the children of God that were scattered abroad. 53 Then from that day forth they took counsel together for to put him to death. 54* **Jesus therefore walked no more openly among the Jews;** *but instead he went unto a country near to the wilderness, into a city called Ephraim, and there he*

---

[250] *The Gospel of St. Matthew,* Ch. 26: 3-4.

[251] *The Gospel of St Matthew,* Ch. 26: 3-4.

continued with his disciples. 55 And the Jews' Passover was nigh at hand: and many went out of the country up to Jerusalem before the Passover, to purify themselves. 56 Then they sought Jesus, and spake among themselves, as they stood in the temple, What think ye, that he will not come to the feast? 57 Now both the chief priests and the Pharisees had given a commandment, that, if any man knew where he were, he should show it, that they might take him.[252]

In order not to fall into their trap, Jesus decided to send someone to bring them to him. So he told his students again: **"Within two days the son of man will be arrested and be crucified"**. This shows that he is trying to fix the time of his arrest and crucifixion. This was not a prediction, it was management of events.

Judas went to them for this purpose:

"4 And he went his way, and communed with the chief priests and captains, how he might betray him unto them. 5 And they were glad, and covenanted to give him money. 6 And he promised, and sought opportunity to betray him unto them in the absence of the multitude."[253]

It means that he was ordered by Jesus to tell them not to try to arrest him by themselves, and that he would arrange it so that he will be brought to him. And this made them happy!

Where were they at the last feast?

It was always Jesus who decided where his disciples would go; it was always his decision. Others were not aware of Jesus' destination and movements when he decided to move from one point to another. It was Jesus who sent his students from place to place, door to door, and

---

[252] *The Gospel of St. John*, Ch.11: 47-57.

[253] *St Luke.* 22

house to house. Nobody was allowed to do anything without the permission of his master. And Jesus, as we have said already, sent his apostles to complete their tasks in pairs. The only exception, as far as we know from the existing texts, was the case of Judas - as we have outlined. For the gathering on Thursday night, Jesus *himself* arranged the place intended for dining. The students asked him: "Where do you want us to go to prepare the food tonight?" Jesus selected John and Peter from the group of the twelve apostles.

> *"8 And he sent Peter and John, saying, Go and prepare us the Passover that we may eat. 9 And they said unto him, Where wilt thou that we prepare? 10 And he said unto them, Behold, when ye are entered into the city, there shall a man meet you, bearing a pitcher of water; follow him into the house where he entereth in. 11 And ye shall say unto the goodman of the house, The Master saith unto thee, Where is the guest chamber, where I shall eat the Passover with my disciples? 12 And he shall shew you a large upper room furnished: there make ready. 13 And they went, and found as he had said unto them: and they made ready the Passover. 14 And when the hour was come, he sat down, and the twelve apostles with him."[254]*

That night Jesus went there in the company of all his apostles. And during this gathering, he did something extraordinary. He stood up, put away his dress, brought water and washed the feet of all of his disciples one by one. He then dried their feet with a towel all by himself.

> *"4 He riseth from supper, and laid aside his garments; and took a towel, and girded himself. 5 After that he poureth water into a bason, and began to wash the disciples' feet, and to wipe them with the towel wherewith he was girded. 6 Then cometh he to Simon Peter: and Peter saith unto him, Lord, dost thou wash my feet? 7 Jesus answered and said unto him, What I do thou knowest*

---

[254] ***The Gospel of St Luke**, Ch. 22: 8-14, **The Gospel of St Matthew**, Ch. 26: 17-18, The **Gospel of St Mark**, Ch. 14: 12-20.

not now; but thou shalt know hereafter. 8 Peter saith unto him, Thou shalt never wash my feet. Jesus answered him, If I wash thee not, thou hast no part with me. 9 Simon Peter saith unto him, Lord, not my feet only, but also my hands and my head. 10 Jesus saith to him, He that is washed needeth not save to wash his feet, but is clean every whit: and ye are clean, but not all.[255]

Jesus said to them: "I wash your feet; you do the same among each other and be kind to each other". This was a new pact that Jesus made with all of them, including Judas, and before sending Judas on his mission! So this removes the possibility of thinking that Judas was a traitor. When they were sitting down and they were eating Jesus told them: "Now I would like to tell you that one of you who are eating with me will give me up to the enemies". They became sad and everybody asked: "Is it me?"

"20 Now when the even was come, he sat down with the twelve. 21 And as they did eat, he said, Verily I say unto you, that one of you shall betray me. 22 And they were exceeding sorrowful, and began every one of them to say unto him, Lord, is it me?"[256]

From the reaction of the disciples we discover that **nobody knew anything about a probable relationship of one of them with the enemies. This shows that only Jesus knew of this contact. It means that this contact was accomplished under the eyes, direction and guidance of Jesus.** The Gospel according to Saint Matthew tells us that they became very sad. Why did they become sad? Because they saw again that Jesus wanted to deliver himself to the enemies. The first time was when he went to Jerusalem.

---

[255] *The Gospel of St. John*, Ch.13: 4-10.

[256] *The Gospel of St. Matthew*, Ch. 26: 20-22. The Greek 'Paradidonai' is commonly translated as 'to betray' but literally it means 'to transfer/ to hand over'.

"18 And as they sat and did eat, Jesus said, Verily I say unto you, One of you which eateth with me shall betray me. 19 And they began to be sorrowful, and to say unto him one by one, Is it me? and another said: Is it me? 20 And he answered and said unto them, It is one of the twelve that dippeth with me in the dish."[257]

Each one asked Jesus: "Who is going to do this?" Jesus remained silent. So Peter asked John by means of a sign, and not by talking, to ask Jesus: "Who is the person?" John asked permission to pose a question and he asked Jesus: "Who is this person?"

""21 When Jesus had thus said, he was troubled in spirit, and testified, and said, Verily, verily, I say unto you, that one of you shall betray me. 22 Then the disciples looked one on another, doubting of whom he spake. 23 Now there was leaning on Jesus' bosom one of his disciples, whom Jesus loved. 24 Simon Peter therefore beckoned to him, that he should ask who it should be of whom he spake. 25 He then lying on Jesus' breast saith unto him, Lord, who is it?"[258]

Each one of them asked: "Is it me?" Nobody asked: "Is it him?" This is a very important point. It is as if Jesus was asking: "I would like one of you to give me to the enemies, and my adversaries". He does not say to them: "One of you would like to do something".

They are sorrowful because they think Jesus will be arrested, but they don't pose any question about the traitor who conspires with the priests. They ask: "who should perform this mission, is it me?" **And nobody casts a suspicious eye on Judas.**

---

[257] ***The Gospel of St. Mark***, Ch.14: 12-20.

[258] ***The Gospel of St. John***, Ch.13: 21-25.

Jesus remains silent. At that moment Judas says: "Is it me?"[259] So it means that Judas asks his master: "Is it time that I realise what you asked me to do?" Everybody waits for Jesus' answer. Judas stretches his hand to take something; Jesus does the same at the same moment. They reach for the same plate. Jesus then says: "It is one who has his hand in the plate with me". This event is extraordinary and of vital importance. **Having their hands in the same plate implies being bound to each other. This is a symbolic act and Jesus was used to talking through symbolic gestures.**

> *"21 But, behold, the hand of him that will hand over me is with me on the table"*[260]

When in the beginning Jesus says: "I will be arrested by my enemies" it means that he knows that somebody is in contact with his enemies. There was no reason for him to wash the feet of this person if he thought he was a traitor. Jesus was a very direct and sincere person. In the case of Peter he told him: "Go away from me, O Satan". This bears witness to the fact that he was very strict and direct. Therefore, if Jesus knew there was a traitor among them, he would not allow him to stay there. He tells of his coming arrest in a certain manner and then he changes his place and starts to wash the feet of the apostles, including Judas'

> *"26 Jesus answered, He it is, to whom I shall give a <u>sop</u>, when I have dipped it. And when he had dipped the sop, he gave it to Judas Iscariot, the son of Simon."*[261]

> *"27 And after the sop Satan entered into him. Then said Jesus unto him, That thou doest, do quickly. 28 Now no man at the table knew for what*

---

[259] *The Gospel of St. Matthew,* Ch. 26: 25.

[260] *The Gospel of St. Luke,* Ch. 22: 21.

[261] *The Gospel of St. John,* Ch.13: 26.

intent he spake this unto him. 29 For some of them thought, because Judas had the bag, that Jesus had said unto him, Buy those things that we have need of against the feast; or, that he should give something to the poor. 30 He then having received the sop went immediately out: and it was night."²⁶²

It shows that there evidently was a plan between Jesus and Judas, and that this was only known to them and no one else. Consequently Jesus told him: "Go and do your mission". St. John's Gospel obviously relates the next set of events to the sop, by saying: "After the sop Satan entered into him". But everybody is aware that Satan has no place in this game. Jesus places a sop with his own hand into the hand of his disciple. But what was the secret of that sop? "Now no man at the table knew for what purpose he spoke this unto him."

Judas and Peter

Judas' mission was not to buy bread and cheese; **it was a secret mission.** After his departure, Jesus again starts to talk about the necessity of love and kindness among the apostles.

*"34 A new commandment I give unto you, **that ye love one another; as I have loved you, that ye also love one another.** 35 By this shall **all men know that ye are my disciples, if ye have loved one to another.**"²⁶³*

Jesus knew that the disciples would ultimately hate Judas. So not only did he give them a new lesson about love, but he also shows a strict face to "Saint Simon Peter".

---

²⁶² *The Gospel of St. John.* Ch.13: 26-30.

²⁶³ *The Gospel of St. John,* Ch.13: 34-35.

"36 Simon Peter said unto him, Lord, whither goest thou? Jesus answered him, Whither I go, thou canst not follow me now; but thou shalt follow me afterwards. 37 Peter said unto him, Lord, why cannot I follow thee now? I will lay down my life for thy sake. 38 Jesus answered him, Wilt thou lay down thy life for my sake? Verily, **verily, I say unto thee, The cock shall not crow, till thou hast denied me thrice.***"*[264]

How can one accept what appears to be the wrong type of action demonstrated by Jesus' advanced apostles? Are Judas, son of Simon, and Simon Peter weak companions and poor disciples? This does not seem to be an acceptable answer. Peter, named Kiefa, was a very advanced apostle, one who was sincere and close to his master. During the night of the arrest, Jesus asked Peter to bring a sword with him, and not to sleep in order to watch everything. He was a very close disciple, and when Jesus returned after three days he appointed him to take care of his limbs.[265] Therefore, Peter must have been very sincere and honest.

Thus, these events show us that Peter was not a wrongdoer and that he had absolutely no intention of denying his master. But in that night and before the eyes of all other disciples Jesus tells him: "You will have denied me three times before the cock crows twice". So Jesus fixes the time for Peter's action.

But Peter is not a liar, nor a denier. It is a manner of talking in coded language about a logical prediction. Jesus gives him a command in the form of a code. Nobody understands what it means, because the code is a secret language between the two. Using the coded language is a way to secure the whole system and make it safe. It is because of these

---

[264] ***The Gospel of St. John***, Ch.13: 36-38.

[265] We remark that there are also opinions which treat the appointment of Peter as the rock of the church a forgery in favour of Roman Catholic claims. Caring of the limbs means being a kind of successor.

types of security measures that the organisation around Jesus could not be easily infiltrated. Jesus says: "O my children, I rest a short while with you[266] and **after I will go to a place where you cannot come with me[267]**". Peter asked: "Where are you going?" Jesus said: "I am going somewhere and you cannot follow me, later you will join me" Peter replied: "Why can't I come with you, **I am ready to sacrifice my life for you**". Jesus Said: "You would like to sacrifice your life for me? You will deny me three times in front of the people, before the cock sings"[268] So when Jesus talks like this he is in fact sending a hidden message to Peter, concerning Peter's task[269].

These actions were all part of a plan. One part was to be carried out by Judas (bringing the enemies to the garden), and another by Peter (by guarding the garden), and so on. However, when these passages are read and taken literally, it appears that 'Peter was not a good person: he denied his master'. But things were not what they seemed. Peter was ready to sacrifice his life for Jesus, and later on Jesus put him in his own place during his occultation. However, at that moment Jesus introduced him as a denier. **So the people took Judas for a traitor and Peter for a denier! All of these are the elements of a very complicated plan devised by Jesus.**

---

[266] *The Gospel of St. John*, Ch. 13: 33.

[267] *The Gospel of St. John*, Ch. 13: 33. They told: does he want go to the Greek-land?

[268] *The Gospel of St. John*, Ch. 13: 36-38.

[269] Here, the reader is referred to the section: **covering the face of the arrested** of this book.

Secret language

"27 And Jesus saith unto them, All ye shall be offended because of me this night: for it is written, I will smite the shepherd, and the sheep shall be scattered. 28 But after that I am risen, I will go before you into Galilee. 29 But Peter said unto him, Although all shall be offended, yet will not I. 30 And Jesus saith unto him, **Verily I say unto thee, That this day, even in this night, before the cock crows twice, thou shalt deny me thrice.** *31 But he spake the more vehemently, If I should die with thee, I will not deny thee in any wise. Likewise also said they all."*[270]

D uring the process of realising his plan, Jesus keeps talking to his apostles in a coded language. The other disciples were not aware of the meaning of these words. St. John's Gospel refers to this fact by mentioning that **nobody understood what Jesus said to Judas**. So the other apostles preferred their own interpretation to the reality of the situation. It is precisely this picture that St. John's Gospel would like to lodge into the minds of the readers concerning the penetration of the Devil in the mind of Judas, when he received the sop from the hand of Jesus.[271] But how did the author of the text know the Devil penetrated the mind of Judas?

So the manner of Jesus' language, saying instead of "I will hide myself for a few days" that "You will not be able to see me for a few days"[272] implies that he is talking in a certain coded manner. The students cannot understand this language and ask him: **"What are you saying? For a while we cannot see you and then after we can see you,**

---

[270] ***The Gospel of St. Mark***, Ch.14: 27-31.

[271] ***The Gospel of St. John***, Ch.13: 27 After taking the sop from the hand of Jesus the Satan penetrated Judas

[272] ***The Gospel of St. John***, Ch. 16: 16.

what does this mean?"[273] After this, the apostles talked to each other to see if anyone could understand what Jesus was saying.[274] It is clear that Jesus explained his plan in a coded style, but they could not understand it and became sad. So when Jesus understood that they wanted to pose another question about his statements he tells them: "You are talking among each other about the subject that **for a while you cannot see me and after a while you can.** I will tell you: that you will cry, be sad, and **the enemy will be very happy, but after a while you will be very happy again".**[275]

> *"21 A woman when she is in travail hath sorrow, because her hour is come: but as soon as she is delivered of the child, she remembereth no more the anguish, for joy that a man is born into the world. 22 And ye now therefore have sorrow: but I will see you again, and your heart shall rejoice, and your joy no man taketh from you."*[276]

Jesus compares his plan to the birth of a child: "You should know that what I am trying to do is very hard. It is like giving birth to a child. It is very complicated but when the child is born there will be only place for happiness". "Nobody can take this happiness from you". "**I am talking to you in parables and indirectly. After a while, I will explain everything directly to you.**"

> *"25 These things have I spoken unto you in proverbs: but the time cometh, when I shall no more speak unto you in proverbs, but I shall shew you plainly of the Father."*[277]

---

[273] *The Gospel of St. John*, Ch. 16: 17-18.

[274] *The Gospel of St. John*, Ch. 16: 19.

[275] *The Gospel of St. John*, Ch. 16: 20.

[276] *The Gospel of St. John*, Ch. 16: 21-22.

[277] *The Gospel of St. John*, Ch.16: 21-25.

The last thing Jesus tells his disciples is "Don't bother about my safety, don't worry about me, I am in control of the entire situation."

> *"33 These things I have spoken unto you, that in me ye might have peace. In the world ye shall have tribulation: but be of good cheer;* **I have overcome the world.** *"*[278]

---

[278] *The Gospel of St. John*, Ch.16: 21-33.

Moving to another place

A fter finishing the Last Supper, Jesus gave his disciples a very particular order.

*"36 Then said he unto them, But now, he that hath a purse, let him take it, and likewise his scrip: and **he that hath no sword, let him sell his garment, and buy one**. 38 And they said, Lord, behold, here are two swords. And he said unto them, it is enough."*[279]

Jesus left the house and his disciples behind him. They knew nothing about his destination, but it was clear that they would likely enter into a complicated situation where use of a sword would perhaps be necessary. They gathered to chant a hymn and to recite the rosary before going towards the Mount of Olives. They reached a point named Gethsemane. Jesus told his disciples: "Rest here. Tonight something will happen to me and all of you. You will all fall into an illusion. I will go to the land of the dead. And then I will come back from that land and I will once again be among you in Galilee. Now come with me."

"26 And when they had sung a hymn, they went out into the Mount of Olives. 32 And they came to a place which was named Gethsemane: and he saith to his disciples, Sit ye here, while I shall pray."[280]

Jesus gave them orders to stay there and to rest for a while. It was night time and they were very tired. When the disciples prepared themselves to rest, Jesus ordered Peter, Jacob, and John not to rest, but to follow him to the Hill of Olives.

---

[279] *The Gospel of St Luke*, Ch. 22: 36 & 38.

[280] *The Gospel of St. Mark*, Ch.14: 26 & 32.

> *"33 And he taketh with him Peter and James and John, and began to be sore amazed and to be very heavy; 34 And saith unto them, My soul is exceeding sorrowful unto death: tarry ye here, and watch. 35 And he went forward a little, and fell on the ground, and prayed that, if it were possible, the hour might pass from him."[281]*

He went to the Mount of Olives and the three selected students followed him.

> *"39 And he came out, and went, as he was wont, to the mountain of Olives; and his disciples also followed him. 40 And when he was at the place, he said unto them, Pray that ye enter not into temptation. 41 And he was withdrawn from them about a stone's cast,* **and kneeled down, and prayed, 44 And being in an agony he prayed more earnestly: and his sweat was as it were great drops of blood falling down to the ground.**"*[282]*

When he reached a particular place on that hill, he said: "Stay here and do your prayers in order that you do not fail the exam and he went away from them to another place. He sat down and started to do his prayers as he used to do, with a lot of energy and movements of the body.

> *"36 And he said, Abba, Father, all things are possible unto thee; take away this cup from me: nevertheless not what I will, but what thou wilt."[283]*

---

[281] *The Gospel of St. Mark*, Ch.14: 33-35.

[282] *The Gospel of St. Luke*, Ch. 22: 39-44.

[283] *The Gospel of St. Mark*, Ch.14: 36. Nowadays, "Abba" is used in Arabic, meaning "O Father", with emphasis. "Ab" mean father, and Aby means 'my father', and Abby means 'O my father' with emphasis.

While he was praying in this manner, his body became very warm and sweat started to drip from it like blood. After a while, he stood up and went back to the place where he had left the three disciples. He found them fast asleep.

> *"45 And when he rose up from prayer, and was come to his disciples, he found them sleeping for sorrow, 46 And said unto them, Why sleep ye? rise and pray, lest ye enter into temptation.*[284]

> *37 And he cometh, and findeth them sleeping, and saith unto Peter, Simon, sleepest thou? couldest not thou watch one hour? 38 Watch ye and pray, lest ye enter into temptation.* **The spirit truly is ready, but the flesh is weak.**"[285]

He said to them: "Why are you sleeping? You shouldn't sleep, but carry on with your prayers."

We read the similar reports in other Gospels as well:

> *'36 Then cometh Jesus with them unto a place called Gethsemane, and saith unto the disciples, Sit ye here, while I go and pray yonder. 37 And he took with him Peter and the two sons of Zebedee, and began to be sorrowful and very heavy. 38 Then saith he unto them, ...tarry ye here, and watch with me. 39 And he went a little further, and fell on his face, and prayed, saying, O my Father,.... 40 And he cometh unto the disciples, and findeth them asleep, and saith unto Peter, What, could ye not watch with me one hour? 41 Watch and pray, that ye enter not into temptation:* **the spirit indeed is willing, but the flesh is weak.** *42 He went away again the second time, and prayed, ... 43 And he came and found them asleep again: for their eyes were heavy. 44 And he left them, and went away again, and prayed the third time, saying the same words. 45 Then cometh he to his disciples, and saith unto*

---

[284] **The Gospel of St. Luke**, Ch. 22: 45-46.

[285] **The Gospel of St. Mark**, Ch.14: 37-38.

them, Sleep on now, and take your rest: behold, the hour is at hand, and the Son of man is betrayed into the hands of sinners. 46 Rise, let us be going: behold, he is at hand that doth betray me.[286]

39 And again he went away, and prayed, and spake the same words. 40 And when he returned, he found them asleep again, (for their eyes were heavy,) neither wist they what to answer him. 41 And he cometh the third time, and saith unto them, Sleep on now, and take your rest: it is enough, the hour is come; behold, the Son of man is betrayed into the hands of sinners. 42 Rise up, let us go; lo, he that betrayeth me is at hand."[287]

After a moment he told them: "It is enough, it is time to leave here. It is the moment that **the son of man** will be arrested by the hand of the wrongdoers. Stand up and come with me. So, they left Gethsemane and went to another house in the middle of a garden on the other side of the desert of Cedron."

"1 When Jesus had spoken these words, he went forth with his disciples over the brook Cedron, where was a garden, into the which he entered, and his disciples."[288]

When they passed the desert and reached the garden, Jesus sent all of them inside the house to sleep because they were all very tired. He ordered Peter not to sleep, but to remain alert in the garden, with his sword.

---

[286] *The Gospel of St Matthew*, Ch. 26: 36-45.

[287] *The Gospel of St. Mark*, Ch.14: 39-42.

[288] *The Gospel of St. John*, Ch.18: 1.

Judas brings the enemies

When Judas left Jesus and the Apostles, he immediately went to the Roman centre and told them he could lead them to Jesus, as he knew where he could be found. He asked them to send a group of soldiers with him. Then, all of them together went to the Pharisees and told them that they wanted go and arrest Jesus. The High Priests and the Pharisees became very angry with Judas because they did not want to arrest Jesus during that night, but on the Sunday instead. They found themselves in a stalemate position and forced to follow Judas and the soldiers. Judas brought the Romans and the Pharisees straight to the garden of Cedron. They were armed with torches and weapons.

> *"2 And Judas also, who betrayed him, knew the place: for Jesus often times resorted thither with his disciples. 3 Judas then, having received a band of men and officers from the chief priests and Pharisees, cometh thither with lanterns and torches and weapons."*[289]

Now we can ask: **How did Judas know Jesus' final destination during that night? How could he be certain where to find Jesus?** On what grounds did he have such certainty to go and bring the soldiers and the Pharisees **directly** to the garden and to the house of Cedron? These questions are highly significant when we consider the fact that Jesus moved three times during that night. First to Gethsemane, then to the top of the hill of the Mount of Olives in Zita, and finally to the other side of the desert of Cedron, inside a garden belonging to a particular house...

When Judas left Jesus during that night, **his mission** was to bring Jesus' enemies to him - but where was he going to take them? We have seen that Jesus was used to moving around and that nobody knew

---

[289] *The Gospel of St. John*, Ch.18: 2-3.

143

anything about his final destination when he started to move. Only Jesus himself knew where he intended to go, and he did not discuss his decisions with anyone else. The Apostles and Jesus' companions followed their Master silently without enquiring where they were headed. Before sending Judas on **his special mission**, Jesus did not discuss with his companions where he wanted to go. However, we read that Judas left Jesus and guided Jesus' enemies **directly** to Cedron.

Only one possibility

There can only be one single explanation for the fact that Jesus went to Cedron and that Judas brought his enemies to exactly the same place: **Jesus himself must have informed Judas about his final destination for that night.** As John explained previously, nobody understood what it was exactly that Jesus said to Judas when he sent him on his mission. We know that Jesus told Judas to go and accomplish **his mission** and that his mission was to bring the Pharisees and the Romans to the garden of Cedron. We are now following the explanation attributed to St. John step by step. And as we observed, St. John was at Jesus' side: during that night on the Hill of Olives and in the garden of Cedron.

However, St. John's Gospel does not provide any explanation of the events that occurred at Cedron. Why should this be so? The reason is clear. During the events inside the house. We know that there was a garden and a house in Cedron and that Jesus had used the house in the garden a few times in the garden of Cedron, St. John himself was asleep on earlier occasions.[290]

It is written in the Gospel of St. John that during the time that they were in the house of the garden of Cedron, Judas, the Romans and the

---

[290] *The Gospel of St. John*, Ch.18, for Jesus often times resorted thither with his disciples.

Jewish priests entered the garden to fetch Jesus. **This is the last time that the name of Judas is mentioned in St. John's Gospel.** The author ceases to mention Judas until the end of his book. He does not make any reference to Judas and it is not clear what happened to him. It would seem that Judas entered the garden and then vanished like a drop of water.

It is written in Barnabas's Gospel: "When Jesus said this, he brought his students to the other side of the desert, where there was a garden. He went with his disciples into this garden. And when he was there Judas brought the Pharisees and soldiers who were armed with torches and weapons. It is certain that during the events of that night in the garden, John was sleeping in the house and so he could not provide us with exact information."[291] According to different documents, all of the apostles were sleeping except Peter Simon (Sham'oun). When the soldiers entered the garden they started to shout: "Who is Jesus? Who is Jesus of Nazareth? Who is Jesus of Nazareth?" They made considerable noise and Jesus' students who were asleep woke up in fear and ran left and right.

"Then all the disciples forsook him, and fled."[292]

All of them abandoned Jesus and ran away. One of them covered his body with a plaid.

> *"50 And they all forsook him, and fled. 51 And there followed him a certain young man, having a linen cloth cast about his naked body; and the young men laid hold on him: 52 And he left the linen cloth, and fled from*

---

[291] *The Gospel of St. Barnabas*, Ch. 216: 2 p.p. 366.

[292] *The Gospel of St. Matthew*, Ch. 26: 56.

them naked. 53 And they led Jesus away to the high priest: and with him were assembled all the chief priests and the elders and the scribes.'[293]

They wanted to arrest him and they gripped his plaid, and it fell from him. So he ran away naked. The Gospel of Barnabas names John as the person who ran away naked.

"John covered himself with a cotton plaid and all of sudden they ran behind him to arrest him and they took his tissue and he let it down and he went away nakedly.'[294]

It is certain that at that moment, Peter was armed with his sword and was watching in the garden. It was unusual for a student of Jesus to carry a sword, so it can only have been part of his mission. Therefore it must have been the order of his Master, as he was certain that something was going to happen during that night. It is clear that Peter was there as a guard, when all of Jesus' disciples were sleeping inside the house.

Where was Jesus?

According to the Gospel of St. John **someone went out of the house** and asked: "Who are you searching for?" They answered: "We are here to arrest Jesus of Nazareth." And then **that person said: "I am Jesus of Nazareth"**.

"4 Jesus therefore, knowing all things that should come upon him, went forth, and said unto them, Whom seek ye? 5 They answered him: "Jesus of Nazareth." Jesus saith unto them: "I am he." And Judas also, which betrayed him, stood with them. 6 As soon then as he had said unto them, I am he, they went backward, and fell to the ground. 7 Then asked he them

---

[293] ***The Gospel of St. Mark***, Ch.14: 50-53.

[294] ***The Gospel of St Barnabas***, Ch. 216: 11-12. p-367.

again: "Whom seek ye?" And they said: "Jesus of Nazareth." 8 Jesus answered: "I have told you that I am he: if therefore ye seek me, let these go their way."[295]

Judas was present: it is written in St. John's Gospel. It is also written that Judas did not speak during this event. The only thing mentioned in the Gospel of St. John is that Judas was standing with the soldiers. He did not present Jesus to them and did not tell them: "Yes, he is Jesus (or No, he is not)."

The only events mentioned in the Gospel following the soldiers' questions are that first **someone walks up to the soldiers and says: "I am Jesus"**. Secondly, someone repeats this and says: **"I am Jesus. Arrest me and leave the others."**

Now the following question arises. Why did the soldiers not arrest the first person who introduced himself to them? The reason is that **nobody attested the validity of this person's identity**. According to Saint John's Gospel **Judas remained silent**. It is clear that for the Pharisees and Romans, Jesus would not be the person who simply stated "I am Jesus" (because they knew that at least eleven other people were ready to introduce themselves in place of their master). They needed solid proof and a witness to confirm the identity of the person claiming to be Jesus. **They needed Judas to present Jesus to them. But this was something he did not do.**

So, they then asked Judas: "Where is Jesus? Who is Jesus?" It is certain that at that moment Jesus and his companions were inside the house, and that **it would be a natural thing for Judas to go inside the house and fetch the wanted person**. So when they saw that Judas

---

[295] *The Gospel of St. John*, Ch.18: 4-8.

was silently observing[296] the situation, they asked him to go and fetch Jesus if that particular person was not Jesus himself.[297]

Subsequently, there was considerable chaos in the garden. It is certain that Peter made use of his sword and cut the right ear of one of the servants of the Jewish priests.[298] This is the last time that Judas is mentioned. Every mention of Judas stops with this moment, during this event and in this place. What happened to Judas?

The enemies did not know Jesus

It is clear that Jesus' enemies came into the garden to arrest him **without knowing what he looked like**. The Roman soldiers did not know Jesus and they did not really care much about him. The Jews had heard different things about Jesus of Nazareth. In each meeting with Jesus in which he claimed to be Jesus of Nazareth, he showed himself to them in a different manner. As Jesus from the very beginning remained very selective with respect to his appearance and his style, it was very difficult for the priests to be certain of his true appearance. All of his actions contained an element of surprise. He would suddenly

---

[296] *The Gospel of St. John*, Ch.18: 5, in *the Gospel of St. Matthew*, Ch. 26 it is written: "51 And, behold, one of them which were with Jesus stretched out his hand, and drew his sword, and struck a servant of the high priest's, and smote off his ear. 52 Then said Jesus unto him: 'Put up again thy sword into his place: for all they that take the sword shall perish with the sword. 53 Thinkest thou that I cannot now pray to my Father, and he shall presently give me more than twelve legions of angels?'"

[297] *The Gospel of St. Barnabas*, Ch. 216: 9 p.216.

[298] *The Gospel of St. Luke*, Ch. 22: 36-50, in *the Gospel of St. Matthew*, Ch. 26 it is written: "51 And, behold, one of them which were with Jesus stretched out his hand, and drew his sword, and struck a servant of the high priests, and smote off his ear. 52 Then said Jesus unto him: 'Put up again thy sword into his place: for all they that take the sword shall perish with the sword. 53 Thinkest thou that I cannot now pray to my Father, and he shall presently give me more than twelve legions of angels?'"

appear among the people, talk with them and then vanish again. **So they did not really have any exact picture of Jesus in their minds**. Furthermore, the resemblance of the apostles and Jesus (their manner of talking, walking, behaving and their dress, for example) made it even more difficult for them. If each apostle introduced himself as Jesus of Nazareth, it was impossible for the Jews and the Romans to accept or to reject this claim, because they could not verify its validity by themselves and without confirmation from his family or friends.

So let us consider all of the above facts and once again return to the garden to follow Judas' and his escorts' actions step by step. At that moment, Judas went inside the house to fetch Jesus and bring him out of the house. However, we note that once Judas and his escorts enter the house another person comes out and addresses the Romans and Jewish priests. He asks them: "Why are you here?" They reply: "We are here to arrest Jesus." He then answers: "I am Jesus." And then there is no more discussion about Judas.

It is not stated in St. John's Gospel that Judas went into the house and came back with Jesus. It is not written that they were both together.[299] The Gospel text mentions that one person appears before the Romans and the Jews. **There is only one individual person claiming to be Jesus. He is not accompanied by anyone else.** So Judas does *not* go inside to bring someone else with him and he does *not* say: "This is Jesus, take him". **Judas goes inside and somebody else comes out and says: "I am Jesus."** One person. And says: **"I am Jesus of Nazareth, arrest me and let the others be in peace."**

---

[299] As we mentioned before, only *The Gospel of St. Barnabas* is precise about the fact that Judas goes into the house where all of the student were sleeping in order to fetch Jesus.

How can we accept that this person was Jesus? The only way to be certain, as we mentioned already, is if someone attested the validity of this person's claim of being Jesus. But the Gospel of St. John makes no mention of any witness. So it seems clear that every one of Jesus' disciples wanted to protect and save the life of his Master and everybody was ready to offer his life for his Master. But **we don't have any evidence that the person who was arrested was in fact Jesus. They arrested somebody under the name of Jesus because of his own testimony that he was Jesus.** Logically speaking, we must accept the fact that we have no evidence proving that the person who was arrested was in fact Jesus.

"This night you all will be slipped about me".[300]

We must first ask ourselves how Judas discovered the place of gathering selected by Jesus and his companions in that garden in the middle of the night and how he guided Jesus' enemies exactly to the right place. Certain Gospels report that Judas went to Jesus and kissed his face to verify to the others the identity of Jesus.[301] But this

---

[300] *The Gospel of St Mark*, Ch.14: 26. Persian translation from Greek (original language), p.80.

[301] 47 And while he yet spake, behold a multitude, and he that was called Judas, one of the twelve, went before them, and drew near unto Jesus to kiss him. 48 But Jesus said unto him: "Judas, betrayest thou the Son of man with a kiss?" *The Gospel of St. Luke*, Ch. 22:47-48. "43 And immediately, while he yet spake, cometh Judas, one of the twelve, and with him a great multitude with swords and staves, from the chief priests and the scribes and the elders. 44 And he that betrayed him had given them a token, saying: "Whomsoever I shall kiss, that same is he; take him, and lead him away safely." 45 And as soon as he was come, he goeth straightway to him, and saith: "Master, master; and kissed him." 46 And they laid their hands on him, and took him. *The Gospel of St. Mark*, Ch.14: 43-46 " 47 And while he yet spake, lo, Judas, one of the twelve, came, and with him a great multitude with swords and staves, from the chief priests and elders of the people. 48 Now he that betrayed him gave them a sign, saying, whomsoever I shall kiss, that same is he: hold him fast. 49 And forthwith he came to Jesus, and said: "Hail, master"; and kissed him. 50 And Jesus

would not be a logical thing to do. Firstly, it is not written in St. John's Gospel and secondly, it is not logical because if we accept that Judas went to take Jesus' enemies to him, it was not necessary for him to go and kiss his face. It was simply enough to point to Jesus and name him, so that he could be arrested.

What is obviously clear to see is that the four canonical Gospels contain quite contradictory statements about this event. Also, the place of Judas in this matter is not at all clear, demonstrating a great number of contradictions and opposing viewpoints.

What we *can* understand from all of this is that during the night of Thursday to Friday, in the middle of a crowd and in a chaotic situation, somebody who pretended to be Jesus of Nazareth was arrested and was taken away by the Pharisees and the Romans at the end of the night. Circumstances were so chaotic that each one of Jesus' companions was running around in a state of frenzy because they were completely taken by surprise and shocked. We do not have any evidence showing whether or not that person really was Jesus. It remains a question.

Another fact is that this signifies the end of the story of Judas Iscariot as far as St. John's Gospel is concerned. St. John's last sentence about Judas describes him as having been there silently. We understand that **Judas enters the garden and then disappears, while someone is brought out of the garden claiming to be Jesus.**

---

said unto him: "Friend, wherefore art thou come?" Then came they, and laid hands on Jesus, and took him. *The Gospel of Matthew*, Ch. 26: 47-50.

A new look at events

As we wrote before, the most complete and comprehensive explanation of that night as represented in the four canonical Gospels is given in the book according to St. John, because St. John was close to his master until the last moments - except during the attack by Jesus' enemies when he was sleeping. Therefore, certain parts of what he explains are what he actually saw and other parts are reports of what he heard.

If we take a new look at that night's events, we see that during that night Jesus and his companions finished their dinner, left the house and changed their location three times. Finally they went to a garden on the other side of the desert of Cedron. Jesus' companions were very tired and sleepy. In the middle of the night Jesus' enemies came to the same place. Judas was with them. Judas was not asleep. And there was another person pretending to be Jesus who was also awake.

This leaves us with three open points to consider:

1. Jesus' enemies did not know what Jesus of Nazareth looked like.

2. Even if they did know Jesus of Nazareth it remained very difficult for them to distinguish him in all the turmoil in the garden during the middle of the night.

3. There were 12 people who looked very similar to Jesus and they were all ready to offer their lives for their Master.

These three points cannot be denied. So why did all of Jesus' enemies go to that garden? The clear answer must be: in order to arrest Jesus. But now there is a new question to consider: How can we be certain that Jesus really was in that house?

St. John explains that Jesus and his companions went to that garden and to that house. The new question is about how we may be certain that Jesus remained in that house when his companions went to rest and to sleep? He knew about the coming arrest as he said to his companions: "In this night you will fall in the trap of a big illusion with regard to me." The only person to know what would happen that night was Jesus himself, because he sent Judas in order to bring his enemies to that place. He knew what would happen. His companions did not know, only he knew.

We do not know exactly what happened in Gethsemane between Jesus, John, Jacob and Peter during the time that Jesus separated these three disciples from the rest of the apostles. What did he tell them? What did he want from them? It is not clear, it is not mentioned anywhere and the author of the Gospel of St. John says that what is written in this book only represents part of an extensive discussion between Jesus and them. The author was only allowed to write down brief parts of these discussions. So, many things were not written down due to a lack of permission.

Ultimately, we do not have any solid evidence whether or not Jesus really was in that garden during all the events. It is possible that Jesus knew of the coming arrest and had left that place before the arrival of his enemies. The fact that the enemies went to that place and that somebody by the name of Jesus was arrested is not convincing enough as evidence to make us accept that Jesus was among them in that garden. The enemies did not go to that place on the basis of their own knowledge of Jesus' location. They went there because they were guided to that place by Judas. And precisely this was Judas' mission. Judas guided all of them to a place in order to arrest a person who was unknown to them. From the first moment they entered the garden they asked everybody: "Are you Jesus of Nazareth?" and the answer was always the same: "Yes I am Jesus of Nazareth." All we know is that the enemies do not leave the garden empty–handed: they arrest somebody who claims to be Jesus of Nazareth. It is written thus: somebody went out of the house and asked them:

"Who are you searching for?"

And they answered:

"Jesus of Nazareth".

That person said:

"I am Jesus of Nazareth. I am telling you, I am Jesus of Nazareth, if you want me, arrest me and let the others go."

And the Roman soldiers and the servants of the High Priests arrested him and took him with them.[302]

Two parallel events

Now it is certain that two events happened parallel to each other. One event is reported in the Gospels and the other event happened outside this report.

The first event

They arrested someone who presented himself as Jesus and then brought him to Hannas, the father in law of Caiaphas, who was the head of the priests in that time. Caiaphas was the person who proposed to the others that it would be better to kill one person than to put the entire community in danger.

"13 And led him away to Annas first; for he was father in law to Caiaphas, which was the high priest that same year. 14 Now Caiaphas was

---

[302] ***The Gospel of St. John*** Ch. 18: 1-12.

he, which gave counsel to the Jews, that it was expedient that one man should die for the people. 15 And Simon Peter followed Jesus, and so did another disciple: that disciple was known unto the high priest, and went in with Jesus into the palace of the high priest. 16 But Peter stood at the door without. Then went out that other disciple, which was known unto the high priest, and spake unto her that kept the door, and brought in Peter. 17 Then saith the damsel that kept the door unto Peter, Art not thou also one of this man's disciples? He saith, I am not. 18 And the servants and officers stood there, who had made a fire of coals; for it was cold: and they warmed themselves: and Peter stood with them, and warmed himself.[303]

When they brought the person arrested under the name of Jesus, Peter and other students followed Jesus' enemies until they reached the house of Hannas. They brought the alleged Jesus inside the house. Peter stood next to the door. The other students went inside the house and Peter talked with the head of the guard so that he could enter as well. At that moment a servant looked at Peter and said: "You are the student of this person who is arrested." Peter denied it: "No, I am not his student."

The second event

When Judas had left the group and came back with the enemies he went inside the house in order to fetch Jesus. Certain documents state that they arrested him because they thought he was Jesus and because all of Jesus' companions also believed him to be Jesus. So with this fact we must accept that he brought something with him which belonged to Jesus and which the companions recognised as being owned by Jesus. And because he had this item in his possession they also thought he was Jesus.

---

[303] *The Gospel of St. John*, 18: 13-18.

It is written in **the Gospel of St. Barnabas**[304] that when Judas went into the house he went towards a certain corner containing a small cave, above which there was a hidden room under the roof.[305] **When he went back again to the garden he looked like Jesus** and he was arrested in place of Jesus.[306] He went there and returned from that corner presumably with the clothes of Jesus on his shoulders. He entered the garden and said: "I am Jesus. Arrest me and let the others go."[307] Jesus' companions woke up in the middle of the dark night and, while running to each side, saw a captured individual whom they assumed to be their master. In short: it was a form of collective psychosis.

Covering the face of the arrested person

Another point of interest is that the soldiers who arrested the alleged Jesus bandaged his eyes to prevent him from running away. But by covering his face with this piece of cloth it became even more difficult to recognize the person behind the blindfold. It is written Gospel: 'They covered his eyes with the blindfold[308].' In one of the documents it is written that the only person who did not believe that

---

[304] *The Gospel of St. Barnabas.* p. 366.

[305] Ibid. This kind of architecture was not unusual. In the ancient monasteries and buildings we can see exactly the same structure. A main place is situated on the first floor with various different small complementary rooms in different corners, with a tunnel into a deep basement, and a hole to a place in the roof. The old part of the Cathedral of St-Taurin, Normandy, France for instance also shows this kind of architecture.

[306] "And God imposed the figure of Jesus on his face" *The Gospel of St. Barnabas.* p. 366. "And God imposed the figure of Jesus on his face"

[307] *The Gospel of St. John*, Ch.18: 8.

[308] *Gospel of Luke*, Chapter 22 Verse 64

this person was Jesus was Simon Peter.[309] Why? **Why only Peter?** It was because Peter was the only the eyewitness to the entire event, from the first moments until the arrest of the alleged Jesus. He had his doubts about the exact identity of the captured person and he denied a relationship to him, just as his master had predicted earlier. But now we see that his master's prediction was a logical observation. From the very onset of the plan, Jesus was certain about Peter's doubts, because he had decided to ask him to take a sword and to keep watching the garden, which Peter did. First, he kept watch all alone and then Judas joined him together with the enemies. Later on, Judas went inside the house to fetch Jesus, and a few moments later a "son of man" came out of the house claiming to be Jesus; and then there is no longer any trace of Judas. Peter felt that something very strange had happened and that the arrested person could be the same person who went inside the house. Peter followed the arrested person, but when they asked him: "Do you know him?" he answered: "No!"(and in this he was right) and he insulted the arrested person. Then the enemies confronted him by saying to him: "You are talking with the same accent, in the same dialect as him." He answered: "No! I swear to God that I am not his student and he is a bad person and a wrongdoer." And he **cursed him** and at that very moment the cock started to crow.

> "70 And he denied it again. And a little after, they that stood by said again to Peter, Surely thou art one of them: for thou art a Galilean, and thy speech agreeth thereto. 71 **But he began to curse and to swear**, saying, I know not this man of whom ye speak. 72 And the second time the cock crew. And Peter called to mind the word that Jesus said unto him,

---

[309] *The Gospel of St. Barnabas* the Spanish/Persian translation, introduction by Dr Khalil Sa'adat, p.26

Before the cock crow twice, thou shalt deny me thrice. And when he thought thereon, he wept".[310]

We can be sure that cursing the arrested person was not out of the fear. Peter was ready to give his life for his Master; and therefore it must have been the consequence of his task during that night.

---

[310] *The Gospel of St. Mark*, Ch.14; 70-72.

Crucify him!

An interesting detail of the arrest is the reaction of the head priest towards the arrested person. He does not ask him: "Are you or are you not Jesus of Nazareth?" but instead he asks him: "Do you pretend to be the King of Israel or not?"[311] And the person alleged to be Jesus replied: "It is what you are telling the others." So the head priest said: "All right, so you do pretend to be the King of Israel. We must kill him. Take him to the Romans."[312]

When they brought him to the Romans, Pilate asked him a series of questions, but the arrested person remained silent. He did not answer and Pilate became highly astonished'.[313] Pilate told the Jews: "Would you like me to let your king free?" He did this because he had discovered that the arrest was due to jealousy towards Jesus on the part of the Jewish priests.[314] This is written in the Gospel of Mark. It is clear that after the interrogation, Pilate the Roman governor decided that the arrested person was not guilty of any crime. He said: "He is guilty of nothing, this person that you have arrested: it is better for you to let him go." But the priests insisted: "He is the person who pretends to be the King of Israel and if you let him go it means that you are not loyal to Caesar. We believe in Caesar. We are obedient to Cesar. If you let him go, it means that you are not loyal to Caesar." So he asked them what they would like to do with him and they replied: "Crucify him!"

Pilate then offered them to free one of the prisoners from the Jewish community as a gesture towards the feast of Passover. "Let me give

---

[311] *The Gospel of St. Mark,* Ch.14: 62.

[312] *The Gospel of St. Mark,* Ch.14: 65.

[313] *The Gospel of St. Mark,* Ch.15: 3-5.

[314] *The Gospel of St Mark,* Ch.15: 9-10.

him his freedom." They answered: "We want another person." They asked Pilate to save the life of Barabbas instead, who was a thief.

Pilate still spoke in favour of the person alleged to be Jesus: "But he is not a guilty. I am not ready to kill him. Take him and bear the responsibility for crucifying him." And he gave him to the Pharisees.[315]

Crucifixion

Pilate gave Jesus to the Jewish community to be crucified. They took the "son of man" who claimed to be Jesus and made him carry his cross to a place named Golgotha. They raised a cross for him in between two other crosses[316].

> *"16 Then delivered he him therefore unto them to be crucified. And they took Jesus, and led him away. 17 And he bearing his cross went forth into a place called the place of a skull, which is called in the Hebrew Golgotha: 19 And Pilate wrote a title, and put it on the cross. And the writing was, JESUS OF NAZARETH THE KING OF THE JEWS."[317]*

The person by whom Jesus was covered

After the sentence of crucifixion had been passed and when the guards untied "the son of man" who gave the impression to be Jesus, this

---

[315] ***The Gospel of St Mark***, Ch.15: 11-15.

[316] ***The Gospel of St. John***, Ch.19: 18 Where they crucified him, and two other with him, on either side one, and Jesus in the midst.

[317] ***The Gospel of St. John***, Ch.19: 16-19. and it continues as follows: 20 This title then read many of the Jews: for the place where Jesus was crucified was nigh to the city: and it was written in Hebrew, and Greek and Latin. 21 Then said the chief priests of the Jews to Pilate: "Write not, The King of the Jews"; but that he said: "I am King of the Jews." 22 Pilate answered: "What I have written I have written.

person created a situation of chaos and disorder and he escaped.[318] People became agitated and the search for the escaped "Jesus" started. The guards, the soldiers, the priests and the Pharisees' slaves stopped people and interrogated them one by one "Are you Jesus"? A few hours later, a "son of man" whose name was also "Jesus" ("Yassou" or "Issu") was captured and delivered into the hands of the guards. It is said that he was one of the leaders of the Jewish masses who had pronounced the sentence against Jesus.

In that atmosphere of collective hysteria, even if that captured person wanted to complain about his arrest, no-one listened to him. People wanted to see a "Jesus" on the cross, and they felt they held one. But he was in fact a cover of the real Jesus: he was his double. The next stages of this strange event show that this "second Jesus" was another secret disciple of Jesus with a hidden mission, to finalise the process of crucifixion. **He spoke a coded language, and he knew how to send Jesus' close friends and family away during the crucifixion.** He was one of the people who were ready to sacrifice their lives for their master, but it was Jesus' plan to save his life at the same time.

The priests immediately and completely undressed the alleged Jesus, covered him with a red robe and put a crown made of thorns on his head. The crown made him bleed and the drops of blood covered his head and face. When they took away his clothes they divided them among them.

> *"28 And they stripped him, and put on him a scarlet robe. 29 And when they had platted a crown of thorns, they put it upon his head, and a reed in his right hand: and they bowed the knee before him, and mocked him, saying,*

---

[318] This version agrees with the explanation found in the Persian book **"Majmal at-Tawarikh wal- Qesas** [Ensemble of the histories and tales]. Majmal al-Tawarikh wa al-Qasas was written in 520 h/1126 A.D. By an unknown author or by Ibn Shady Asad Abadi.First editor Mohammad Taghi Bahar- Tehran 1939. New edition Tehran-Donyaye ketab, 1996. Ali Ashar Abdollahi.

Hail, King of the Jews! 30 And they spat upon him, and took the reed, and smote him on the head."[319]

Jesus Christ - "Soul of God" - had a "contemporary double". This "son of man" was also named Jesus. He was also born in Jerusalem around two thousand years ago, in a Jewish family. He was also a son of parents named as Mary and Joseph. He also had a brother named Jose. He also knew a woman known as Mariamne (Mary Magdalena), and a man (a child) named as Judas. There were many similarities between Jesus, son of Mary, and his double.

When Jesus (son of Mary) was claimed by St. John the Baptist to be "Christ", and when his enemies wanted to eliminate John the Baptist and Jesus Christ, the double of Jesus decided to sacrifice his life for his master in order that his master could accomplish his divine mission.

Judas Iscariot was a missionary Apostle of Jesus Christ. He was told by Jesus: "Judas! Your mission is to sacrifice the man who clothes me". And Judas accomplished his mission with the aid of "Jesus' double" and thus was to receive the hate and blame from all generations until the end of time. Jesus Christ's enemies believed they had crucified him. However, he was in fact taken to a high place in the sky for a period of three days, and later he continued with his mission to spread the seeds of Spirituality across the world. The recent discovery of an old Jewish family tomb in Jerusalem fits in with the explanation presented in an Old-Persian book named "Tarikh Bal'ami" (Bal'ami's book of history") which discusses a second Jesus, who was a contemporary of Jesus Christ and who was crucified in his place. This book is the second-oldest manuscript ever written in the Persian language (352 of hegira/ 973 A.D.). It is the translation of another Book of History written by Mohammad Jarir Tabari (310/ 931 A.D.) who was an expert in "the tales of Prophets and Kings" in the Qur'an. Writers like Tabari,

---

[319] *The Gospel of St. Matthew*, Ch. 27: 28-30.

Bal'ami and Ibn Shadi Asad Abad had a more than thorough knowledge of the content of the New Testament concerning the crucifixion of Jesus Christ, but they introduced another version of the event: in their books they state that the Romans and Pharisees by mistake crucified "Jesus' double". They did not catch Jesus Christ, they did not crucify him and they did not kill him.[320]

---

[320] See Conclusion and Appendix.

The final round

The event of the crucifixion is the final moment of this process. Until then, everything had happened according to Jesus' plan. But each moment a possibility existed that a spontaneous and unpredictable event would occur that would jeopardise the success of this process. A large crowd had gathered on the scene because people had been told that the king of Israel was going to be crucified. This was the same person who pretended to be the promised Christ. Not many people knew Jesus well, but most had heard about him. The companions, the Apostles and Jesus' family were present, but they could not recognise the face of the "son of man" as it was covered by blood and the person was dressed in a red robe.

Recognising the "son of man" was not at all easy. It is important to realise that someone took Jesus' companions and family away, into the distance and far from the cross. This is written in all of the Gospels. All of the women saw the crucifixion from a distance. These women were Maria Magdalena, Maria the mother of Jesus, Maria the mother of Jacob, Salomé mother of John, another lady who was the mother of Joshua and finally various other women who were present.[321] They were kept away from the scene of the crucifixion[322] and later St. John left the place with St. Mary.

---

[321] *The Gospel of St. Mark.* Ch 15. 40-41 "40 There were also women looking on afar off: among whom was Mary Magdalene, and Mary the mother of James the less and of Joses, and Salome; 41 (Who also, when he was in Galilee, followed him, and ministered unto him) and many other women which came up with him unto Jerusalem."

[322] *The Gospel of St. Matthew.* Ch. 27: 55-56. *The Gospel of St. John.* Ch.19: 25 and 27: "25 Now there stood by the cross of Jesus his mother, and his mother's sister, Mary the wife of Cleophas, and Mary Magdalene. 27 And from that hour that disciple took her unto his own home". As of this moment, there are no direct eyewitness reports attributable to St. John's Gospel. The content of this book concerning the matter could be a collection of the sayings of the other witnesses.

I am thirsty, Ily, Ily lama sabagtani

The "crucified Jesus" is said to have proclaimed: "I am thirsty." According to some of the other Gospels he did not express his thirst, but said this very strange verse: "*Iluni, Iluni, lama sabaghtani*". Whatever it was, it does not matter whether he expressed his thirst[323] or whether he exclaimed this peculiar verse: it was a secret code he used to signal that he wished to end his time on the cross. Then an unidentified man went out of the crowd and returned with a certain liquid which he subsequently brought to the mouth and nose of the "crucified Jesus" with a sponge.[324] And he says: "I do this to see if Elias comes **to bring him down from the cross**."[325] According to St. Matthew's Gospel Jesus was given a liquid mixed with gall. The gallnut is a poison with a bitter taste. Merely smelling the sponge (without drinking) would be enough for the person on the cross to lose consciousness and appear to be dead.

> "There they offered Jesus wine to drink, mingled with mirrh; but he received it not."[326]

---

[323] As we mentioned on the preceding pages, the jar of water near the cross was not filled with water, but with another liquid. According to *St Matthew's Gospel*, ch.27-34, it was vinegar mixed with gall which must have been a very powerful anaesthetic that caused a type of cataleptic coma simply by smelling it. This report reminds us exactly of the passages mentioned in the book "Samak e Ayyar". According to this book, people lost their consciousness only by smelling the vapour of a medicine named Bihoushaneh mixed in the wine. *The Samak's city*, by P.N. Khanlary, Tehran, 1988. Agah, p.77-78. See also the appendix about **Bihoushaneh & the path of Ayyari.**

[324] *The Gospel of St. John.* Ch.19: *The Gospel of St Marc.* Ch.15: 36.

[325] *The Gospel of St. Mark.* Ch.15: 33-38.

[326] *The Gospel of St. Mark.* Ch. 27:34. p.46, English version edited by The Gideons International.

This goes to show that among the people who were present, there were many disciples of Jesus who were not known to the Apostles but who were nevertheless involved in this event.

So, we must discover who was responsible for preparing this liquid, for putting it next to the cross, and for bringing it to the mouth and nose of the person on the cross with the help of a sponge and the necessary tools. And we must also discover why using this liquid caused such an immediate reaction on the body of the crucified person.

By smelling the liquid solution, the person on the cross lost consciousness. His head dropped and he fell into a coma. However, the other two people who had also been crucified and were situated next to him remained conscious and aware.

It seems certain that **the death of the person on the cross, assumed to be Jesus, was in fact not due to being crucified but due to smelling the potion**[327]. And the period from the start of the crucifixion until the moment he lost consciousness lasted only three hours, from six to nine o'clock. At 9.00 it was finished.

After he had lost consciousness the person on the cross had to be brought down very quickly because the effects of the potion might

---

[327] There is no doubt about this case. Robert B. Greenblatt, M.D. writes in his book *"Search the Scriptures. Illustrated Modern Medicine and Biblical Personages"*; pp 107-109 that the theologians from diverse branches of Christianity and the scholars maintain that the liquid was offered to Jesus by the Daughters of Jerusalem. It was a group of Jewish women dedicated to Jesus. *"And there followed him a great company of people, and of women, which also bewailed and lamented him. But Jesus turning unto them, said: Daughters of Jerusalem, weep not for me ..."* (Luke 23: 27-28). According to Robert B. Greenblatt the particular effect of wine-**vinegar**, when mixed with different **herbal drugs** such as **gall,** myrrh, frankincense, mandrake was well known in the Biblical time. He adds that gall – (Papaver somniferum), known in the Holy Land- was a kind of "opium-poppy plant" which was used to extract a powerful drug to **reduce suffering and to induce sleep**.

fade and because he would then start to regain consciousness whilst he remaining on the cross. And then, contrary to plan, people would see that he was still alive.

Another risk of resting on the cross too long was that he could actually be killed by the crucifixion. Thus, it was necessary to bring him down immediately once he had lost consciousness.

How was he brought down from the cross?

As we mentioned earlier, Joseph of Arimathea was one of Jesus' disciples who had access to the High Priests and who was also close to Pontius Pilate, the Roman governor of the region. Joseph went directly to Pilate for permission to bring down the dead body of Jesus from the cross.[328] Pilate was astonished: **"First you ask me to crucify them and now you ask me to bring them down! You must wait at least twelve hours. They must die; they will run away if we take them down too early**." Joseph replied: "No, Jesus has died already. In order not to let the other two run away it is better to give the command to break their legs."[329]

Joseph also persuaded the Jewish community not to let the bodies stay on the cross on Saturday. He insisted that the Shabbat should be kept clean. They accepted his request and Joseph went to Pilate. He asked him to break the feet of the two thieves who had been crucified next to Jesus and to allow them to be brought down. So the soldiers went and broke the legs of the first man and the third man, but when they came to Jesus, they saw that he was dead, and they did not break his legs.

---

[328] *The Gospel of St. Matthew.* Ch. 27: 57.

[329] *The Gospel of St. John.* Ch.19: 31-33; *The Gospel of St. Mark.* Ch.15: 44-45.

Pilate was astonished at how quickly Jesus had died and asked **"Are you certain that he died so quickly?"** Joseph replied: "Yes. But you can send someone to verify it." And Pilate then sent his trustee to go and verify things for himself. He went, and when he returned to Pilate he said: "Yes, he is dead:" So they brought him down and they gave the body to Joseph. The crucifixion had started at six o'clock and was finished by nine o'clock. And at nine o'clock the night had already set in and it was dark.[330]

The burial of the body

As we mentioned in the previous chapters, it is certain that during the second part of Jesus' disappearance, the events that occurred became the responsibility of friends of Jesus who were not among the twelve Apostles. The person who brought down the body was Joseph. It was Joseph who took down the body and covered it with white linen. It was not Jesus' Apostles or his family who took back the body. It was this man, Joseph. **The Apostles and Jesus' family did not see the body and did not even verify his identity.** In addition, we do not have access to Joseph's report concerning the event of the crucifixion In fact, we do not even know if such a commentary exists. The only certainty we have, according to the Canonical Gospels, is the fact that from the moment of arrest until the burial moment the family and the eleven Apostles of Jesus rested in the background.[331]

The arrest and the subsequent crucifixion took place quickly, but the burial was even quicker. The speed of the last part of the event did not leave any time, neither for friends and family, nor for the enemies and adversaries to verify anything with respect to the buried person.

---

[330] *The Gospel of St. Luke.* Ch. 23: 44-45.

[331] *The Gospel of St. Matthew.* Ch. 27: 55-56. The only person who was involved for a short while in this affair was Simon Peter.

When the women in the house of St. John heard that the crucifixion was over and that the body of Jesus was going to be buried, they were highly astonished and they collected perfumes to go and prepare the body of Jesus, **but it was already too late.**[332] Joseph advised them to go back and to return on Sunday morning.[333] So, the women looked at the burial process from a distance.[334]

Now, is the speed with which the entire process was completed not peculiar? Does it not signal an act which should be kept secret? It was Jesus' will to keep this secret. He intended to give everyone the impression, or rather illusion, that everything had been completed.

After the night of crucifixion and throughout the following Saturday, Jesus' entire family and all of his friends rested in their houses to pray and cry, and to console each other.

Opening the tomb

As we mentioned earlier, the person who had been crucified had fallen into a deep coma as result of being given a narcotic potion. He was then brought down from the cross and his body was given to Joseph. The tomb contained enough air for the person inside[335] to breathe and

---

[332] *The Gospel of Mark.* Ch. 15. 43-47.

[333] *The Gospel of St Luke.* Ch. 23: 51-56.

[334] *The Gospel of Mark.* Ch. 15: 43-47. *The Gospel of Matthew.* Ch. 27: 60-61.

[335] There was no coffin involved, only a linen shroud. The burial practice of the Jews in the region of Jerusalem, from 10 B.C to 60 A.D., involved laying down the dead body on a stone bench, where it was left to decay. After a year the bones would be collected and put into an ossuary, i.e. a little limestone bone-chest. Read for instance S. Jacobovici and C. Pellegrino, *The Jesus Family Tomb*, San Francisco 2007; and Jacob Slavenburg, **Het Graf Van Jezus – Het Mysterie van de Tomb van Jezus, Maria Magdalena en Judas**, Walburg Pres. 2007 Zutphen

stay alive until it would be reopened. For this particular purpose the tomb had been custom-built.

The Gospel of St. Luke reports that Joseph participated in the assemblies of the Sanhedrin. Joseph was a pleasant and sincere man. His birthplace was a small town named Rame. Joseph was waiting for the apparition of the divinity of God. He was a student of Jesus. He went to Pilate and asked for Jesus' body. He covered this body with white linen[336] and he put him into a new tomb that he had prepared and that no one had used previously. After everybody had gone back home Joseph went to the tomb and asked the guards to go home, too, because everything was quiet. The guards knew he was very close to Pilate. So they accepted his request and went back home. In the early morning of the following Sunday, the women from Galilee went to the tomb of "Jesus". What they found was an open tomb, with a heavy stone removed from its entrance and white linen inside the tomb: no body was found in the tomb.

> *"1 Now upon the first day of the week, very early in the morning, they came unto the sepulchre, bringing the spices which they had prepared, and certain others with them. 2 And they found the stone rolled away from the sepulchre. 3 **And they entered in**, and found not the body of the Lord Jesus."*[337]

One of the logical explanations for this strange mystery is that after the departure of the tomb guards, Joseph opened the tomb, brought out the body of the "crucified man" and gave him

---

[337] *The Gospel of St. Luke.* Ch. 24: 1-3 The phrase: "They entered in" shows that the Tomb was deep and big, not an ordinary one but a special sepulchre.

another potion which would reverse his cataleptic coma.[338] **The tomb was left open with the white linen inside it.**

The women saw the empty tomb but could not take it in or accept it. According to all the Gospels it is clear that everybody who had witnessed the event never believed in any miracles. Nobody is quoted as saying that it was a miracle. They did not consider this form of explanation acceptable. When the women went back to their houses and explained that there was no body in the tomb, they were met by great general disbelief, and their report was regarded as a product of their imagination.

> "9 And returned from the sepulchre, and told all these things unto the eleven, and to all the rest. 10 It was Mary Magdalene, and Joanna, and Mary the mother of James, and other women that were with them, which told these things unto the apostles. 11 And their words seemed to them as idle tales, and they believed them not. 12 Then arose Peter, and ran unto the sepulchre; and stooping down, he beheld the linen clothes laid by themselves, and departed, wondering in himself at that which was come to pass."[339]

Peter quickly left the house, went to the tomb and found it opened with white linen inside it. He verified and saw that it was true.[340] He then left the community and returned to his house.

---

[338] It may well have been the extract of a particular plant and a medicine named Mohrgh. Thus, the body regained awareness. In the jargon of the knights this narcotic potion is named "bi-houshaneh" and the anti-dote is named "Pad bihoushaneh". Also see appendix.

[339] *The Gospel of St. Luke.* Ch. 24: 9-12.

[340] It seems that Peter went into the tomb to check whether it could contain a secret hole or a hidden corner.

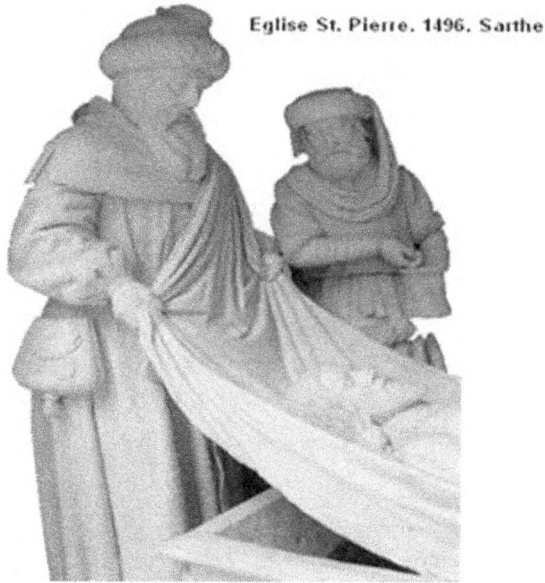

Figure 4 - Eglise St. Pierre, 1496, Sarthe

When the body of the crucified person was going to be buried, all family, friends, followers, companions and apostles became extremely sad and upset. And then, on the Sunday morning, they discovered that there was no body. First they had been astonished, depressed and shocked by the events of the arrest followed by the crucifixion, and now they were shocked again by this new development. At that moment they obviously did not recall the conversation with Jesus in which he told them: "For a short while I will hide myself from your eyes. You will be very sad, but quickly I will come back to you and you will become very happy."

They had forgotten that Jesus had told them that the entire process would resemble the birth of a new child. It is a complicated affair, but afterwards they would become very happy. They forgot all of this; they were overawed and in a state of utter shock. Some of them went back to their houses and some to their villages in order to think about what they had experienced. They felt extremely saddened because they attached a great deal of hope to the apparition of Christ. It had been written in the old documents that Christ was the King of the Israelites and that when he appeared the problems of the Israelite community would be solved. In the beginning, they had been very happy and enthusiastic but now they had become hopeless and depressed. It is in this state that they returned to their own villages.

Let us now consider the Sunday morning, a few hours after the event. We find astonishment and depression among Jesus' companions. After the crucifixion had been completed, the Pharisees returned to their homes and felt satisfied. Jesus' friends were very sad and astonished. We may conclude that **the process which began by one of "Jesus' disciples fulfilling his mission by contacting the Pharisees" had been successful up to this point.**

Judas, the disciple who undertook this mission, led a group of Jesus' enemies to Cedron. This group, believing to have captured the "wanted person" then went from Cedron to the hill of Skull, where "the person who clad Jesus" had been crucified.

According to our explanations, extracted from various different texts, the arrested person in Cedron was not "Jesus son of Mary", but someone who claimed to be him. According to the Gospel of St. Barnabas the captured person in the garden of Cedron was "Judas". According to "Balami's book of history"[341] and "Majmal ot tawarikh wal Qesas,"[342] on the basis of reactions from the crowd, the "arrested

---

[341] *The History of Abu Ali Mohamad ibn Mohamad Balami* is the translation of the extract of the book of *History of the prophets and kings* written by Mohammad Jarir Tabari. The book of the history of Balami is the second-oldest text ever written in the Persian language. 352 of hegira/ 973 A.C; corrected by Malek o-sho'ara Mohamad Taghi Bahar. Tehran, 1385/ 2006. Publisher: Zowwar/ Mohammad Parvin Gonabadi 224- 230.

[342] *Majmal ot tawarikh wal Qesas,* Ibn shadi asad Abadi, p. 216-219.

person" escaped on the hill of Skull and a person named Jesus was arrested and crucified. The event of the crucifixion showed that the "second Jesus" who clad the "Jesus son of Mary" was not captured accidentally. He was one of Jesus' disciples, and his arrest was one element of that highly complicated puzzle. He was arrested and brought on the cross, and in the eyes of the people he died. After the crucifixion he was buried[343] and everything was finished quickly.

Now it is clear that, after the crucifixion, the danger was removed of enemies tracing Jesus in order to arrest him. Jesus could return to his people and restart his activities in a manner that was based on his own calculations and plans.

---

[343] And of course he was brought out of the tomb a very short while later, after which he left that place for another.

The mysterious destiny of Judas

Let us face the question concerning the whereabouts of Jesus and Judas. It must be remembered here that everything had happened so quickly.

Do not fear blame!

A care–free attitude with regard to blame is one of the guiding principles of *Fotowwat* (knighthood) and of Esoterism in general (including Gnosticism and Sufism). It means that the seeker continuously acts in accordance with the principle of Knighthood and that he is not afraid of being blamed or insulted by others. This principle is included in one of the chapters of Jesus' teachings to Judas. Jesus tells his Apostles that all of them, including Judas, are like the twelve hours of the day and that he is the sun which gives light to each one of them in each hour.[344]

It is also highly remarkable that during a personal teaching of Jesus to Judas, the former tells the latter: "You will be person number 13." It means that your destiny is to go out of this circle. Being number 13, or being out of the circle, means that Judas will be blamed by others as a diabolical person. Only the Gospel of Judas mentions this. It is clear that Judas dearly loved his Master and that because of this love he accepted to become the target for the arrows of those who did not know or appreciate the subtlety and depth of the Jesus' plan.

"Jesus told Judas: "You will become the thirteenth of twelve and you will be hated until the end of time. But in the other universe you will have a place above all the Saints."[345]

---

[344] ***The Gospel of St. John,*** Ch.11: 910.

In order to study the hatred and resentment towards Judas we need to compare and evaluate the contents of the Gospel of Matthew, Chapter 26, verses 20-25, Chapter 27 verses 3-10, the Gospel of Mark, Chapter 14 verses 17-21, the Gospel of Luke, Chapter 22 verses 21-23, the Gospel of St. John, Chapter 13 verses 21-30 and the Acts of the Apostles written by Paul, Chapter 1, verses 15-20.[346]

It is clear that Judas was hated by all of the disciples. The underlying reason could be that Judas was already, before this event occurred, at the highest place in the eyes of Jesus. It shows that Judas was a person with an enormous spirit and soul. And the only thing that was important to him was the satisfaction of his Master, without asking anything in return. He was generous and unselfish. His only interest lay in being next to his Master in **the other world**, and not in becoming a hero as a result, because he truly believed in the continuity of the journey of the soul after being separated from the body.

It is written in the Gospel of St. John, Chapter 15, verses 17-23 that Jesus said:

"I command you, before everything else: be kind to each other. Be full of love towards each other. If the world takes you for its enemy it is not important because before being an enemy of yours it was an enemy of mine. If you are a part of this world you are loved by this world. But because you are not from this world and because I selected you from this world, the world hates you and takes you for its enemy. Remember the commands and the teachings that I am

---

[346]Jesus responded to Judas:" Tu deviendra le treizieme, et tu sera maudit par les autres generations, et tu regneras sur elles. Lorsque viendront les derniers jours, elles [...] et tu ... vers le haut vers la generation sainte". *l'Evangile de Judas*, French version. p.37. Sur la malediction de Judas, comparer avec les evaluations de Judas dans L'Evangile de Matthieu (26, 20-25; 27, 3-10) Evangile de Marc (14, 17-21), Evangile de Luc (22, 21-23); Evangile de Jean (13, 21-30); et les Actes (1, 15-20). Il est ici suggeré que Judas est meprise par les autres disciples, mais qu'il sera exalte au-dessus d'eux comme disciple preeminent. Ibid- Footnote p.37.

giving you. You are my students and a student cannot be in higher place than his Master. If they bother you be indifferent, for they bother you more than me. If they accept to respect me they will also respect you. But they do not respect me. Everything they will do against you it is because of me, not because of you. They do all this to you because they don't know who has sent me".

*"17 These **things I command you, that ye love one another.** 18 If the world hates you, ye know that it hated me before it hated you. 19 If ye were of the world, the world would love his own: but **because ye are not of the world, but I have chosen you out of the world, therefore the world hateth you.** 20 Remember the word that I said unto you; The servant is not greater than his lord. If they have persecuted me, they will also persecute you; if they have kept my saying, they will keep yours also. 21 But all these things will they do unto you for my name's sake, because they know not him that sent me. 22 If I had not come and spoken unto them, they had not had sin: but now they have no cloke for their sin. 23 **He that hateth me hateth my Father also.**[347]*

The question may be asked here why we do not usually relate the images of a generous character and a knight to the person of Judas. Actually, the canonical Gospels, and particularly the book according to St. John, are mainly aimed - without any concrete evidence - against Judas, even though none of them ever mentions any negative comments that Jesus may have made concerning Judas. We read in the Gospel of St. John:

*"They were eating and **Satan entered into the heart of Judas** the son of Shamoun of Iscariot."[348]*

---

[347] *The Gospel of St. John,* Ch. 15: 17-23.

[348] *The Gospel of St. John,* Ch.13: 3.

But – again, without providing any evidence - how could one see the penetration of Satan into the heart of somebody else? The same book adds that:

> *"During the supper Jesus gave to Judas a piece of food and **just in that moment Satan** penetrated the heart of Judas."*[349]

It is not in any way a concrete form of evidence. If you were to present this type of evidence to a judge in court he would reject it on the grounds that it does not present any sound evidence. The reader must be aware of this and instead consider the real events as they occurred in the physical world. The reader should not fall into the trap of the personal judgments expressed by the authors of the Gospels. In fact, certain convincing proof undeniably exists that exonerates Judas.

Jesus wanted to accomplish an extremely complicated mission to triumph over his enemies. St. John's Gospel confirms that Jesus and Judas had a long private conversation before Jesus sent Judas on his mission. We must assume that all Jesus' Apostles were in love with him, that they respected him as their Master and that they were ready to follow his orders - even though they did not fully comprehend their meaning.

The important point here is that Judas does not leave the supper table of his own accord: Jesus sends him away. If Judas had had the intention to carry out certain acts against Jesus he would not wait; he would go out very quickly by himself and bring the soldiers to arrest Jesus. Judas does not do any of this. Jesus sends him away and says: "Go and do your mission."[350] Furthermore, St. John reports: "No one understood what Jesus told to Judas."[351] However, there is nothing

---

[349] *The Gospel of St. John*, Ch.13: 27.

[350] *The Gospel of St. John*, Ch.13: 27.

[351] *The Gospel of St. John*, Ch.13: 28.

unusual about this affair. There is absolutely nothing that appears to be out of line, and it is not at all clear why John accuses, something that becomes even more unlikely when we consider the fact that Judas felt himself to be under the orders of his own master.

Our first piece of evidence is there: Jesus tells them "Now I would like to tell you that one of you who are eating with me will give me up to the enemies". The students looked at each other and became astonished and said: "Which one of us?"[352] St. John's Gospel says: "Peter asked by means of a sign to ask Jesus for more clarification about what he had said" and he went and sat down on the ground between Jesus' feet and asked him: "O Rabbi, tell us which one of us". And Jesus said to him: "The person whom I give a piece of food" and he gave it to Judas Iscariot, the son of Shamoun.[353] Judas was sitting down with his master just like the other Apostles, without looking for any pretext to leave the gathering by himself. During that particular night there was nothing to be done in the city or elsewhere, apart from the gathering. If Judas wanted to betray Jesus, then why did Jesus send him away? And if there was something else to be done somewhere else in the city, why did Jesus send Judas rather than somebody else? And before sending him away, why did Jesus wash and dry his feet? And even before this, why did Jesus let him attend to and rest among the Apostles during the Last Supper? Jesus was used to escaping from the traps set by the Pharisees, so for him it was very easy to escape from Judas' trap – should there have been one. It was very easy for Jesus not to allow Judas to be among his apostles. This is exactly what he did to his own brothers when he did not permit them to go to Jerusalem with him.[354]

---

[352] *The Gospel of St. John*, Ch. 13: 21-22.

[353] *The Gospel of St. John*, Ch. 13: 25-26.

[354] *The Gospel of St. John*, Ch. 7: 5-10. 3 His brethren therefore said unto him: "Depart hence, and go into Judaea, that thy disciples also may see the works that

The task of Jesus' agent was to hand over the "man who clad Jesus" to the Romans and the Pharisees. And Judas performed his mission in line with the orders from his master, even though he himself did not fully understand the exact reason for his action.

And we also have a second piece of evidence. How Judas was instructed where to bring the soldiers? This is not clear. It is like a miracle or some form of very strong telepathy if we believe that Jesus did not *tell* Judas where he was going in that night. But in that case, if we accept that everything was carried out by Jesus as part of a very complicated plan, then we must look at things objectively. We mentioned previously that Jesus moved around considerably, going from place to place without fixing his final destination. His actions had a covert style about them. It is therefore not logical to assume that he left that house twice and changed his location many times and yet, through mere coincidence, that Judas arrived at exactly the same place where Jesus was staying at that moment.

Therefore we are left with only two logical possibilities:

1. Judas was a very powerful telepath who had established a strong connection with his Master and who was thus able to follow his Master from a distance. Judas knew where Jesus was going. But if this was actually the case, it would be impossible

---

thou doest. 4 For there is no man that doeth anything in secret, and he himself seeketh to be known openly. If thou do these things, shew thyself to the world." 5 For neither did his brethren believe in him. 6 Then Jesus said unto them: "My time has not yet come: but your time is always ready. 7 The world cannot hate you; but me it hateth, because I testify of it, that the works thereof are evil. 8 Go ye up unto this feast: I go not up yet unto this feast; for my time is not yet full come." 9 When he had said these words unto them, he abode still in Galilee. 10 But when his brethren were gone up, then went he also up unto the feast, not openly, but as it were in secret.

for Judas to be an evil person because - if he was evil - he would definitely have lost this type of heart connection.

2.   Judas was told by his Master to bring his enemies to that place.

There is no other choice.

This latter possibility is to be favoured over any other, as it is the most logical one. In this case Judas acted exactly in accordance with his Master's wishes.

Nobody knew what was going to happen in that night. As we mentioned, Judas brought the enemies from the city to Cedron and afterwards to the hill of Skull on which a man "who clad Jesus son of Mary" was hanged and killed.

If we accept that Jesus talked with his friends and explained to them what was going to happen (in coded language), and if we study the chronological development of his plan objectively, all of the issues which are usually regarded as predictions suddenly become pieces of a rational and exact puzzle. Jesus did not surrender himself to fate. He wanted to impose his own will and decisions on his adversaries to overcome their conspiracies and to give his adversaries the illusion that he had been arrested and crucified in order to be free from their conspiracies and traps. If we view this event objectively, it may be concluded that Jesus becomes a greater and a more important figure as well as a more realistic person.

And what happened to Judas?

We are certain that Judas accomplished his mission to avert the shadow of danger from the head of his master, but we are not certain about the consequences of his actions. **He felt responsible for the lost life of the sacrificed person, because he did not yet know what the following steps of the event would entail.** Like the other apostles, he only knew about part of the actions, and not the whole plan. He was ready to receive the blame in the eyes of all generations until the end of time, but to see someone else on the cross was not easy for him to bear.

We do not know if Judas knew that the crucified person was not really dead but only in a coma. The Gospel of St. John and the Gospel of St. Luke are silent about Judas. The Gospel of St. Matthew spends a few sentences on the disinterest of Judas for the 30 silver coins of money (his pretext to achieve his purpose). It is written in this Gospel that, after the crucifixion, people found the body of Judas who had hanged himself (without giving any details about where and how).[355]

Further investigation into the case of Judas is needed. Still, this may not be possible at present - especially because we lack further information and because the documents obtained from the Gospel of Judas are incomplete.

---

[355] *The Gospel of St. Matthew*, Ch. 27: 3-10: 3. Then Judas, which had betrayed him, when he saw that he was condemned, repented himself, and brought again the thirty pieces of silver to the chief priests and elders, 4 Saying, I have sinned in that I have betrayed the innocent blood. And they said, What is that to us? See thou to that. 5 And he cast down the pieces of silver in the temple, and departed, and went and hanged himself. 6 And the chief priests took the silver pieces, and said, It is not lawful for to put them into the treasury, because it is the price of blood. 7 And they took counsel, and bought with them the potter's field, to bury strangers in. 8 Wherefore that field was called, The field of blood, unto this day. 9 Then was fulfilled that which was spoken by Jeremy the prophet, saying, And they took the thirty pieces of silver, the price of him that was valued, whom they of the children of Israel did value; 10 And gave them for the potter's field, as the Lord appointed me.

Jesus' minor-occultation

Let us recapitulate here. The event started in the night of Friday to Saturday, the burial - following the crucifixion - took place in the night of Friday to Saturday, and the occultation of Jesus lasted until Sunday morning when he reappeared. According to the Qur'an, at that time Jesus left to a high point placed in the sky.[356]

> *"When the soldiers and Judas approached the place in which was Jesus (Yassou), Jesus went carefully into the house while the eleven disciples were sleeping. And when God saw his creature in a dangerous situation, He ordered his messengers Gabriel, Michel, Oril, and Refail to take him from the world. Therefore those pure angels came down and caught Jesus from a hole (of the house) situated facing the South direction, and they took him up and brought him to the sky, and posed him in the third sky in company of the angels who are busy by the eternal God-worshiping."[357]*

It is not clear where exactly Jesus was hiding at the time. The occultation of Jesus started during the period that his companions were sleeping inside the house in the garden of Cedron which contained a small hole towards the Southern direction. With his apostles remaining unaware, Jesus went to that corner to go somewhere else later.[358] It was a hidden little cave.[359] When the soldiers and the Pharisees left the garden with the alleged Jesus, Peter, John and all of the companions followed the group. So they left the house. Nobody was interested in the house any longer. All attention was

---

[356] ***The Gospel of St Barnabas,*** Ch. 216: 1-6. p.215. And 4 angels have taken out him from his body and brought him to the divine sky.

[357] ***The Gospel of St.. Barnabas,*** Ch. 215. 1-6, Persian version, p. 366.

[358] ***The Gospel of St. Barnabas,*** ibid.

[359] In ***the Gospel of St. Barnabas*** is written that "it was a Ghorfeh = little place, from which Jesus was brought up". Ch.216. 1, p.366.

focused on the arrested person. Once he was taken away, the danger subsided and Jesus was free to realise the last part of his plan.

Three days after the event of his arrest, Jesus re-joined his followers on a road between Jerusalem and Emmaus, in a small village just two kilometres outside Jerusalem. Perhaps the place was a quiet hidden cave on a mountain near that village, or on the top of the Hill of Olives. In this respect, it is useful to analyse here the "anti-gravitational phenomenon" of Jesus' transfiguration happening on top of this high hill in order to gain a better understanding of the event that took place in Gethsemane on the Thursday night.

The silence of the Gospel of St. John

As we mentioned in the preceding pages, it is not clear what happened on the Mount of Olives. What happened to the three students? What happened to Jesus? It is certain that John was one of the three people who followed Jesus and who had been with him. He was an eyewitness to that event, but the Gospel remains silent in this matter. Why should this be so? It must be because this is one of those moments that Jesus gave the order not to talk about those experiences with anybody else as long as he was alive.[360] Even though John's Gospel is supposed to be written long after that event, it does not mention anything about what happened that night - which **goes to show that Jesus was still alive**.

An anti-gravitational phenomenon

Nevertheless, the question remains what happened on that night. Other documents write that Jesus took Peter, Jacob and John after six days and that he went to the top the hill into a quiet and secluded corner. It would seem that Jesus was performing a Gnostic act. While

---

[360] *The Gospel of St .Matthew*, Ch.17: 9 "Tell the vision to no man, until the Son of man be risen again from the dead".

he was performing his practice, a powerful stream of energy ran through his entire body and his astral vehicle was in a state of levitation, witness by the fact that he stated "My soul is ready, but the flesh is weak". He was sweating and perspiring.[361] All of sudden, the three eyewitnesses saw him go up in the air.[362]

"1 And after six days Jesus taketh Peter, James, and John his brother, and bringeth them up into a high mountain apart, 2 And was transfigured before them."[363]

It could not have been a vision, because a vision is a personal experience through extra-sensorial perception. When three people witness an event occurring in front of their eyes, they are exposed to a real phenomenon. According to the existing written texts and documents, the three disciples discovered their master in the air. They did not see two Jesuses, one in the air (astral body) and another one on the rocks (elementary body). They saw him in the air, shining as the sun.

"And his face did shine as the sun, and his garment was white as the light."[364]

At that moment, an extraordinary new phenomenon happened. They saw that two other individuals joined their master in the air: Moses and Elias.

---

[361] *The Gospel of St. Luke*, Ch. 22: 44.

[362] In paintings of the "transfiguration", Jesus is inside a kind of egg which is comparable to an electro-static sphere. Often, the transfiguration of Jesus is interpreted as a "dedoublement" or a kind of "out-of-elementary-body experience", but the levitation of the material body is also possible because of its polarisation due to the effect of certain frequencies of vibration caused by the particular Zekr.

[363] *The Gospel of St. Matthew*, Ch.17.

[364] Ibid.

"3 And, behold, there appeared unto them Moses and Elias talking with him."[365]

The transfiguration could not have been a dream or a vision, but an anti-gravitational phenomenon, since Peter talked with the figures.

"4 Then answered Peter, and said unto Jesus, "Lord, it is good for us to be here: if thou wilt, let us make here three tabernacles; one for thee, and one for Moses, and one for Elias."[366]

At that moment another extraordinary phenomenon was witnessed. In the darkness of the night, a huge bright cloud appeared in the sky above all of them, and the sound of a voice was propagated from the Mountain replying to Peter about Jesus[367].

"5 While he yet spake, behold, a bright cloud overshadowed them: and behold a voice out of the cloud, which said, "This is my beloved Son, in whom I am well pleased; hear ye him".[368]

So what did happen in reality on the Mount of Olives? Here, a mysterious event can be linked to Elias. We should not forget that Jesus often talked about Elias and that during his speeches he constantly referred to him. And now we hear from Elias in the Canonical texts

---

[365] Ibid.

[366] Ibid.

[367] To learn more about the sudden appearance of the "bright cloud" in the darkness of the night we can study the books of Dr. Allen Hynek: *The new reports about the U.F.O*, edited in French. *Nouveau rapport sur les O.V.N.I.* by "J'ai lu" Paris. 1981; and other literature such as *Du nouveau sur les socoupes volantes*. Frank Edwards. Edited by "J'ai lu". France. 1978; *Confrontation*. Jacques Vallee. "J'ai lu" France. 1992; *Les O.V.N.I*. Michel Dorier & J.P. Troadce. Edited by "Que sais-je?". Presses Universitaires de France. France. 1992.

[368] Ibid

"6 And when the disciples heard it (that voice), they fell on their face, and were sore afraid. 7 And Jesus came and touched them, and said, Arise, and be not afraid. 8 And when they had lifted up their eyes, they saw no man, save Jesus only. 9 And as they came down from the mountain, Jesus charged them, saying, Tell the vision to no man, until the Son of man be risen again from the dead".[369]

We may state that during the time of the crucifixion Jesus was somewhere else, achieving the same kind of experience, perhaps on the top of the Mount of Olives again. It was not in vain that he often mentioned the name of Elias.

*"And as they came down from the mountain, Jesus charged them not to talk about their experience ... 10. And his disciples asked him, saying: "Why then say the scribes that **Elias must first come**? 11. And Jesus answered and said unto them: '**Elias truly shall first come**, and restore all things. 12. But I say unto you, that **Elias is come already and they knew him not** ...*"[370]

Even "the crucified person" uttered a remarkable sentence, which was interpreted by the witnesses as an appeal to Elias. We are not certain about the exact structure of the last sentence of "the son of man" on the cross. It is said that he proclaimed "Ilouni", as it is said he spoke "Ily, Ily". "Il" can be understood to denote God in Hebraic. But this word can also be "Ely". Ely means Elias. This supports the idea that

---

[369] ***The Gospel of St. Matthew***, Ch.17: 1-9. This event is also reported in the ***Gospel of St. Mark*** Ch. 9. 1-14.

[370] ***The Gospel of St. Matthew***. Ch-17. 10-12. A similar report is written in the ***Gospel of St. Mark*** ch. 9 . 9-13: " And as they came down from the mountain ... they asked Jesus, saying: "why say the scribes **that Elias must first come**? And Jesus answered: "**Elias verily cometh first**, and restoreth all things ... but I say you that **Elias is indeed come** ..."

"the son of man" on the cross wanted to tell people that he had achieved his mission according to the will of Elias.

Elias: a brief biblical explanation.[371].

According to the Bible, Ely (or Elias) was a prophet – living as a hermit on the top of Mount Carmel. After a 40 day period of seclusion in a cave, where he was regularly nourished and comforted by the hospitality of a raven, he left the earth towards the high sky. The Bible writes that a powerful celestial vehicle appeared in the sky and abducted him (bodily) in the middle of a fiery whirling stream and that it brought him high forever.

Figure 5 - Picture of Prophet Elias been fed by a Raven

---

[371] Ely/ Elijah lived in Israel in the 9th century BC. The names symbolize, says the Church, **Elijah's whirlwind assumption to heaven in a chariot of fire drawn by horses of fire**. The name of this Hebrew prophet is now very common in Greece. His shrine is always situated on mountains and hilltops where Helios, the heaven-born flaming charioteer, was worshipped.
http://www.britannica.com/biography/Elijah-Hebrew-prophet.

"When God took His decision to bring up Elias to the sky by a whirling-wind-stream ...[372] *he was walking and talking with Elysee... all of a sudden a fiery vehicle propelled by the fireful horses appeared and separated them from each-other, and Elias ascended to the sky by a whirling wind-stream..."*[373]

Figure 6 - Greek Icon showing Prophet Elias flying to heaven in a fiery chariot

Elias never died but left the earth with his body. The bodily ascension of Elias (Idris) is also mentioned in the Qur'an.

"And commemorate Edris (Elias) in the Book (Qur'an), for he was a man of truth, a Prophet, and **We uplifted him to a place on high**"[374]

In the Gospel of Barnabas, the point of departure for Jesus towards the sky is a hidden room, with a hole facing the southern direction, in

---

[372] ***Book of Kings***, Ch.2 – 1.

[373] Ibid. Ch. 2 - 11.

[374] ***The Qur'an***. s.19, 56-57 The Muslim documents and especially the Qur'an version concerning the event of Jesus remind us of the event of Elias. It suggests that Elias came back with his celestial vehicle and picked up Jesus from the Mount of Olives or the house of Cedron, towards a high point placed in the sky, all of which lasted for a period of three days. .

191

the house situated in the garden of Cedron. In that document it is written:

> *"And Judas broke into that* **little room, from which Jesus was** **picked up to the sky.** *And all of the students were sleeping. So God did a very strange affair. Judas changed in talking and looking and he seemed like Jesus, by a manner that we all believed him to be Jesus. Judas awoke us and asked us one by one to know where is Jesus. We wondered and replied but you are your-self our teacher! Do you forget this fact? He smiled and replied how foolish you are! You don't know Judas Iscariot? In that discussion, the soldiers came into the room and caught Judas under their hands. When we heard the explanation of Jus/Jesus, and the presence of the soldiers in the room, run away as the mad men. And Youhanna (St. John) escaped with a cotton-towl around his body, and one soldier tried to capture him, and he let down his cover and escaped naked."*[375]

The same occurrence is reported in St. Mark's Gospel which does not mention the name of St. John:

> *"And there followed him a certain young man, having a linen cloth cast about his naked body; and the young-men laid hold on him, and he left the linen cloth, and fled from them naked."*[376]

The text of the Gospel of Barnabas makes clear that the soldiers and Jesus' students did not find any trace of Jesus and took Judas in place of Jesus. Jesus was lifted up towards the sky completely, both with his elementary and his astral body. Meanwhile, Judas was arrested in his place because of his resemblance to his master.

---

[375] *The Gospel of Barnabas.* Ch. 216. 1-12, pp.366-367.

[376] *The Gospel of St. Mark.* Ch.14- 51-52.

The fresco of the Visoki Decani in Kosovo

A fresco entitled *The Crucifixion* was painted in 1350, above the altar at the Visoki Decani Monastery in Kosovo. Two flying fiery celestial vehicles, with their pilots, are painted in the air in the two extremes of the picture, above the roofs of the buildings and temples. The pilots are looking at each other and one of them points at "a son of man on the cross". Above the crucified man there are two couples of angels, as is described in the Gospel of Barnabas.[377] This wall painting is truly unique in its kind and attests that from an ecclesiastic perspective various different beliefs were held with respect to all the events surrounding Jesus.

Figure 7 - Crucifixion – 14th Century wall painting of crucifixion in an old church – Kosovo

---

[377] http://uk.youtube.com/watch?v=RcrzD0PfyPs the flying objects in this painting is perfectly designed! Their aeronautical shapes have nothing to do with usual vehicles of 700 years ago

Figure 8 - Enlarged upper left section of a 14th century wall
painting in a church in Kosovo

If we examine the Qur'an on this topic we find that verse 185 of Surat
3 mentions that Jesus left the earth for a certain period of time and was
taken up to the sky.

*"Remember when Your Lord told O Jesus I take you up and I bring you high
to Myself."*[378]

---

[378] **The Qur'an,** s. 3: 55. Here we would like to introduce the term of 'Tohfee-eh'.
Tohfee-eh can be translated as 'taking away', 'being taken off'. This is the case for the
self-awareness (soul + astral body) in the voluntary death, where in a state of deep
meditation, in a coma, and in deep sleep the soul is separated from the physical body.
In different verses of the Qur'an we find references to this type of out- of-body
experience where one leaves his/her body —or in other terms the awareness places
itself out of the brain and body. A man is able to leave his body during sleep, a
voluntary "death" or physical death. **The Qur'an,** s. 39: 42 "Allah takes up the souls
in the moment of their death, and who dies during their sleep". Surat 32: 11 "Tell the
angel of the death takes you up who is missioner to you". Surat 6: 60 "He is who
takes you up during the night". Surat6: 61 "His soul is taken away by the angels and if
it is only a dream he comes back to his body. But if it is the definite physical death

The Bodily Ascension

"When God found his Man in danger, He commanded his messengers Gabriel, Michael, Rafael, and Oriel to take up Jesus from the world. So those pure angels came down and took Jesus from a tunnel which was on the northern side and they brought him toward the sky and posed him in the third sky."[379]

The Gospel of St. Barnabas does not include a report stating that the body of Jesus was found somewhere in the house of Cedron! His travel to the sky was a physical journey.

"And they did not kill him, nor crucify him, but they made an error about that affair, and certainly they did not kill him, but Allah brought him up to a high placed point."[380]

The Qur'an verses about Jesus show that he was literally (bodily) picked up and brought to the sky.[381] The reader can then ask himself the question "But where? There is no fixed place in the sky." Here, we

---

his soul doesn't return". In the moment that the death comes to one of you our messenger takes him up and they don't pass the borders. The death of Jesus could be interpreted as a voluntary death. This is a usual phenomenon for mystics of the Gnostic path, where, through certain physical, mental and energetic exercises during a state of deep meditation, they can reach a point at which they are able to leave their physical body. The exercises which preceded the meditation occurred on the mountain of Zita, when the companions of Jesus were sleeping.

[379] *The Gospel of St Barnabas*, 4th edition, P. version- pub. Alma'I, Tehran 1383, Ch. 215: 4-6 In the Spanish edition - in place of Oriel - the fourth angel is Azril.

[380] *The Qur'an* s. 4, v.157; s.19 v-57.

[381] A near-death experience. This could be the equivalent of "the Voluntary Death" in Gnostic-Sufi jargon. "Die before dying!" In a N.D.E the physical body remains accessible to be visited by the witnesses. But in the case of bodily ascension, no trace of the abducted person remains! The person involved distances himself from the earth and its inhabitants.

remind the readers of the appearance of the huge cloud above the mountain of Zita (mentioned on the preceding pages).[382]

The content of the Gospel of St. Barnabas and the Qur'an support the bodily travel of Jesus toward the sky, while the "double of Jesus" was on the cross. The wall painting in a monastery in Kosovo reminds us of the same.

> *"And the Jews had a leader whose name was also Jesus (Ishou'). When they untied Jesus to hang him on the cross, Allah made Jesus disappear from their eyes, and imposed the figure of Jesus on the face of second Jesus (Ishou') who was their leader. The Jews told he disappeared by magic. Let's wait one hour, and we'll find him back... After a short while waiting they saw Ishou who looked like Jesus. They arrested him and did not accept at all his opposition,... and hanged him on the cross. And God the biggest one brought the real Jesus to the sky ..."[383]*

---

[382] We also remind the reader of the ascension of the body and soul of Elias with a very powerful celestial vehicle, as is written in the Bible.

[383] ***Tarikh e Balami*** p.224-230.

Jesus' Return

O n Sunday, before noon, Jesus returns and shows himself to his companions. However, they do not believe it is Jesus of Nazareth, the son of Mary. Initially, they do not know him and fail to recognize him, and finally they do not believe in the possibility of him returning after thinking that he had been crucified. Afterwards, they grew extremely anxious and thought that he was a phantom or the ghost of a dead person. But Jesus warns them: "No. I am not a phantom. I am Jesus in my physical body. I am not a soul. Come and touch my body and be certain that I am myself. I am extremely hungry because during these days I have not eaten anything. Bring something, I would like to eat."

> *"22 When therefore he was raised from the dead, his disciples remembered that he had said this unto them; and they believed the scripture, and the word which Jesus had said."*[384]

Jesus joins his disciples

During the Sunday morning, two of Jesus' disciples were walking from Jerusalem towards Emmaus. On the way, they were talking with each other about all of the events that had occurred. In the midst of their discussions a third person joined them. It was Jesus himself. They did not recognise him. He interrupted their discussion to ask them why they were sad and why they were walking so wearily. One of them was Keliophas. He replied: "It seems that you don't know Jerusalem, you don't come from Jerusalem, and you don't know what has happened during the last three days in Jerusalem. You are not aware of all the events that have occurred." And Jesus asked them: "What has

---

[384] *The Gospel of St. John*, Ch. 2: 22.

happened?" Keliophas started to report: "There was a man, called Jesus of Nazareth, he was a prophet.

He was an able speaker and a teacher, he was close to God. But the Pharisees and the Romans arrested him and gave the order to kill him and he was crucified. We attached a great deal of hope to him, that he came to us as Christ and thus would free us from the Romans. Now it is two days after his death, and this morning we became even more astonished when the women returned from his tomb and told us they did not find him in his tomb. The only thing they found in the tomb was white linen that he was wrapped in. We sent some of our friends to verify what the women had reported and they confirmed it."

"13 And, behold, two of them went that same day to a village called Emmaus, which was from Jerusalem about threescore furlongs. 14 And they talked together of all these things which had happened. 15 And it came to pass, that, while they communed together and reasoned, Jesus himself drew near, and went with them. 16 But their eyes were holden that they should not know him. 17 And he said unto them: "What manner of communications are these that ye have one to another, as ye walk, and are sad?" 18 And the one of them, whose name was Cleopas, answering said unto him: "Art thou only a stranger in Jerusalem, and hast not known the things which are come to pass there in these days?" 19 And he said unto them: "What things?" And they said unto him: "Concerning Jesus of Nazareth, which was a prophet mighty in deed and word before God and all the people: 20 And how the chief priests and our rulers delivered him to be condemned to death, and have crucified him. 21 But we trusted that it had been he which should have redeemed Israel: and beside all this, today is the third day since these things were done. 22 Yea, and certain women also of our company made us astonished, which were early at the sepulchre; 23 And when they found not his body, they came, saying, that they had also seen a vision of angels, which said that he was alive. 24 And

certain of them which were with us went to the sepulchre, and found it even so as the women had said: but him they saw not."[385]

Jesus replied: "You really are fools!" and he started to talk about Moses, other Prophets, the things that were written in other books, and about what he had taught them himself. They were in deep discussion until they reached Emmaus. He told them: "My path goes on. I must keep on going." But they invited him to stay because the night was approaching. So he accepted, and entered their house. Then they sat down at the table together and they brought the bread to Jesus. He broke it into three pieces and passed them the bread. Then, suddenly, they recognised him. They became very happy, but Jesus told them: "I must go as I told you. I must go elsewhere." So he left them.

"25 Then he said unto them: "O fools, and slow of heart to believe all that the prophets have spoken: 26 Ought not Christ to have suffered these things, and to enter into his glory?" 27 And beginning at Moses and all the prophets, he expounded unto them in all the scriptures the things concerning him-self. 28 And they drew nigh unto the village, whither they went: and he made as though he would have gone further. 29 But they constrained him, saying: "Abide with us: for it is toward evening, and the day is far spent." And he went in to tarry with them. 30 And it came to pass, as he sat at meat with them, he took bread, and blessed it, and brake, and gave to them. 31 And their eyes were opened, and they knew him; and he vanished out of their sight.

32 And they said one to another: "Did not our heart burn within us, while he talked with us by the way, and while he opened to us the scriptures?" 33 And they rose up the same hour, and returned to Jerusalem, and found the eleven gathered together, and them that were with them, 34 Saying: "The Lord is risen indeed, and hath appeared to Simon." 35 And they told what things

---

[385] *The Gospel of St Luke*, Ch. 24: 13- 24.

were done in the way, and how he was known of them in breaking of bread."[386]

The two people began to talk to each other became very sad and they may have said to each other: "When he walked with us and talked to us about the books we didn't recognize him. We didn't know him and now that we have discovered his identity, he left us: it is too late." So they decided to go back to Jerusalem to join the gathering of Jesus' eleven Apostles and talk with them. So they went back and reported what they had experienced, saying that: "We really met Jesus, he came with us to our house and he gave us bread." The other disciples were again astonished and said: "But what you are saying is not possible, it is only a product of your imagination."

They were all involved in this type of discussion when all of a sudden Jesus appeared to them and said to them: "Peace be unto you" Once more, they were shocked and astonished and they thought they were talking to a ghost or a dead person.

*"36 And as they thus spake, Jesus himself stood in the midst of them, and saith unto them: "Peace be unto you." 37 But they were terrified and affrighted, **and supposed that they had seen a spirit.** 38 And he said unto them: "**Why are ye troubled?** and why do thoughts arise in your hearts? 39 **Behold my hands and my feet, that it is I myself: handle me, and see; for a spirit hath not flesh and bones, as ye see me have.**" 40 And when he had thus spoken, he shewed them his hands and his feet. 41 And while they yet believed not for joy, and wondered, he said unto them: "**Have ye here any meat?**" 42 And they gave him a piece of a broiled fish, and of a honeycomb. 43 **And he took it, and did eat before them.** 44 And he said unto them: "These are the words which I spake unto you, while I was yet with you, that all things must be fulfilled, which were written in the law of Moses, and in the prophets,*

---

[386] ***The Gospel of St. Luke**, Ch. 24: 25-35.*

and in the psalms, concerning me." 45 Then he opened their understanding, that they might understand the scriptures."[387]

Jesus asked them: **"Why are you troubled? Why are you in doubt? Come and touch my feet, my hands and feel that I am here with my physical body. I am alive. The soul doesn't have meat and bones; but I have meat and bones, come and touch me**." He went to each one of them and made them touch his feet and his hands. They became very happy, but absolutely astonished and could not accept what they saw.

Jesus let them verify that he was not a ghost

A very well-known story exists about Thomas, who is reported to have touched Jesus' wounds in order to convince himself that Jesus is alive. In this case, we assume this story to be a later addition. We cannot find any supporting evidence for it. **Jesus, however, clearly invited people to examine his physical reality so as to assure them that he did not die on the cross.**

Jesus intended to prove that he was physically present, as he was before the event of the crucifixion. They touched his body to verify that he was no ghost. It is important to note here that the wound is not mentioned at all. **Jesus did not proclaim "Come! And see my wounds!" but "Come! And by touching my body, see that I am real, not a ghost".** We see this as a very powerful sign. Jesus showed them all of his body to make them fully aware of the fact that he never rested on the cross. Jesus, after letting his companions verify that he was not a ghost, asked for something to eat because he was very hungry. So they brought him freshly prepared fish and honey, and Jesus sat down and ate. "It is as I told you in the beginning. I go and after three days I will join you again. You can find it written in the

---

[387] *The Gospel of St. Luke*, Ch. 24: 36-46.

Thora in the book of Anbia and in Zabour (psalms) of David." At that moment their minds became clear about the written passages in those books concerning Jesus. The Gospel of St. John writes that Jesus left his disciples after finishing the meal and that after a while he came back to them. Upon his return, he appointed Peter as his successor among his people.[388]

According to the writings of Marcus he says: "Go to different corners of the world and talk with the people and give them the teachings of the evangelium.[389] After the separation of Jesus from the group, Peter gathered all of the companions of Jesus together and allowed somebody else to take the place of Judas in the circle of twelve. At that moment Paraklit, or the Holy Ghost, appeared to them and ran through the bodies of all of them. Afterwards, they left each other and went to different places in Jerusalem. Saint Mary, Saint John and some other women went to Ephesus and it is possible that Jesus went to that same destination. Lazarus went to Lefkana and stayed there for thirty years in order to guide people to the teachings of Jesus. Barnabas went to Cyprus, Syria and Jerusalem before returning to Cyprus, and he died in the land where he was born. Peter went to Rome and was crucified there. Paul went to different cities of Byzantium. And Thomas went to Edessa – present-day Orfoe. All of them went in different directions and started to deliver Jesus' teachings to the people. God was among them. He ran through their hands and provided them with signs in order to prove the validity of their teachings.[390]

---

[388] *The Gospel of St. John*, Ch. 21: 14 -17.

[389] *The Gospel of St. Mark*, Ch. 16: 15.

[390] *The Gospel of St Mark*, Ch. 16: 20.

Where did Jesus go from Jerusalem?

After appointing Peter as his successor in the gathering of the Apostles (according to St. John's Gospel), Jesus told them: "I will go far from this place". Why? Maybe because it was no longer possible for him to stay there in accomplishing his mission (educating students and writing spiritual teachings) Maybe he wanted to avoid making people jealous of him or maybe he refused to let the same nightmare start all over again. So he had to go elsewhere. But where did he go?

As we mentioned earlier in our discussion about the Pharisees, they were certain that Jesus wanted to leave Jerusalem and go to **the land of the Greeks** to establish his work there.

> *"35 Then said the Jews among themselves: "Whither will he go, that we shall not find him? Will he go unto the dispersed among the Gentiles, and teach the Gentiles?" 36 What manner of saying is this that he said: "Ye shall seek me, and shall not find me: and where I am, thither ye cannot come?"* [391]

Certainly Jesus would have wanted go to the land of the Greeks in order to teach the Greeks. It is possible that by 'Greek land' they are referring to Ephesus (in present-day Turkey). In line with this assumption, it is possible that Jesus started to teach different students. He went to a new land offering new potential. From the very beginning in Jerusalem, **he chose his students** among Gnostics and Jews, Tsadokits, Esseniens, Greeks, Zealots and numerous other sects and groups that were present at the time.

But most of the people attracted to him were much more interested in having someone to liberate their country from the Roman rulers. But

---

[391] ***The Gospel of St. John***, Ch. 7: 35-36. From the Greek translation. The Persian version writes "...he would like to go and stay among the Greeks".

Jesus was a real Christ and a soul saviour; he was not a country liberator. **By carrying out his subtle plan successfully he made the leaders of the Jewish community believe that his life was finished. Thus, he could rid himself of popular expectations involving him as a country liberator. Instead, he could now follow his mission of teaching people how to free their souls and how to develop their substance.** In the new land Jesus could select new students among the Western people, the Gnostics, and the students of Philo. This is probably how Gnosticism became linked to teachings of Jesus.

Ephesus[392] and the cave

As was mentioned on the preceding pages, it is almost certain that part of the Christian community went to what was known as *Greek-land* and stayed there. Some of the early Christian texts were written in that place. The most important elements of those texts included the works of St. John the apostle. Moreover, his tomb is supposed to be situated there (in a place named ZanJan), in the region of Ephesus in Cappadocia.

In the same area, we find a chapel assumed to be St. Mary's praying place. If we take the particular closeness of St. John to Jesus into consideration, we can understand why the early Christians, the apostles and the members of Jesus' family stayed in that place. It is because they followed their Beloved Master.

The Qur'an confirms the fact that Jesus was living, talking and teaching in this world until he was old, without detailing exactly where this took place. But it prominently places the case of the companions in the cave in the picture. One may very well argue that in the coded

---

[392] For more information consult *Smith's Bible dictionary*, p.306.

language of the Qur'an it is related to the continuity of the event of Jesus and his life.

Many things happened in the region of Ephesus and Cappadocia. A wealth of treasures has been found in the form of old wall paintings dating back to the flourishing period of early pre-Byzantine Christianity. Also, other historical pieces of evidence remain from that period, testifying to the transition from Mithraicism to Christianity. **All developments resemble the eruption of a huge spiritual volcano, spreading its streams all around the world. How could this happen if the source of inspiring energy was not there personally?** The caves of Cappadocia presented the best natural spot to help the new Christian community stay alive, grow and mature.

If we travel to Ephesus, we can find the cave of the Seven Sleepers. It is written in the Qur'an and in the report of Al-Birouni that seven companions and a dog stayed in a cave for a period of 300 years (in the solar calendar) or 309 years (in the lunar calendar). We know that the event of the crucifixion took place between 33 and 35 A.D. We also know that Christianity became the official religion of the Roman Byzantine Empire during Constantine's reign in 345. Thus, it corresponds with the time spent in hibernation by the companions in the cave in Ephesus.[393] It gives us the same date (35 and 309 add up to exactly 344). This is the time that Constantine experienced his first dream[394] about Jesus and about Christianity.

---

[393] According to the solar calendar they spent 300 years in the cave and 309 years according to the lunar calendar. Albirouni. *Asar ol baghieh,* p.451.

[394] The dream is only an individual and personal experience. One cannot give any importance to a dream or consider the dreams of others without foundation. We don't know if Constantine really had a dream or whether he pretended to have had one. Nevertheless, the date should be about 344 A.D. A majority of researchers considers the whole story of Constantine having a dream to be a pretence, used by

So, the seven companions went into the cave during the time of Darianus[395] and came out of it in the period of Constantine. This event occurred among the Greek people who were living in Ephesus at that time. The commentaries of the Qur'an do not hesitate to introduce the Seven Sleepers as Jesus' disciples.[396] The reader will find adequate explanations about this part of Jesus' life in the second volume of this study.

In sum, it is certain that this new place became the new centre or school for Jesus to teach, but it was not without consequence. We know that Jesus himself had been circumcised in line with Jewish rules, but in the Gentile world people were not used to that tradition. This fact caused a problem, harming the ritual rules and finally becoming one of the reasons for the break-up between two famous apostles of Jesus: Barnabas and Paul.[397]

---

him (and his mother Helena) to gain more power. He was not interested in religion, only as a political factor. Thus, they could create that myth.

[395] Daghaltianous proceeds the period of official Christianity in Byzance. In the 19th year of the reign of Constantine, the high archbishops gathered in the Council of Nicea and determined the definitions of Christianity. Al Birouni. *Asarol baghieh*, p.136.

[396] Al Mo'tasam, the Kalif of the Abbasid dynasty, sent somebody in the company of his ambassador in Byzance to Ephesus to visit the Cave of the Seven Sleepers. Mohammad ibn Moussa Shaker went and touched them with his own hand, but he doubted if the cadavers were those of the famous seven sleepers of the tale in the Qur'an" Abu Reyhan: *Asar ol Baghyeh*, p.450. "The Gnostics used to live in a particular style, and when they died, their bodies rest complete for long while. Sometimes you can see once they have died their bodies are left alone, and in different monasteries when they die their bodies are left standing up supported by their sticks and they rest there in that position for a long time." Ibid 451. This testimony is important. It shows that many Gnostics used to go to the caves in the mountain of Cappadocia and in the region of Ephesus, and rest and meditate in different caves, and leave their physical bodies.

[397] The reader is referred to the second volume of this research project.

Going back to Jerusalem

During that period, Jesus sent several apostles and disciples to different corners of the world (Lazarus to Lefkana, Barnabas to Syria, Jerusalem, Cyprus, Paul to Jerusalem and Roman land) where they successfully continued their missions until the end of their days. Saint John the apostle probably died in the region of Ephesus, but according to certain sources Jesus himself went back to Jerusalem in the company of his family, after having stayed in Ephesus for a while. Jesus spent his old age in that place.

The elementary body can be harmed or destroyed at each moment and it is Fani, 'not-remaining', but the soul is "remaining", Baghi (eternal). So, the soul is eternal but the body is not.

> *"When Jesus understood that his students were talking about him, he said: "Why do you argue with each other? If you see "the son of man" who goes up in his first place, lo, that it is only soul which goes up." And there is not any use of the body."*[398]

---

[398] *The Gospel of St. John*, Ch. 6: 62.

Conclusions

What we can conclude from the Christian documents is that the event of the crucifixion was a real event. It is certain that Jesus' enemies had made a plan in order to arrest and kill Jesus. It is certain that they built the wooden cross in order to crucify Jesus. It is also certain that "a son of man" under the name of Jesus was really crucified. The question is: was it really Jesus himself or not? This question cannot be answered with a definite 'Yes' or 'No', according to the contents of the existing Gospels.

On the basis of the existing official Gospels we cannot reach a definite conclusion. Nor can we draw the conclusion that the person who was crucified died as a result of the crucifixion.

The official Gospels mention that **Jesus certainly was alive before and after the event of the crucifixion. He was alive both spiritually and physically** and he was living among his people before and after the event of the crucifixion.

Through rational and logical thought we can draw the following three conclusions.

1. The person who was crucified did not die on the cross, but only lost consciousness. He was brought down from the cross with a complete body without serious injuries. He then regained awareness and left the place.

2. The person who was crucified at the time experienced some sort of NDE (near-death experience). It means that his heart started to beat very slowly (low arterial pressure) and that his body went to a state of cataleptic coma. Because of this situation, he was brought down from the cross. (People can have this experience in a state of deep hypnosis and "dead-

209

asana" in Hatha-Yoga.) He then left that place, coming out of that "voluntary death" and going somewhere else.

3. In the two cases described above, and even contemplating the idea that the person on the cross could have been Jesus himself, the fact that people saw him alive after the event of the crucifixion can be due to one of these two possibilities. Both are probable and acceptable. But as we have seen, according to the official Gospels it is not certain that the crucified person was in fact Jesus. The act of crucifixion was a sacrifice in order to keep the life of Jesus bodily and spiritually safe from being harmed by his enemies and non-believers. And there are **certain recent discoveries** which prove these possibilities.

Troubling discovery

"Israeli construction workers-building an apartment complex in Jerusalem's east Talpiot district - first uncovered ten of the 2,000-year-old ossuaries - or limestone coffins - in a tomb in March 1980. **This tomb belonged to "Jesus and his family"**. Statistical tests and DNA analysis testify the age of this tomb to be about 2000 years. There is no doubt about the nature of this discovery: it is a familial tomb with highly interesting names carved on the grave-stones. According to the Israelian Antiquities Authority, six of those coffins were marked with the names Mary, Matthew, **Jesua son of Joseph**, Mary, Jofa (Joseph, Jesus' brother) **and Judah son of Jesua**. Another grave is said to be of Mary Magdalene - "**Mariamene" is Mary Magdalene**.

Archaeologists said that the burial cave was probably that of **a Jewish family with similar names to those of Jesus' family**. Israeli archaeologist Amos Kloner, who was among the first to examine the tomb when it was first discovered, said the names marked on the coffins were very common at the time. "I don't accept the news that it was used by Jesus or his family". The discovery of the tomb does not undermine the key Christian belief that Jesus was resurrected three days after his death. Academic Stephen Pfann, a scholar at the University of the Holy Land in Jerusalem, said: "I don't think that Christians are going to buy this ..." The tests on samples from two of the coffins show Jesus and Mary Magdalene were likely to have been buried in them and to have been a couple. The coffin marked "Judah son of Jesua" contains probably the son of Jesus and Mary."[399] **But** the combination of names found on the tombs is an extraordinary coincidence! It is not only a person named Jesus, but an entire family with the famous and well-known names. And there is another strange coincidence: Jesus is presented as the son of "Joseph"! [400]

Whose is this tomb? Jesus' or his double?

We do not know to which "Jesus' family" this tomb belongs. The question remains (and he the reader is here referred to the appendix), but the familial tomb of Jesus either belongs to "Jesus son of Mary" (the real one) or to "Jesus son of Mary" (his double)!! This is an irrefutable fact. In this book, we extensively discussed the idea that a certain person acted as the double of Jesus, and now the archaeologists talk about an extraordinary discovery.

The similarity between Jesus' double and the real Jesus is not merely limited to their names (which was very common in the Jewish community in that period), but to many other aspects as well. Jesus' double was a contemporary of the real Jesus; he was the son of Mary; the husband of Mary the mother of the double of Jesus was named

---

[399] A documentary about this subject did by James Cameron the Oscar-winning Titanic director.

http://news.bbc.co.uk/1/hi/world/middle_east/6397373.stm

[400] See: Jacob Slavenburg, **Het Graf Van Jezus – Het Mysterie van de Tomb van Jezus, Maria Magdalena en Judas**, Walburg Pres. 2007 Zutphen

Joseph; the double of Jesus had a brother named Jofa; the double of Jesus had a wife named Maria Magdeleine, and finally the double of Jesus had a son named Judas! …

So if he cannot be considered to be the real Jesus, he can definitely be considered to be the double of Jesus! This is now a historical fact.

This double of Jesus lived in the same city and in the same period (2000 years ago) as the real Jesus. Now, at least with all the available evidence, we should accept the idea that the tomb found in Jerusalem is owned by the double of Jesus, and thus that the double of Jesus in fact really existed. It is beyond any doubt that this person was an "existing person" who, as a result of the many similarities, could be the best person to "clothe" the real Jesus.

Appendix

a) Iranian Christianity

Now let us consider the following question: which evangelium is the Qur'an talking about? It must be an evangelium in which the crucifixion of Jesus is denied. The book 'evangelium' mentioned in the Qur'an is not the Gospel of Barnabas. We know that the Gospel of Barnabas was never mentioned in the history of Islam. No mention of this Gospel can be found in the Qur'an. It seems that long before Islam, maybe even as early as the 4th century, every reference to the evangelium of Barnabas vanished and or was eliminated. This book was removed from the hands of the people.

Still, a few copies of this book may have remained in the library of Constantinople in the Byzantine Empire. Still, the general public and 'ordinary' people would never have been able to access this book. Therefore, it is not very likely that a connection between the Christian world and the Islamic world could have been established via the book of Barnabas. The Gospel of Barnabas is a completely unknown book in the Islamic world. So when the Qur'an speaks about the 'evangelium', it is not the Gospel of Barnabas. Surat 5, verse 110 of the Qur'an writes that God talks to Jesus and tells him: "I taught you wisdom, the Torah and the Evangelium".[401]

The Qur'an also talks about another aspect of the evangelium: according to Surat 5 verse 46 God proclaims 'We gave him the evangelium in which was guidance and light'.[402] This evangelium, according to the Qur'an, was used by the group of Christians

---

[401] *The Qur'an* s. 5: 110.

[402] *The Qur'an* s. 5: 46.

(Nasara)[403] named in the Qur'an as the "Ghessis" and "Rohban", ('the esoteric seekers'). These people had "a pure heart and the source of pure water opened from their eyes when they were exposed to the verses of the Qur'an".[404]

The Qur'an describes another book attributed to Jesus. It contains many errors and numerous additions which raise Jesus and his mother to a high place equal to that of divinity and equal to the place of the unique God.[405] The Qur'an criticizes the trinity and the divinity of Jesus and Saint Mary and also criticizes the evangelium and its commentaries for making such comparisons. For the Qur'an, the one and only evangelium is that which is based on the unity of one God.

In order to investigate which evangelium the Qur'an is referring to, we must look for an evangelium in which there is no place for any trinity.

In the Qur'an, the Nasrani community (Surat 3 Al-Emran, 7) is composed of two categories:

1. The official community (the Constantinist Christianity of the Byzantine Empire (Surat 30 Ar Roum/ 2-3) or Western Christianity, based on trinity of God (Surat 5 Maedeh/ 73)' exaggeration about Jesus (Surat 9 Towbeh/ 30) & his mother/ (Surat 5 Maedeh/ 77), and crucifixion of Jesus 4 Nessa'/ 157). The Qur'an draws a strict line between the Muslims and this

---

[403] **The Qur'an** s. 5: 82. The Christian Community is divided into many branches. The first is named "Maleka'ieh" The population of Byzantium follows this branch and in the Roman territories there are no followers of any other branch. Other branches include Nestorians, Jacobins and Erosions. The beliefs of these branches have more in common with Muslim beliefs than any other. Al-birouni **Asar ol Baghieh,** p.438.

[404] **The Qur'an,** s. 5: 82.

[405] **The Qur'an,** s. 9: 30.

category of the Christian community[406]. "Western Christianity"[407] introduces Jesus in a halo of an unbelievable paradox. On the one hand, the believers of Jesus bring him to a state of divinity where he is placed next to God and on the other hand they bring him down from divinity in order to nail him on a wooden cross. This kind of Christianity became the official state religion in the Byzantine Empire in the fourth century A.D., under the influence of Constantine and his mother Helena. In this religion, the four canonical Gospels are accepted but emphasis is placed largely on numerous other theological books.

2. "Gnostic" communities named 'Rahbanniat'[408] (Gnosticism), related to the discipline of the apostles of Jesus who are described as 'Rahban' (monk) and 'Ghessiss'[409] (Gnostics). The Qur'an considers this category of Christians to be the closest people to the Muslim community.[410] Here, this form of

---

[406] *The Qur'an*, s. 5 Maedeh: 51: "O believers! Take not the Jews or Christians as friends. They are but one another's friends. If any one of you taketh them for his friends, he surely is one of them. Allah will not guide the evil-doers."

[407] Al-Birouni, *Asar ol baghieh*. 438-507, the book was written in Khorasan in 360-440 of hegira.

[408] It is explained that Rahbaniat is the path that a seeker selects in order to please Allah as much as possible and to the best of the seeker's abilities. Rahbaniat can be interpreted as the best name for the discipline of Mani: it is an Old Persian word, mentioned in *the Qur'an* - 57/ hadid/ 27.

[409] 1st of 5 steps of the hierarchy of the seekers in the discipline of Mani was the level of Ghessis. *Qur'an*, s. 5 Maedeh: 82.

[410] *The Qur'an*, s. 5 Maedeh: 82 - 86:" and had you will certainly find those to be nearest in affection to those who believe [Muslim community] who say "we are Christian [Nasara]". This because some of them are "Ghessiss" [Gnostic] and "Rahban" [monk, mystic], and because they are free from pride. And when they hear that which hath been sent down to the Messenger [Mohammad], thou seest their eyes overflow with tears at the truth they recognise therein, saying "O Lord! [Rabbana] we

Christianity is named **the Iranian Christianity or 'A'in e Tarssaii'**, based on unity and in which there is no place for the crucifixion and the holiness of Jesus. In this Christianity there are direct references to advice and teachings offered by Jesus, who invites mankind to pray to the unique God. Neither he nor his mother is introduced as being divine. This category of Christianity was a continuation of the Gnostic tradition that was common among the apostles of Jesus, named the school of 'ruhbaniat' or Gnosticism.[411] In continuation of these types of teachings, a school of Christianity came into being in the city of Babel (Babylon) in the third century A.D. This school exerted its influence on many parts of the world. This kind of Christianity was introduced to the world by the Iranian Prophet Mani. Mani appeared and he introduced himself as 'Paraklit'[412], 'the promised person by Jesus' who was sent to

---

believe. Write us down therefore with those who bear witness to it. And why should we not believe in Allah and in the truth which has come down to us, and crave that our Lord would bring us into Paradise with the just? Therefore hath Allah rewarded them for these their words, with gardens' neath which the rivers flow. They shall abide therein for ever."

[411] *The Qur'an*. s. 57: 27.

[412] Perkelit means "comforter". This word is about a person whose arrival was announced by Jesus before his occultation, and it is mentioned in all of the 4 canonical Gospels and the Acts of St Paul. *The Gospel of St. John*, Ch.15: 26 "26 But when the Comforter comes, whom I will send unto you from the Father, even the Spirit of truth, which proceeded from the Father, he shall testify of me" More details about Perkelit are given in *The Gospel of St. John*, Ch.16: 7-14: "For if I go not away, the Comforter will not come unto you; but if I depart, I will send him unto you. 8 And when he is come, he will reprove the world of sin, and of righteousness, and of judgment: 9 Of sin, because they believe not on me; 10 Of righteousness, because I go to my Father, and ye see me no more; 11 Of judgment, because the prince of this world is judged.12 I have yet many things to say unto you, but ye cannot bear them now. 13 Howbeit when he, the Spirit of truth, is come, he will guide you into all truth: for he shall not speak of himself; but whatsoever he shall hear, that shall he speak: and he will show you things to come. 14 He shall glorify me:

spread the right evangelium and who was connected to Gabriel, the angel of revelation of the right book. He said that his mission was to reveal the correct version of the evangelium of Jesus Christ, based on the unity of the Creator (as it is written in the Gospel of St Mark)[413] and the duality of the dialectics of light and darkness in creation (as it is mentioned in the Gospel of St. John)[414], without any exaggeration and without any errors. The Creator of all creatures and establisher of the dynamism of his creation must be recognized, on the basis of the eternal antagonist dialectic principle of light and darkness.

---

for he shall receive of mine, and shall show it unto you." In the Qur'an, Jesus is presented as the announcer of an "adorated man". In this case the word should be read Paraklit, and not Perkelit.

[413] *The Gospel of St Mark*, Ch.12: 28-33; 29 And Jesus answered him, The first of all the commandments is, Hear, O Israel; The Lord our God is one Lord: 30 And thou shalt love the Lord thy God with all thy heart, and with all thy soul, and with all thy mind, and with all thy strength: this is the first commandment. 31 And the second is like, namely this, Thou shalt love thy neighbour as thyself. There is none other commandment greater than these. 32 And the scribe said unto him, Well, Master, thou hast said the truth: for there is one God; and there is none other but he: 33 And to love him with all the heart, and with all the understanding, and with all the soul, and with all the strength, and to love his neighbour as himself, is more than all whole burnt offerings and sacrifices. 34 And when Jesus saw that he answered discreetly, he said unto him, Thou art not far from the kingdom of God. And no man after that, dears ask him any question.

[414] *The Gospel of St. John*, Ch.1: 1 & 4 1 In the beginning was the Word, and the Word was with God, and the Word was God. 2 The same was in the beginning with God. 3 All things were made by him; and without him was not anything made that was made. 4 In him was life; and the life was the light of men. 5 And the light shineth in darkness; and the darkness comprehended it not.

Rahbaniat[415] resembles the teachings of Mani

The Qur'an argues that Rahbaniat is neither the order nor the commandment of God to the people (through Jesus), but that it is only a pure invention of a part of the Christian believers because of their extreme love towards God.[(34)] The discipline of Rahbaniat is accepted in the Qur'an and the seekers of this discipline, "rahban" and "Ghessiss", are mentioned in a very respectful manner.[416]

Enjil and Zabour [417] in the Qur'an

"Those who follow the apostle, the unlettered Prophet, whom they find mentioned in the Torah and the Injil..." (Surat Al A'raf 7:157),[418]

---

[415] It is a very hard task to develop the seed of the soul [Sophia] by rejecting worldly desires, becoming vegetarian, practising long periods of ascetic behaviour and living like a hermit in a cave or living lonely in the monasteries, forbidding oneself any conjugal relationship and familial contacts.

[416] *The Qur'an*, Surat 5 Maedeh, 66 "if that they observe the *Torah* and the *Enjil* and what hath been sent down to them from their Lord, they shall surely have their fill of good things from above them and from beneath their feet." Here there is talk about another book/other books than *Torah* and *Enjil*. It could be an allusion to Zabour.

[417] *The Qur'an*, s. 54/43, s.35/25, s.26:196, s.16: 44, s.3:184: the holy book named *Zabour* is cited in plural, and in the following surats in singular: s.17: 55, s.4: 163, s. 21: 105. Twice, the book named Zabour is attributed to David, and once it is regarded as a holy book – part of Torah. In other cases it is added to a shiny book. Once, the Muslims are guided to the "persons who are the people of "reminding" [zekr], if they cannot understand the verses of the Qur'an. In s. 16 Nahl: 44 and in another verse there is mention of the **Zabours** of the ancients. s.26:196. This can be interpreted as the books used by the Gnostics and the followers of Mani.

[418] According to the Qur'an, the *Enjil* predicted the coming of a new prophet under the name of Ahmad: "...Jesus, the son of Mary said: "O children of Israel! I am the apostle of Allah (sent) to you, confirming the Taurat (which came) before

218

Enjil (Surat Al A'raf 7:157), mentioned in *the Qur'an* as the book of Jesus (Surat Al Saff 61:6), should not be taken for the New Testament. The followers of Mani also refused to accept the New Testament as the exact teachings of Jesus. They were persuaded that their Enjil contained the pure teachings of Jesus revealed to them again by Mani.[419]

So, the Qur'an does not accept the theology and the world view propagated and expressed by Western Christianity[420] as they had developed in Constantinople and spread across the world since the 4th century. The Qur'an considers the trinity to be a form of 'non-belief' in God.[421] To believe in Jesus and his mother as Divine beings is also viewed as a form of idolatry.[422] Mohammad invites the priest of Nadhjran, who did not want to accept the Qur'an verses related to Jesus, to go and to curse each other and to ask God who is right and who is wrong.[423] So it is clear that Mohammad and the Qur'an were strictly against 'Western' Christianity and that they did not accept the validity of this ideology and world view. Moreover, it was felt that it was the Qur'an which accepted and introduced the only right evangelium, free from any exaggeration or any doubt about the unity of God.

---

me and giving glad tidings of an apostle to come after me, whose name shall be Ahmad' "

[419] Al-Birouni, *Asarol baghieh*, p.33. Another book of Mani was named *Zabour*. In other books of Mani, which formed the basis of Iranian Christianity, the factual case of the crucifixion of Jesus is rejected but nevertheless accepted as a Gnostic principle with many esoteric meanings.

[420] Roman-Christianity, Maleka'ieh. Al-Birouni, *Asarol baghieh* p.494.

[421] *The Qur'an*. s. 5: 73.

[422] *The Qur'an*. s. 5: 16.

[423] *The Qur'an*. s. 3: 61.

The Qur'an accepts the validity of an evangelium expressed by a group of followers known as 'Rahban e Ghessiss'. We should not forget that 'Rahban' is a Persian word meaning 'the seeker of the esoteric path' or 'the seeker of the substantial evolution path', and that 'ghessiss' is an Iranian word used among the followers of **Iranian Christianity** which constitutes one of the five levels of substantial evolution, according to Mani's definition.

Thus, Iranian Christianity is the form of Christianity that is introduced by the Qur'an under the name of 'Rouhbaniat'. Followers of this form of Christianity are considered in the Qur'an to be the friends of God who do not want anything else but to be near to God. **It is certain that Mani absolutely rejected the crucifixion of Jesus but a more than considerable resemblance can be distinguished between Mani's Gnostic teachings about Jesus and the content of the Qur'an concerning the rejection of the crucifixion of Jesus.** On this powerful basis, we can deduce that the real evangelium of Jesus, which is introduced several times in the Qur'an, corresponds to a far greater extent with the version that Mani used to present as the evangelium of Jesus in comparison with the official and unofficial Gospels propagated in the Christian world.[424]

So, from all of the above discussions we can see that Jesus sent his apostles everywhere in the world, as stated in the Gospel of St. Mark, to invite people to follow the Evangelium[425], and that the Qur'an talks about the 'real Christianity' resembling the Christianity of Mani rather than Western Christianity and its various different branches.

---

[424] The *Nag Hammadi Scriptures* do not refer to the Trinity in the traditional sense with Jesus as the third member, nor to Mary as a divine person. We know that the Kathars in Southern France were still using these scriptures in the 12th century: they were able to quote the *Gospel of Thomas* by heart, for instance.

[425] *The Gospel of St. Mark*, Ch.16: 15.

Unity and duality

The books of Mani, '**Enjil e Pak**' and '**Zabour**' are based on the unity of God[426] and contain many important facts that need to be reviewed in due course, so that we may be able to establish a link between **Gnosticism in Christianity and esoterism in the Islamic world**. The Zoroastrian monks, who rejected the religion of Mani, condemned a world view based on duality. Instead, they interpreted the dialectics of light and darkness as 'duality' and argued that Mani did not believe in the unity of God.

However, the dialectics and the duality between light and darkness in the created universe correspond exactly to the verses of the Qur'an.[427] It is not against the principle of unity. **Iranian Christianity** cannot be regarded as a dualistic or '**Manicheistic**' religion. It is wrong to see Iranian Christianity as a dualistic religion or Mani-religion. Manichaeism is the explanation of the dialectics in the created world; not in the existential aspect of the entire universe.[428] The entire

---

[426] *The Qur'an* talks about the book of David named *Zabour* (s. 7: 55 & s. 4: 163). But *the Qur'an* also mentions other divine holy books '**Zabour**' in the plural form **Zobor**, and the Qur'an advises Muslims, if they experience difficulties to understand correctly the meaning of the verses of the revelation, to go to the persons named "The companions of reminding", owners of the evidence and the **Zabours**. S.16: 44, In other verses, the word **Zabour** is used in plural form as well: see s. 54: 43 and s. 35: 25, for instance.

[427] *The Qur'an*. s. 35: 1 "All thanks to Allah, creator of the skies and the earth, the poser of darkness and light." The opposite direction of the way toward darkness and its travellers, and the path toward light and its passengers are explained in *the Qur'an* s. 2: 254.

[428] *Zand* and *Pazand* are the names of two books by followers of the Iranian prophet. The compilers of these books are named *Zandik* and *Zanadekeh* in plural form. The follower of the religion of Mani was named also "Sabe'in" (Al Birouni/ Asar ol Baghieh: Sabe'in are the followers of the religion of Mani living in Samarkand: p.310) and they are cited under the same name in the Qur'an. Jebrail Nouh Nasrani (Christian author) wrote an answer to a Christian whose name was

universe is based on unity, the unity of the creator and the duality of the creation. But this is a very complex topic within Mani's overall philosophy: one which was misunderstood by the Zoroastrian monks as well as by the Muslim theologians. Perhaps the monastery of Bosra in southern Syria had been visited by Mohammad from the age of 12. This monastery was under the influence of the Iranian Christianity community; *not* the Western form of Christianity. This is one of the contributing factors for the development of Islam in Iran and also of Sufism in the West of Iran and in city of Babel (present-day Baghdad).

b) Bihoushaneh & the Path of Ayyari [429]

b-1) ANAESTHETIC (bi-hushaneh)[430]

Myrrh/ gall, bang, diverse herbal drugs (opium)

The particular effect of wine-**vinegar**, when mixed with different **herbal drugs** such as **gall,** myrrh, frankincense, mandrake was well known in the Biblical time. Gall – (Papaver somniferum), known in the Holy Land- was a kind of "opium-poppy plant" which was used to extract a powerful drug to **reduce suffering and to induce sleep.**[431]

Yazdan-bakht, and explains that Mani had a book in which he predicted his final destiny, that he would be arrested and tortured and killed in the worst possible manner. Asarol baghieh, p. 310. Some important chapters are dedicated to Mani in the second volume of this book.

[429] For more information read the book by Arjani Faramarz Khodadad: *Samak Ayyar.* First published in 5 volumes by Parviz Natel Khanlary, Tehran 1368, and later in 3 volumes by M. Rowshan. Ed: Seday e Mo'aser. Tehran. 1382.

[430] Bang/ opium. *Samak Ayyar.* Vol.4, p. 412. Edited by Khanlary, **and Darab Nameh.** Mowlana Mohammad Bighami. Vol.1 p.239 & 784. See also http://www.babylon.com/definition/anesthetic/Farsi

Myrrh is a reddish-brown resinous material, the dried sap of a tree named *Commiphora Myrrha*, native to Yemen, Somalia and the eastern parts of Ethiopia. The sap of a number of other *Commiphora* and *Balsamodendron* species are also known as myrrh, including that from *C. erythraea* (sometimes called East-Indian myrrh), *C. opobalsamum* and *Balsamodendron kua*. The name entered English via Ancient Greek μύρρα, which is probably of Semitic origin. Myrrh is most commonly used in Chinese medicine for rheumatic, arthritic and circulatory problems. **It is usually combined … with alcohol**, for both internal and external use. **Mixing myrrh gum with vinegar** increases its ability to remove blood congestion and to relieve pain.

Myrrh exudes as a fluid from resin ducts in the tree bark when the bark splits naturally or is cut in tapping. Galls are rich in resins. The larvae in galls serve a useful purpose as food for survival and as fishing bait, resembling nuts and therefore called "gallnuts" or "nutgalls'. Pyrethrum (Amorr) is a natural insecticide which attacks the nervous system of insects, causing paralysis and death. Myrrh has slight antiseptic, astringent, and carminative properties. It has been employed medically as a carminative and in tinctures to relieve sore gums and mouth. An essential oil distilled from myrrh is a constituent of certain heavy perfumes. **In the alchemical mixtures of the Ayyar Myrrh, bang (opium), and gall were used to make a powerful "Bihushaneh"** [432]

b-2) Ayyar and Fotowwat (knighthood)

In ancient times, there was a group of secretly operating men with specific professions who had special skills and knowledge. These

[431] Robert B. Greenblatt, M.D. *"Search the Scriptures. Illustrated Modern Medicine and Biblical Personages"*; The Parthenon Press. 1985. pp 107-109

[432] http://www.independent.co.uk/news/prozac-opium-and-myrrh-the-ancient-arts-of-anaesthesia-are-unlocked-1238659.html

people could act as kidnappers. The name of their brotherhood was Ayyar. For more information the reader is referred to the book by Arjani Faramarz Khodadad: **Samak Ayyar.** For many centuries, the tale of Samak Ayyar had been a story in the oral tradition until a writer (kateb) named "Arjani" put it down into writing - in an unknown period. It may well have been written in the Saljokid period (about 9 centuries ago). This book was edited and published in 5 volumes by Dr P.N. Khanlary in Tehran, about 50 years ago. Khanlary also added a complementary additional work to this ensemble, entitled "**Shar e Samak**" (The Samak's city) in which he dedicated an entire chapter to the Path of Ayyari (A'in e Ayyari).

The path of Ayyari is based on brotherhood between the members of the community. Its members retain the secrets of the path until the end of their lives. They made the plans to help the wreakers by generosity. And in another chapter Khanlary explains the Ayyar's manners, including how **they kept changing their face & clothes** (pp. 79-81), and **how they used a narcotic medicine named "Bihoushaneh"** (pp. 77-79) ...

Ayyar were usually able to change their looks, go into the streets and frequent people, sometimes disguised as men and sometimes as women. Arresting an Ayyar was by no means an easy affair, because the Ayyar always adopted an unknown identity and a changing face. The group of Ayyar included people who knew how to dig tunnels from their hidden places to the places of their adversaries. Without any modern equipment they were able to trace the right direction in digging the tunnels to their targets. They would then appear in the night, climb steep walls with the help of their ropes, apply a certain dose of a poison to the person they wanted to abduct, rendering them in a totally unconscious state of mind, and finally disappear silently with their victim. The Ayyar knew very well how to apply the extract from a particular nut and concoct some sort of "unaware-maker solution (sleeping potion)", an anaesthetic called "Bihushaneh" in their jargon. They knew about the correct dose and the time a person could remain in this state, and they also knew how to prepare the antidote to let their victims wake up again. Khanlary writes:

"Ayyar has a bag with him, containing a medicine called "Bihoushaneh". It is one of the important elements of the success of Ayyar in carrying out the mission. It could have been a kind of opium that Ayyar used to solve in a jar of wine…" **Merely smelling the vapour of this medicine was enough to anaesthetize anybody.** .."The vapour of the medicine mixed in the wine penetrated the brain of "Magogar". He lost his awareness, and the cup fell down from his hand …His head turned, and without any control he fell down in a coma (bi-houshi)"[433]

The secret knowledge concerning the various different poisons and their subtle practice was passed on to future followers over the centuries. We assume that there were people gathered around Jesus who also knew this secret and who applied it at the moment of the crucifixion of the person mistaken for Jesus, dissolved in what we hear may have been vinegar or a strong wine.

An ancient oral story exists about a popular hero who is a member of a knightly brotherhood. This tale, recited by professional story tellers for thousands and thousands of years, was written down in the Persian language in an unknown period (probably in the Slajokid-period), under the title of Samak Ayyar. *Samak*" means "fish and *Ayyar* means naked. The book of Samak Ayyar is the mirror of the Ayyar's lifestyle. It shows that a long tradition existed in the Middle East involving certain skills. The circle of brotherhood was named Fotowwat. The

---

[433] P.N. Khanlary. *The Samak's city,* Tehran. 1988. Agah, p.77-78. This passage reminds us exactly of the event of the "crucified Jesus" and his last moments on the cross.

pact of "Fotowat" entails a link between master and disciple in line with the traditions of "brotherhood" and "knighthood". The knights-cum-brothers are prepared to help the weak, and they are ready to sacrifice their wealth and their lives in their mission.

During daytime, the Ayyar, members of this clandestine community, acted as workers, shop-keepers, merchants and traders. At night, however, they gathered in the ruins outside the cities and formulated their plans of action. The prophet Mohammad discusses this circle of *Fotowwat* and brotherhood in the Qur'an. The Qur'an tells us about a group of knights (Fetyeh) who were living in Ephesus. They were the Christian Gnostics who spent a period of 300 years in meditation in a cave, in the suburb of Ephesus. One of their methods was to dig horizontal tunnels during the night and pass through them to the castle keepers in order to kidnap the governors and the oppressors. They were masters at presenting illusions, and experts in the art of disguise. Under different covers, they managed to infiltrate protected places, taking the place of the usual cupbearers. It was the best option for them to use their narcotic solution by mixing it in the jar of wine and to cause everybody in the gathering to fall asleep. The following step would then be to lead the governor out of the palace or to open the gates of the castle to their friends and let them enter ...

c) Blame and generosity within the circle of brotherhood (Sufi community) of Baghdad (9th century A.D.)

Now, we would like to present an example of the tradition of generosity: one of the underlying principles of Iranian Christianity which was based on the relationship between Jesus and his apostles. It happened during the times of the first Sufi generation in Baghdad. As we know, Baghdad replaced the city of Madaen, which itself replaced the city of Babylon. All of them were the capitals of different kingdoms. Since the time of Mani, Babylon, Madaen and Baghdad were regarded as the centre of spirituality by the followers of the Mani religion. They were famous under the title of Zandik and Zanadegheh (plural of Zandik). The Zanadegheh were persecuted by different dynasties before and after Islam. The Islamic Gnostics, known as Sufis, were also traced and persecuted by the fanatics because they were also accused of being Zandiks and followers of the Mani religion who disguised themselves under the Muslim esoteric name of Sufis.[434]

The Sufis of Baghdad followed the esoteric message of the Qur'anic teachings and they interpreted the verses of the Qur'an in an esoteric manner. This was not acceptable to the theologians of that time. They were strongly opposed to the Sufis. They believed that the Sufis were non-Muslims and considered them to be more or less Manichaean.

The theologians went to the Caliph of the Abbasid dynasty and talked to him so that he would provide them with a governmental decree, backed by a religious fatwa, which allowed them to eliminate the Sufis. The reason they used for wanting to kill them was the fact that the Sufis used to go to the 'Sardabeh', the underground places, to talk about the hidden secrets which were considered against the outer aspects of Islam. When they wanted to eliminate the Sufis of the first generation, one of the Sufis decided, in an act of generosity, to give his life, in order to allow the others of this school of thought to escape. This person was known as Mansour Hallaj. He did exactly what Judas did. So he volunteered to die or to be executed in order to save the school of the esoteric Islam. In order for us to gain a full understanding of this type of knighthood, we must consider the backgrounds of this affair.

It is written in an old document that there was a person whose name was Golam e Gahlil and who was opposed to the Sufis. He went to the Caliph of Baghdad and told him that there was a new kind of people among the Muslim Community who named themselves Sufis. Instead of reading the Qur'an they

---

[434] ***Asar ol baghieh,*** p. 308-312.

performed the Sama. They would sit in circles, sing songs, whirl around and discuss topics that are wrong and do not correspond with the religious laws (shariat). They would sit down in their place and meditate for a long period of time and go to the underground rooms to talk with each other in secret. Thus, they certainly are the followers of Mani, the 'zandir'. (**Zandik** *is the name of the evangelium of Mani and 'zandik' means 'follower of zand').*

So this person asked the Caliph to provide him with the order to kill all of them and to abolish the religion of zandir for good. He told the Caliph "if you give us permission to kill the leaders of this group, the whole group will be eliminated". Golam e Gahlil was a very famous religious person and he wanted the governmental order in support of his religious Fatwa. So the Caliph ordered the execution of the leaders of these orders, including people like Abu Hamse, Aram, Chebly, Nuri and Junaid. Thus, an executioner was sent with a sword in order to cut their heads one by one. At that moment, Nuri, one of the Sufis, ran towards the executioner and asked: "Please cut my head before you cut the heads of the others". Another person, whose name was Arham, said: "No, please kill me first before the others". Both of them were very happy, singing and not at all sad. The executioner tells them: "The caliph asked me to cut the head of Arham first. After I have killed him I will come to you. Be patient, it is not your moment. The sword is not a thing to play with". Nuri replies: "No, my school is based on generosity and I am a teacher of this school, and in my school I advise others to be generous and to give away the dearest thing in their life. And as I only have a few breaths before the end of my life, I would like to give these breaths for my friends in order to be generous and set an example to my students. So please cut off my head first".

The executioner was deeply touched by this gesture and started to cry. He left the group, went to the Caliph and said: "I cannot kill them, they are very strange people". The caliph asked him what had happened and he explained what he had seen. The caliph said: "Indeed they are very strange and very sincere and honest in their beliefs. So, he consulted the judge and said that he could not explain the reasons why these people had to be killed. He told the judge: "Talk with them and fix a sentence".

Appendix

The judge knew Junaid: Junaid was not only a very advanced seeker in Sufism, but he also had a great knowledge of religious law. Pazi, the judge, understood that he could not challenge Junaid on his knowledge of the Islam. And he could not challenge Nuri because this man had even more knowledge than Pazi. So he went to Shebly: Shebly was a friend of Mansour Hallaj who did not know much about religious science. So the Judge thought this was his best chance of finding an excuse to kill them. He asked Shebly: "If you have 20 pieces of money, how much religious tax must you pay?" Shebly answered: "21 pieces!" The judge exclaimed: "How is this possible, why?" Shebly said: "Why does one need to have 20 pieces of money? This is your punishment for owning so much. If you are a seeker you must be empty-handed, so you cannot have money".

The judge posed a question to Nuri and Nuri answered. The judge bowed his head to his knowledge about religious science. Then Nuri said to the judge: "Now I want to ask you a question. You asked me a great deal about religion but you did not ask me about the people who are taking their breaths for God, those who are walking and staying for God, and those who are living for their Beloved. These are the people who are ready to give the two worlds (the visible and the invisible) for one moment of seeing God's light in their hearts. They are living for and are doing everything in order to reach this light of God in their hearts. The moment you reach this light is the moment of real science and real conviction. Not what you ask from us. Go and learn this science". The judge was astonished and turned his head to the Caliph and said: "If these people are the followers of Mani, if these people are outside religion, then in the entire world there is no real Muslim. If these people are not Muslims then in the whole world there are no Muslims". After this, the Caliph invited them and said to them: "Ask me anything you would like and I will give it to you". They told him: "The only thing we would like is to ask you to forget us forever. We don't need anything, let us be free. We do not want your acceptance or your rejection. Your acceptance is like a rejection and your rejection is like acceptance".

The Caliph was deeply touched by these comments, started to cry and let them go.[435]

This shows that the first generation of Sufi seekers in Baghdad were students of the school of Gnosticism, and thus that they were linked to the esoteric tradition of Jesus through the bridge of Iranian Christianity, or the School of Mani. They learnt from Judas the lesson of generosity and sacrifice. And the actions demonstrated by Mansour Hallaj and his sacrifice for his brothers, sisters, friends and his school reminds us of what Judas Iscariot & the second-Jesus did in order to save the life of their master.[436]

d) Elias, The Hebrew prophet

The Israelite king Omri had allied himself with the Phoenician cities of the coast, and his son Ahab was married to Jezebel, daughter of Ethbaal, king of Tyre and Sidon. Jezebel, with her Tyrian courtiers and a large contingent of pagan priests and prophets, propagated her native religion in a sanctuary built for Baal in the royal city of Samaria. This meant that the Israelites accepted Baal as well as Yahweh, putting Yahweh on a par with a nature-god whose supreme manifestations were the elements and biological fertility, celebrated often in an orgiastic cult. Jezebel's policies intensified the gradual contamination of

[435] Attar Nishabouri, *Tazkeratol Aowlia,* Mohammad Ghazvini, Tehran. Second vol. p. 8-9.

[436] Jesus said: - "[Come], that I may teach you about [secrets] no person [has] ever seen. For there exists a great and boundless realm, whose extent no generation of angels has seen, [in which] there is [a] great invisible [Spirit], [hidden heaven] which no eye of an angel has ever seen, no thought of the heart has ever comprehended, and it was never called by any name". *Gospel of Judah,* Electronic version of the National Geographic publication.

the religion of Yahweh by the Canaanite religion of Baal, a process made easier by the sapping of the Israelites' faith in Yahweh.

Elias/Elijah is a Hebrew prophet who ranks with Moses in saving the religion of <u>Yahweh</u> from being corrupted by the nature worship of <u>Baal</u>. Elijah's name means "Yahweh is my God" and is spelled Elias in some versions of the Bible. The story of his prophetic career in the northern kingdom of Israel during the reigns of Kings Ahab and Ahaziah is told in 1 Kings 17–19 and 2 Kings 1–2 in the Old Testament. Elijah claimed that there was no reality except the God of Israel, stressing <u>monotheism</u> to the people with possibly unprecedented emphasis. He is commemorated by Christians on July 20 and is recognized as a prophet by Islam.[437]

Elias' shrine is always on mountains and hilltops where Helios, the heaven-born flaming charioteer, was worshipped. They symbolize, says the Church, **Elijah's whirlwind assumption to heaven in a chariot of fire drawn by horses of fire.**[438]

e) Garden of Gethsemane

The Garden of Gethsemane lies across the Kidron Valley on the Mount of Olives (Hebrew *Har ha-Zetim*), a mile-long ridge paralleling the eastern part of Jerusalem, where Jesus is said to have prayed on the night of his arrest before his Crucifixion. The name Gethsemane (Hebrew *gat shemanim*, "**Olives** press") suggests that the garden was a grove of Olives trees in which an oil press was located.

---

[437] The different parts of this text are extracted from the Encyclopaedia **Britannica** Online, and Wikipedia Online (http://www.britannica.com/biography/Elijah-Hebrew-prophet).

[438] **Wikipedia**. Hundreds of lofty peaks all over the Greek world still commemorate this personification of the Sun-god (equivalent of Apollo/ Helios/ Elias

- https://en.wikipedia.org/wiki/Elijah)

Though the exact location of Gethsemane cannot be determined with certainty, Armenian, Greek, Latin, and Russian churches have accepted an Olives grove on the western slope of the Mount of Olivess as the authentic site, which was so regarded by the empress Helena, mother of Constantine (the first Christian emperor, early 4th century A.D.). An ancient tradition also locates the scene of the prayer at Gethsemane and betrayal of Jesus at a place now called the Grotto of the Agony, near a bridge that crosses the Kidron Valley. At another possible location, south of this site in a garden containing old Olives trees, is a Latin church erected by Franciscan monks on the ruins of a 4th-century church.[439]

Gethsemane[440] was the garden where, according to the New Testament and Christian traditions, Jesus and his disciples retreated to pray after the Last Supper, the night before he was crucified. According to Luke 22:43–44, Jesus' anguish in Gethsemane was so deep that "his sweat was, as it were, great drops of blood falling down to the ground". Gethsemane was also where Christ was betrayed by his disciple Judas Iscariot. Furthermore Orthodox tradition holds that Gethsemane is the place where the Apostles buried the Blessed Virgin Mary, after her Dormition.

The garden identified as Gethsemane is located at the foot of theMount of Olives , now within the city of Jerusalem in the Kidron valley. Located by the garden is the Church of All Nations, also known as the Church of the Agony. The ancient church was destroyed by the Sassanids in 614. The church rebuilt on the site by the Crusaders was finally raised, probably in 1219. Also on the Mount of Olivess is the Russian Orthodox Church of St. Mary Magdalene with its distinct

---

[439] The text is extracted from **Encyclopaedia Britannica** Online & **Wikipedia** Online

[440] Greek: Γεθσημανι, *Gethsēmani* 'Hebrew:גת שמנים, from Aramaic גת שמנא, *Gaṯ Šmānê*, meaning 'oil press'

golden, onion-shaped domes (Byzantine/Russian style). It was built by Russian Tsar Alexander III in memory of his mother.

In the Gospels the name *Gethsemane* is given in Greek (Matthew 26:36 and Mark 14:32) as Γεθσημανι (Gethsēmani). This represents the Aramaic גת שמנא (Gaṯ-Šmānê), meaning 'the oil press' or 'oil vat' (referring to olive oil). It would appear from this that there were a number of olive trees planted around the area at the time. The Gospel of Mark (14:32) calls it *chorion*, "a place" or "estate"; The Gospel of John (18:1) speaks of it as *kepos*, a "garden" or "orchard".

The Garden of Gethsemane was a focal site for early Christian pilgrims. It was visited in 333 by the anonymous "Pilgrim of Bordeaux", whose *Itinerarium Burdigalense* is the earliest description left by a Christian traveller in the Holy Land. In his *Onomasticon,* Eusebius of Caesarea notes the site of Gethsemane located "at the foot of the Mount of Olivess", and he adds that "the faithful were accustomed to go there to pray".[441]

f) Jesus' familial tomb[442]

This tomb was unearthed in 1980 during construction of an apartment building and was first connected to the Jesus family in a 1996 BBC

---

[441] Wikipedia - https://en.wikipedia.org/wiki/Gethsemane

[442] Stuart Laidlaw. This is the extract from the report by Stuart Laidlaw (faith & ethics reporter), Feb 26, 2007, about *The Lost Tomb* which *was* aired on Discovery Channel in the U.S., on Channel 4 in the U.K. and on Vision TV in Canada on March 6.

The complete report by Stuart Laidlaw can be accessed at:

http://www.thestar.com/News/article/185708

documentary. Jacobovici's [443] documentary uses scientific methods, including DNA testing, statistical analysis and forensic examination.

Archaeologists were given three days to document the tomb and excavate it for treasures. Inside, they found ten ossuaries and three skulls. Six ossuaries had names etched into them – Jesus son of Joseph, Judah son of Jesus, Maria, Mariamne, Joseph and Matthew – all Jesus family names. Still, those were names most commonly found among Jews in the first centuries.

Figure 9 - The Jesus' family tomb in Jerusalem

"The names that are found on the tombs are names that are similar to the names of the family of Jesus"[444].But while the names are common, the chances of them being found together are 600 to one.[445]

---

[443] Toronto documentary director Simcha Jacobovici. Jacobovici said to the **Star** that " the discovery should not shake anyone's belief in the resurrection of Jesus", and that he consulted several theologians in making the film. Cited by Stuart Laidlaw. The book was published by Jacobovici in collaboration with Charles Pellegrino, who wrote a book "The Jesus Family Tomb" prefaced by Titanic director James Cameron.

http://www.thestar.com/news/2007/02/26/jesus_tomb_claim_sparks_furor.html

Probably Maria – mentioned on one of the ossuaries - is the mother of the Jesus. A name found on another box, Mariamne, points to his wife; and the name of Joseph (inscribed as the nickname Jose) points at his brother. [446]

"Maria is the Latin form of Mary, and is how Jesus' mother was known after his death as more Romans became followers. Mariamne is the Greek form of Mary. Mary Magdelene is believed to have spoken and preached in Greek. Jose was the nickname used for Jesus' little brother. Also, the Talpiot Tomb is the only place where ossuaries have ever been found with the names Mariamne and Jose, even though the root forms of the name were very popular and thousands of ossuaries have been unearthed.

This is not, however, the first time a Jesus ossuary has been found. The first was in 1926. Another famous ossuary, inscribed James son of Joseph brother of Jesus, is also featured in the documentary.[447] **If James is added to the equation, there is a 30,000 to one chance that the Talpiot Tomb did not belong to the holiest families in Christianity.**[448]

James Tabor, an experienced archaeologist, chairman of the Department of Religious Studies at the University of North Carolina and an expert whose book **The Jesus Dynasty** last year raised many

---

[444] Kloner, cited by Stuart Laidlaw. "It's a beautiful story but without any proof whatsoever," Amos Kloner, professor at Israel's Bar-Ilan University, told Deutsche Presse-Agentur. Kloner researched the tomb for the Israeli periodical Atiqot in 1996.

[445]According to the calculations made by the University of Toronto statistician Andre Feuerverger and cited by Stuart Laidlaw.

[446] According to Andre Feuerverger and cited by Stuart Laidlaw.

[447] Stuart Laidlaw.

[448] Feuerverger calculated for Jacobovici, as cited by Stuart Laidlaw.

questions, says that as an academic he has seen enough to convince him of the evidence, but admits to some trepidation about claiming that the tomb of Jesus has been found." There's a part of you that says it's too amazing. How can it be right?"[449]

Tabor states that the discovery of the tomb could even strengthen the belief of anyone who doubted that Jesus even existed. "To have a material link to Jesus ... is wonderful. It is an archaeological dream... I think we can say, in all probability, Jesus had this son, Jude, presumably through Mary Magdalene."[450]

DNA tests conducted for the documentary at Lakehead University on two ossuaries – one inscribed Jesus son of Joseph and the other Mariamne, or Mary – confirm that the two were not related by blood, so they were probably married.[451]

---

[449] Tabor told the Star, cited by Stuart Laidlaw

[450] Tabor cited by Stuart Laidlaw

[451] See also: Jacob Slavenburg, **Het Graf Van Jezus – Het Mysterie van de Tomb van Jezus, Maria Magdalena en Judas**, Walburg Pres. 2007 Zutphen

Bibliography

Arjani Faramarz ibn Khodadad Kateb. *Samak Ayyar*. Published by P.N.Khanlary. edition Agah. Tehran-1988 in 6 volumes. Other publication in 3 volumes by M. Rowshan. Ed: Seday e Mo'aser. Tehran. 1382/2003.

M. Abegg. E. Cook, M.Wise. *Les manuscrits de la mer Morte*. Published by Tempus. 2003, France. p.20.

E. Ayati. *Tarikh Ya'ghobi*. (Persian translation) edition Elmi 6th publication; Tehran. 1366.

S.M. Azmayesh J. V. Shaik. *Een ontmoeting met Jezus in Christendom en Islam*. Ten Have. 2008.

M. T. Bahar. *Majmal at-Tawarikh wal- Qesas* (Ensemble of the histories and tales)written in 520 .h/1126 A.D. by an unknown author or by Ibn Shady Asad Abadi. First editor Tehran 1939, new edition Tehran-Donyaye ketab- 1996 by Ali Ashar Abdollahi.

M. Boyce. *The Manichean Hymn cycles in Parthian*. London, 1954, *& A reader in Manichean Middle Persian and Parthian*. Leiden. 1975 & *A word-list of Manichean middle Persian and Parthian*. Leiden 1975 & *Parthian writings and literature*. Cambridge history of Iran: Vol 3, part II. Cambridge. 1983.

Abu Reyhan El- Byrouni. *Al-Fehres*. (written in 377- 4th century of hegira, 10 th A.D.) edition Asatir. Tehran 1381.

A. Esmailpour. *The poems of light*. Edition Ostoureh. Tehran 2007. G. Flugel. *Mani, Seine Lehre und seine Schriften*. 1862.

A. Dana Seresht. *Asarol Baghieh An el Ghoroun el Khalieh* (The remaining traces from the lost centuries). This is on the books written by El-

Birouni (940-1020 A.D./ 360-440 H.) in Gazneh in Arabic language. Tehran, Amir Kabir. 1363.

M. Dorier & J.P. Troadce. *Les O.V.N.I.* Edited by "Que sais-je?'. Presses universitaires de France. France. 1992.

F. Edwards. *Du nouveau sur les soucoupes volantes.* Edited by "J'ai lu". France. 1978.

M. Ghazvini. *Tazkeratol Aowlia.* Attar Nishabouri. Tehran. 1310.

N. Golb. *Who wrote the Dead Sea Scrolls?* New York, 1995.

E. Goodspeed. *The original language of the Gospel.* Published by Thomas Kepler. N.Y. 1944.

M. P. Gonabadi: *Tarikh e Bal'ami.* Abou Ali Mohammad ibn Mohammad Bal'ami/ the translation and commentary of *Tarikh e Tabari/* by M. T. Malek o sho'ar Bahar/Tehran-1341. *The History of Abu Ali Mohamad ibn Mohamad Balami* is the translation of the extract of the book *History of the prophets and kings* written by Mohammad Jarir Tabari. The book of the history of Balami is the second oldest text ever written in the Persian language. 352 of hegira/ 973 A.D.; corrected by Malek o-sho'ara Mohamad Taghi Bahar. Tehran. 1385/ 2006 – publisher: Zowwar Mohammad Parvin Gonabadi W.B. Henning: *The disintegration of the Avestic Studies.* Acta Iranica 15, Leiden 1977, & *A Pahlavi Poem* Acta Iranica15. Selected Papers. Leiden. 1977;

Robert B. Greenblatt, M.D. Search the Scriptures. Illustrated Modern Medicine and Biblical Personages. The Parthenon Press. 1985

A. Hynek. *The new reports about the U.F.O,* edited in French language . *Nouveau rapport sur les O.V.N.I.* by "J'ai lu" Paris. 1981.

R. Kasser. *Complements au dictionnaire copte de Crun*, Le Caire. 1964, Bibliotheque des etudes coptes.

R. Kasser, M. Meyer, and G. Wurst, in collaboration with François Gaudard. *L'Evangile de Judas*. Edition "J'ai lu"/ Flammarion.2006. from *The Gospel of Judas*. The National Geographic Society. 2006.

W. Klassen. *Judas, Betrayer or friend of Jesus?* Minneapolis, Fortress. 1996.

King, Karen L. *The Gospel of Mary of Magdala, Jesus & the first woman Apostle*. Santa Rosa, California, Polebridge press. 2003.

E. M. Laperrousaz. *L'attente du Messie en Palestine a la veille et au debut de l'ere Chretienne*. edition A. et Picard. 1982. *Quomran et ses manuscrits de la Mer Morte*. edition Mon lieu, 2006 – France; *"Les Esseniens selon leur temoignage direct"*. edition Desclee. 1982; *Qoumran. L'etablissement essenien des bords de la mer Morte. Histoire et archeologie du site*, 1979, edition A. et Picard. *Les manuscrits de la Mer Morte* edition P.U.F. (Que sais-je), Paris-2003.

J.Y. Leloup. *The Gnostic wisdom of Jesus*, Amazon.com

M. Mayer: *The Gnostic Discoveries. The impact of the Nag Hammadi Library*. San Francisco. Herpersanfransisco. 2005.

M. Mayer. *The Gnostic Gospels of Jesus. The Definitive Collection of Mystical Gospels and Secret Books about Jesus of Nazareth*. San Francisco. Harper San Francisco. 2005.

M. Mayer. *The Gospel of Thomas. The Hidden Saying of Jesus*. San Francisco. Harper, San Francisco. 1992

F. Mebarki – E. Puech. *Les manuscrits de la mer Morte*. Edition "du Rovergue". 2002.

K. Paffenroth. *Judas, Images of the Lost disciple.* Kentucky. Westminster John Knox Press. 2001.

C. Pellegrino. *The Jesus Family Tomb.* San Francisco 2007

Khalil Sa'adat. *The Gospel of St Barnabas.* Persian translation, 4th edition, Alma'i, Tehran 1383.

T. C. Skeat. *Irenaeus and the Four-Gospel Canon.* Novum Testamentum, Vol. 34, Fasc. 2 (April 1992).

Jacob Slavenburg. *Het graf van Jezus, het mysterie van de tombe van Jezus, Maria Magdalena en Judas.* Walburg pers. 2007.

W. Smith. *Smith's Bible Dictionary.* edition Pyramid Books. N.Y. 1967.

Sundermann. *The Manichean Hymncycles Huyadagman & Angad Roshnan in Parthian and Sogdian,* London. 1990.

J. Tabor. *La veritable histoire de Jesus.* French version published by Robert Laffont- Paris 2007.

J.A. Thompson. *The Bible a la lumiere de l'archeologie.* Edition L.L.B. 1988.

H. Yaghmai. *Tarjomeh tafsir Tabari.* (The translation of the commentary of Tabari) edition university of Tehran/ 1339 J. Vallee. *Confrontation* "J'ai lu" France. 1992;

A.H. Zarin Koub. *The poetry of Khaghani,* explained By Minoresky. translated in Persian - edition Farhang Iran Zamin, 1332.

Some complementary books

Qur'an (Arabic version, translation done by the author- not yet published-); *The Qur'an.* English version, translated by J.M. Rodwell. Forwarded & introduction by Alan Jones (The Oriental Institute, Oxford). Edited by Phoenix. London. 1994.

Qur'an's vocabularies (Al-Mo'jam ol Mofahras, Arabic version). M.F. Abdol Baghy. Edited by Esmailian. Tehran. 1978.

Qur'an's vocabularies (*Kalemat ol Qur'an*/ Arabic version). H.M. Mahlouf. Edited by Dar on nadouh ol Jadideh. Beyrout. 1959.

Qur'an's commentary (*Tafsir ol Jalaleyn.* Arabic language.) Edited by Dar ol Ma'refah. Beirut.

Nag Hammadi scriptures & Manichaean Studies, n. 54. 2002.

Bibliotheque copte de Nag Hammadi. Edition Peeters.

National Geographic Magazine. May 2006.

National Geographic (DVD). May 2006.

New Testament (4 Canonical Gospels) on line.

New Testament. French, English and Dutch translation. Association Internatinale des Gedeons. 1956.

The holy book/ Old and New Testaments. Translated into Persian language, from the Original Greek and with the former translations diligently compared and revised by his Majesty's special Command/ authorizing King James version, with explanatory notes and cross references to the standard works of the church of Jesus Christ of Latter-day Saints./ *New testament.* Persian translation from Greek, Latin, and Hebraic languages, reproduced in 1982 by photography from the Edition 1904.

The encyclopaedia Britannica. **www. Britannica.com**

Easton's Bible Dictionary, originally published in 1897.

Schaff-Herzog Encyclopaedia of Religious Knowledge, 1914.

Scholars Version translation of *the Gospel of Thomas* taken from *The Complete Gospels:* Annotated Scholars Version.* Copyright 1992, 1994 by Polebridge Press.

L'Evangile selon Thomas. Neuchatel, delachaux & Niestle. 1961; The *Gospel of St. Thomas.* http://www.allaboutjesuschrist.org

The Gospel of Philip. NHC II.3, codex page 81, Robinson.

The Gospel of Judas. The website of the National Geographic publication on internet.

Pictures

Figure 10 - Master of justice and four apostles – France

Figure 11 - Maria Magdalene - Leader of the daughters of Jerusalem - Lisbon

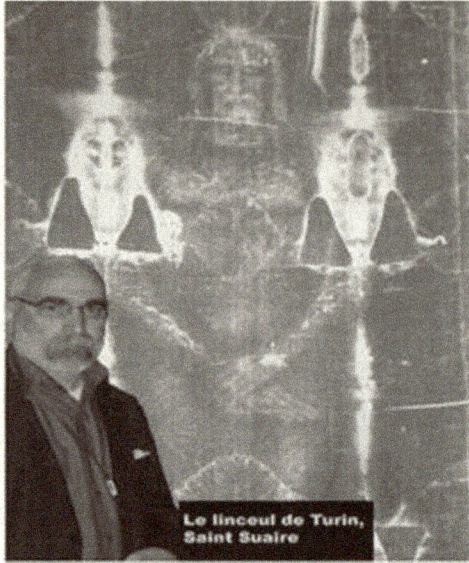

Figure 12 - The Shroud of Turin

Leonardo da Vinci's Last Supper

Figure 13 - Leonardo da Vinci's last supper, Milan, Italy.

Leonardo da Vinci was initiated into esoteric knowledge. Like Michelangelo, he added secret meaning to his paintings. He also added special symbols. So far, a great part of da Vinci's hidden meaning has been revealed.

The Da Vinci Museum in Tongerloo, near Antwerp in Belgium, owns a copy of Leonardo's Last Supper, painted in his time by his students - under his approval and probably with his cooperation. This huge copy shows the entire fine and delicate details which have long disappeared from the original fresco in Milan. Visitors can clearly discern what lies on the plates on the table, the apples, the pieces of bread, the glasses filled with wine, the carafes with water, a salt tub pushed over by Judas.

In April 2008 I visited this masterpiece and sat in front of it for nearly three hours. I am familiar with the content of the recently found Gospel of Judas, where Judas is presented as an initiate of Jesus rather than a traitor. Knowing this, I could all of a sudden see how – in the painting – the hands of Jesus and Judas exactly mirror each other, while reaching for an empty plate at the same time. This mirroring is no accident. The artist deliberately painted the scene this way. Leonardo is one of the first artists *not* to place Judas on the other side of the table, all alone, as was common practice in the art of his days. Instead, he included Judas in the group of disciples and gave him a special place among them, close to Jesus. Judas' entire figure mirrors Jesus, from the position of their feet, their sandals, to the colour of their undergarments and robes. This is no coincidence. The crowning touch is the clearly visible link between them represented in the folded hands of John /Maria Magdalena right in between their reaching hands. How much clearer could Leonardo have presented his idea to us in showing that these two persons are closely related? Take a close look: the evidence is staring us in the face.

Leonardo was an initiate harbouring a divergent opinion with respect to Judas. He knew the esoteric and hermetic scriptures. He had learned about them at the Medici's Court in Florence, probably through Marsilio Ficino, who translated these texts. Leonardo used his knowledge in the composition of his paintings, just as Michelangelo did with his cabbalistic knowledge in the frescos of the Sistine Chapel. Both genius artists painted secret heretical messages right in front of the eyes of their Roman Catholic patrons - something which these same eyes were unable to see.

Dr. Willem Glaudemans

List of Figures

www.ingramcontent.com/pod-product-compliance
Lightning Source LLC
Chambersburg PA
CBHW021223090426
42740CB00006B/353